Neoliberal Legality

Neoliberalism has been studied as a political ideology, an historical moment, an economic programme, an institutional model, and a totalising political project. Yet the role of law in the neoliberal story has been relatively neglected, and the idea of neoliberalism as a juridical project has yet to be considered. That is: neoliberal law and its interrelations with neoliberal politics and economics has remained almost entirely neglected as a subject of research and debate. This book provides a systematic attempt to develop a holistic and coherent understanding of the relationship between law and neoliberalism. It does not, however, examine law and neoliberalism as fixed entities or as philosophical categories. And neither is its objective to uncover or devise 'the law of neoliberalism'. Instead, it uses empirical evidence to explore and theorise the relationship between law and neoliberalism as dynamic and complex social phenomena. Developing a nuanced concept of 'neoliberal legality', neoliberalism, it is argued here, is as much a juridical project as a political and economic one. And it is only in understanding the juridical thrust of neoliberalism that we can hope to fully comprehend the specificities, and continuities, of the neoliberal period as a whole.

Honor Brabazon is an Assistant Professor in the Centre for Criminology and Sociolegal Studies, University of Toronto, Canada.

Neoliberal Legality

Understanding the role of law in the neoliberal project

Edited by Honor Brabazon

Routledge
Taylor & Francis Group
LONDON AND NEW YORK

First published 2017
by Routledge
2 Park Square, Milton Park, Abingdon, Oxon, OX14 4RN

and by Routledge
711 Third Avenue, New York, NY 10017

First issued in paperback 2018

Routledge is an imprint of the Taylor & Francis Group, an informa business

British Library Cataloguing in Publication Data
A catalogue record for this book is available from the British Library

Library of Congress Cataloging-in-Publication Data
Names: Brabazon, Honor, editor.
Title: Neoliberal legality: understanding the role of law in the neoliberal project/edited by Honor Brabazon.
Description: Abingdon, Oxon; New York, NY.: Routledge, 2017. | Includes bibliographical references and index.
Identifiers: LCCN 2016024999 | ISBN 9781138684171 (hbk) | ISBN 9781315544106 (ebk)
Subjects: LCSH: Law–Economic aspects. | Law–Political aspects. | Neoliberalism.
Classification: LCC K487.E3 N46 2017 | DDC 340/.115–dc23
LC record available at https://lccn.loc.gov/2016024999

ISBN 13: 978-1-138-60613-5 (pbk)
ISBN 13: 978-1-138-68417-1 (hbk)

Typeset in Baskerville
by Wearset Ltd, Boldon, Tyne and Wear

I must tell you that what we have got is an attempt to substitute the rule of the mob for the rule of law, and it must not succeed. It must not succeed. There are those who are using violence and intimidation to impose their will on others who do not want it. … The rule of law must prevail over the rule of the mob.

Margaret Thatcher, Prime Minister of the United Kingdom, on picketing during the 1984–5 miners' strike

This book is dedicated to the mining families of 1984–5 and to all others who have stood against neoliberalism.

Contents

Notes on contributors ix
Acknowledgements xi

Introduction: understanding neoliberal legality 1
HONOR BRABAZON

1 **Law, development, and political closure under neoliberalism** 22
TOR KREVER

2 **Neoliberalism and economic sovereignty: property, contracts, and foreign investment relations** 43
NICOLÁS M. PERRONE

3 **Neoliberal law and regulation** 61
ANDRÉS PALACIOS LLERAS

4 **Law, social policy, and the neoliberal state** 77
KENNETH VEITCH

5 **Law, neoliberalism and the constitution of political subjectivity: the case of organised labour** 92
ROBERT KNOX

6 **Continuity and rupture in restraining the right to strike** 119
NTINA TZOUVALA

7 **The promise of rights: international indigenous rights in the neoliberal era** 140
KRISTIN CIUPA

8 **Dissent in a juridified political sphere** 167
HONOR BRABAZON

9 **Alegality: outside and beyond the legal logic of late capitalism** 190
VANJA HAMZIĆ

Index 210

Notes on contributors

Honor Brabazon is an Assistant Professor in the Centre for Criminology and Sociolegal Studies at the University of Toronto and has been a Visiting Researcher at the Institute for Global Law and Policy at Harvard Law School and a Visiting Student in the School of Law at Birkbeck, University of London. Her research theorises shifting conditions and strategies of social change based on research she has conducted in Bolivia, Sweden, the United States, India, and Canada.

Kristin Ciupa is a PhD candidate in the School of Politics and International Relations at Queen Mary, University of London where she researches the connections between Venezuelan oil development and anti-neoliberal regionalisms in Latin America.

Vanja Hamzić is a Senior Lecturer in Legal History and Legal Anthropology SOAS, University of London, Faculty at the Institute for Global Law and Policy at Harvard Law School, and a Member of the School of Social Science in the Institute for Advanced Study at Princeton. He is author of *Sexual and Gender Diversity in the Muslim World: History, Law and Vernacular Knowledge* (I.B. Tauris, 2016) and co-author with Ziba Mir-Hosseini of *Control and Sexuality: The Revival of* Zina *Laws in Muslim Contexts* (Women Living Under Muslim Laws, 2010).

Robert Knox is a Lecturer in the School of Law and Social Justice at the University of Liverpool. He works primarily in the Marxist and critical legal traditions. His research touches on the relationship between international law, empire and imperialism (with a particular focus on questions of racialisation), on the relationship between law and social change and the role that legal processes play in shaping collective subjectivity.

Tor Krever is a Visiting Research Fellow at the Centre for Social Studies, University of Coimbra, Portugal and a PhD candidate in law at the London School of Economics and Political Science. His research focuses on the history and theory of international law. He has worked on development issues at the United Nations in New York, human rights in the occupied Palestinian territories, and international criminal law at the Special Court for Sierra Leone in the Hague. He is Assistant Editor of the *London Review of International Law.*

Andrés Palacios Lleras is a PhD candidate in the Faculty of Laws at University College London where he researches the advent and evolution of competition law in Latin America. He has worked in Estudios Palacios Lleras S.A.S. and in the Colombian competition authority.

Nicolás M. Perrone is a Lecturer at Durham Law School in Durham University, Junior Faculty at the Institute for Global Law and Policy at Harvard Law School, and a Research Fellow at the Centre of Interdisciplinary Studies of Industrial and Economic Law at the Universidad de Buenos Aires. He has worked for the OECD Directorate for Financial and Enterprise Affairs, the UNCTAD Division on Investment and Enterprise, and the Argentine federal judiciary.

Ntina Tzouvala is a post-doctoral fellow (Laureate Fellowship) at Melbourne Law School. Her research interests include history and theory of international law, with an emphasis on socio-economic history of international law.

Kenneth Veitch is a Senior Lecturer at Sussex Law School in the University of Sussex. He is the author of *The Jurisdiction of Medical Law* (Ashgate, 2007) and co-editor of *Social Rights in the Welfare State: Origins and Transformations* (Routledge, 2016).

Acknowledgements

This project began as a conference I organised at the University of Oxford in 2013. I am very grateful for the conference funding provided by the Department of Politics and International Relations, for the assistance of Margo Kirk, Jason Hussain, Rasangi Prematilaka, Kate Candy, and Professor Lois McNay in the Department, to Mansfield College, and to Dave Lappano for assistance on the day of the event. I am also grateful to all participants in the conference, whose rich and compelling response to my idea of 'neoliberal legality' motivated this book.

The volume would obviously be nothing without the contributions found herein, but I am additionally grateful to its authors for elaborating the concept of neoliberal legality in directions that impressed and inspired me, and which I am proud to include in this collection. I also wish to thank Routledge for making this book possible, particularly Colin Perrin and Laura Muir, as well as those who worked on the production of the book, including Penny Harper, Lucy Buchan, Hannah Riley, and Emma Critchley.

I extend my heartfelt thanks to everyone who has expressed interest in this project along the way, particularly Mariana Valverde, Davina Cooper, Sarah Lamble, Ruth Buchanan, Illan Wall, Sundya Pahuja, and Matt Craven. Additional thanks is owed to several people for insightful discussions with me about the themes of the book, including Liam McHugh-Russell and Rob Knox.

I am very lucky to have the benefit of knowing Peter Brogan, Alex Levant, Leslie James, Dave Lappano, Kheya Bag, Blair Ogden, Sarah Dulmage, Paul Jackson, and Ryan James, whose friendship, love, encouragement, and generosity has made this project (and me) stronger in many ways. Finally, thank you to my proud Baba, to my brilliant sister Greer, and to my also-brilliant, also-proud, and incredibly patient parents for all their love and support. This is for you.

Introduction

Understanding neoliberal legality

Honor Brabazon

Introduction

Neoliberalism has been studied as a political ideology, an historical moment, an economic programme, an institutional model, and a totalising political project. Yet the role of law in the neoliberal story has been relatively neglected, and the idea of neoliberalism as a *juridical* project has not been considered. Neoliberalism generally has been understood as an economic phenomenon: it celebrates the supremacy of the market, it is justified using economic rationales, and it is measured through economic or socio-economic indicators. Scholarly analysis has begun to examine the political components of neoliberalism, but this remains largely in relation to the success of its economic programme. Even critiques of neoliberalism have centred either on the economics of its goals or on its socio-economic outcomes without due attention to how these goals are devised or these outcomes reached, beyond the mere insertion of 'neoliberal' content into policymaking.

Meanwhile, the role of law and its interrelations with the politics and economics of neoliberalism has remained almost entirely ignored as a subject of research and debate. Even critical political and economic writing tends to characterise law merely as an institutional vehicle through which neoliberal reforms can be effected (when law is mentioned at all). Some legal scholarship has considered changes in specific areas of law in relation to neoliberalism, such as rule of law in the international development context (Dezalay and Garth, 2012), international trade law (Lang, 2011), property rights (McIntosh and Hatcher, 2010), and law in the post-communist transition (Glinavos, 2010). Several critical legal scholars have discussed the possibility of a more active and central role of law in discussions that relate such specific areas of law to broader processes of empire or globalisation (Bartholomew, 2006; Buchanan and Pahuja, 2004; de Sousa Santos and Rodríguez-Garavito, 2005; Goodale, 2005; Kennedy, 2006; Rittich, 2006). And, on a few occasions, scholarship of international relations has mentioned an expanding and intensifying role for law more generally in the neoliberal period (e.g. Cutler, 2003; Harvey, 2003).

However, nowhere has there been a systematic attempt to understand how these divergent threads are woven together in order to develop a holistic and coherent understanding of the relationship between law and neoliberalism. This volume hopes to initiate such a discussion.

The volume does not examine law and neoliberalism as fixed entities or as philosophical categories, however, and its objective is not to uncover or devise 'the law of neoliberalism'. Nor is this volume about all manner of changes to the discipline of law in the neoliberal period. Instead, it uses empirical evidence to explore and theorise the relationship between law and neoliberalism as dynamic and complex social phenomena. It concerns itself specifically with the *role* law plays in the neoliberal project. It asks not just what about law has changed but also *why, why now, why law, and to what end.* The volume explores and advances the following principal arguments. It contends that law takes a particular shape in the neoliberal period that is consistent with, but also more specific than, the liberal-capitalist legal form. It demonstrates that certain aspects of law have enabled it to play a crucial role in conceiving, constructing, and cohering neoliberalism in a way that other social institutions, structures, or sets of norms could not. It illustrates how law fundamentally shapes neoliberalism and argues that neoliberalism should be considered a juridical project, in addition to a political, ideological, and economic one. Finally, it underlines that the relationship between law and neoliberalism is not automatic but presents and embodies contradictions and vulnerabilities in the law and in the neoliberal project that highlight possibilities for emancipatory change.

As it constructs these arguments, the volume introduces the concept of 'neoliberal legality' to denote the specific form, mode, and role that law assumes in the neoliberal period. This concept builds upon the idea of 'liberal legality' which represents the particular historical form law takes in liberal capitalist societies. In this formulation, law is conceived as a system of generalised rules that are interpreted through reason and applied equally to all following rational procedural formalities in a manner void of political concerns and outcomes (Klare, 1979). These ambitious and decontextualising claims to law's neutrality, equality, and rationality are widely known in critical legal scholarship to legitimise the legal order, but they also foster a particular world view and facilitate certain types of relationships and interactions whilst restricting others. This volume contends that the logic and legitimacy of the legal form have played an active, unique, and essential role in the construction of the neoliberal world order.

In this view, it is not only the content of neoliberal law that has helped to create the neoliberal order but also the very fact that law has been used in its creation. It is even possible to speculate that neoliberalism might not have become so powerful, at the current time, or in its current form if liberal legalism had not enjoyed a particular degree of hegemony in the same moment as the political and economic conditions of neoliberalism occurred. The volume thus argues that neoliberalism must be seen as a convergence of intertwined and mutually influential political, economic, *and juridical* trajectories. Neoliberalism is as much a juridical phenomenon as a political and economic one, and it is only in understanding the juridical thrust of neoliberalism that we can hope to fully comprehend the specificities (and continuities) of the neoliberal period as a whole.

Neoliberalism

'Neoliberalism' is the often ill-defined shorthand that has come to represent the dominant ideology, political economy, and policy approach internationally from the 1980s onward. Although by exploring the juridical component of neoliberalism and the specifics of the dynamics that evidence it, the volume ultimately is aimed at uncovering with more precision the nature of neoliberalism, its authors seek to avoid getting mired in determining a definitive definition of something so complex and contradictory. These authors opt instead to explore neoliberalism as a contested and multi-faceted phenomenon in order to engage with a set of questions about how the ideas, policies, and social relations made visible from these different angles operate and interact, and the impact of these interactions (Chadwick, 2016).

The chapters thus combine different approaches to understanding neoliberalism, particularly neoliberalism as a utopian-epistemological theoretical project and as a class-based political project – projects that are productive of particular subjectivities in both cases. These approaches are not exhaustive and are complementary, overlapping, and at times contradictory.

The first is the view of neoliberalism as an internally disputed intellectual current that began as a small thought collective in the 1930s in Europe (mainly known as 'ordoliberals') and in the United States (mainly known as the 'Chicago School'). From this angle, it is an attempt to avoid the mistakes of classical *laissez-faire* liberalism, socialism, totalitarianism, and the welfare state (Mirowski, 2009) by articulating a utopian vision of the ideal configuration of social relations for the realisation of freedom, which is understood by neoliberals not as a quality to be possessed but as the ability to pursue individual self-interest through autonomous market transactions (Friedman, 1962; Mirowski, 2014: 437). From this perspective, neoliberalism is a normative theory about the nature of freedom and democracy as much as it is about the market. As Palacios Lleras puts it in his chapter, neoliberalism is not just 'an account of … how markets work or the nature of regulation; it aims to reconceive how political, economic and legal relations should take place in a society founded upon individual liberty'.

The second angle represents a view of neoliberalism as a class-based political project. Drawing from Harvey (following Duménil and Lévy), neoliberalism is a pragmatic and adaptive project initiated by the upper fractions of economic elites in the last quarter of the twentieth century to re-establish the conditions for capital accumulation and profitability and to restore their economic and political power following its decline during the post-war period (Duménil and Lévy, 2011; Harvey, 2006; McNally, 2010).

The third angle draws from Dardot and Laval (based on Foucault) who consider neoliberalism to be a totalising rationality that is not only destructive of the welfare state apparatus but also productive of particular subjects and social relations (Dardot and Laval, 2013: 3). Here it also draws from Althusser and Gramsci who likewise invite analysis of subjectivities and social relations. From this angle, it can be argued that the construction of neoliberal subjects and neoliberal social relations is integral to both of the above projects, and indeed can be understood as a goal of those projects in itself.

Much remains to be elaborated from each of these perspectives, but this multi-faceted view is generative. For instance, the analyses in the book demonstrate that an explanation of neoliberalism referring only to class interests is simplistic. Neoliberalism cannot, as Dardot and Laval warn, be reduced to the inevitable product of an autonomous, external 'logic of capital', or a mere repetition of pre-existing capitalist dynamics (Dardot and Laval, 2013). Likewise, neoliberalism is not a return to classical liberalism. And it is not solely ideational; rather, these ideas and subjectivities came to the fore in a particular way, at a particular time, with considerable political and economic power behind them, and they have furthered particular interests over others. In her chapter, Tzouvala argues that appreciating neoliberalism as both a theoretical and political project sheds light both on the ascent of neoliberal ideas from a marginal intellectual pursuit in the 1930s to a dominant orthodoxy worldwide and on what differentiates neoliberalism from other moments of capitalism. She also points out how inclusion of these different dimensions of neoliberalism presents commonalities amongst otherwise eclectic and at times opposing neoliberal thinkers and policymakers. Furthermore, the authors' attention to subjectivities usefully counters the impression that society is akin to a billboard that can simply be changed from one ideology to the next and that the people in that society are not invested in, affected by, or contributors to one paradigm or another.

The chapters thus explore the complexity of the novelty and continuity; structure and agency; micro and macro; ideas, subjectivities, and materialities that neoliberalism presents, and they invite further investigation of the interrelationships between these angles of analysis.

The neoliberal conceit

From this hybrid perspective, several principal ideas of neoliberalism are highlighted throughout the volume, which can be understood to be conceived and brought to bear through the legal form. One is the importance of a strong state in neoliberal thought. Neoliberal rhetoric rehearses the claim that neoliberalism represents the scaling back of the state and return to a free market. In contrast, neoliberal thinkers actually shared the conviction that individual freedom follows from explicit political choices – that the conditions for their vision of the good society will not unfold naturally, as classical liberal theories posited, but must be constructed (Mirowski, 2014: 53). Neoliberal policy thus requires a strengthening of the state in order to implement the material rules necessary for market competition and to develop the subjectivities required for a neoliberal social order (Wacquant, 2012).

If the state is increasingly acknowledged – at least in academic circles – to have been restructured in the neoliberal period rather than restrained, this is typically seen as a re-orientation of the state away from social concerns and toward facilitating market transactions: 'profit over people'. In his examination of regulatory changes, for instance, Palacios Lleras depicts the state's shift from a direct provider of goods and services to a regulator of competing private interests, supporting the contention that state regulation has in fact increased. Likewise, in his discussion of the second wave of neoliberal development policy in the 1990s, Krever describes the replacement of initial anti-state, pro-market policy with policy based in an understanding that the state could be used to facilitate market transactions through particular legal institutions, such as securing property rights and ensuring the enforcement of contractual obligations. Law and the state are reduced to servicing market-based business activity.

However, the book's chapters illustrate that the state has been reconfigured not just toward the market directly but that it has also been reconfigured as part of a broader shift toward a particular method of social organisation. This social order foregrounds, amongst other priorities, 'the efficiency of market competition, [and] the role of individuals in determining economic outcomes' (Palley, 2005: 20). In fact, in neoliberal thought, the market is to some extent portrayed merely as an information processor (Mirowski, 2014: 54) that facilitates self-interested decision-making and competition. In neoliberal thought, society is meant to be seen not as a composite of socio-economic classes, interests, or communities engaging in conflict, collaboration, or even market exchange but as a collection of atomised individuals engaging in market-based competition. An extension of the centrality of competition lies in the acceptance of inequality – of winners and losers – and even in the celebration of inequality as a necessary 'motor for progress' (Mirowski,

2014: 63). Neoliberalism strives to *manage* difference and inequality, rather than to *address* them.

The chapters thus challenge the common tendency to define neoliberalism solely as an extension of the reach of markets and instead explore which aspects of markets, and of capitalist social relations more broadly, are actually being extended – and how. It is here that the role of law is elucidatory.

Juridification

Perhaps the most noticeable juridical change in the neoliberal period is the more active role of law, which mediates further areas of social life, and more intensively (Cutler, 2003). In the book, this juridification is documented in Knox's account of the shift in the regulation of trade unions in the UK from legal abstentionism (workplaces governed by unions) to direct state involvement through 'a flurry of *juridification*' (emphasis his). Likewise, Tzouvala demonstrates how legislation restricting the right to strike in Greece, which had previously marked only the outer limit of political confrontation, is now far more central to labour relations, directly targeting the actions of union members. In my chapter, I indicate that street protest has been increasingly juridified and hyper-regulated in the neoliberal period, whilst Hamzić underscores the near-ubiquity of law. Moreover, several chapters provide examples of social activism and political grievances that previously took the form of industrial action or street protest but increasingly have been channelled toward the courts.

The significance of the increased reach of law extends beyond the content of the laws in question to the form of law itself, which this volume contends has been essential to the development and spread of the neoliberal social and economic order. In doing so, the book departs from previous attempts to understand the role of law in relation to political-economic systems which simply tack law on to existing political-economic analysis. Instead of seeing law as an institutional vehicle for a predetermined neoliberal programme, the book contends that law is *constitutive* of neoliberalism. In this respect, it builds on Marxist texts of the 1970s and 1980s that began to sketch a more robust and nuanced relationship between law and capitalism than determinist accounts that relegated law to economics' inferior superstructural counterpart (notably Balbus, 1977; Hay, 1975; Klare, 1979; Thompson, 1975). These analyses argue convincingly that capitalist economic and juridical relations developed in tandem as two equally essential expressions of capitalist productive relations (Fine, 1984: 207) and proffer that the legal form is co-constitutive of capitalist relations.

As above, the legal form in the capitalist period projects the image of a system of generalised rules that are interpreted through reason and applied equally to all following rational procedural formalities in a manner void of political concerns and outcomes, creating 'the guise of an impartial, determinate, and humane rule of law' (Klare, 1979: 130–132; also Pashukanis, [1929] 1978). Laws appear to be universal and fixed, independent of historical conjuncture and political will, and legal decisions appear to be technical matters of the interpretation of universal and fixed legal texts in a very formalist sense. In this view, law is a principal means of mediating social relations and shaping subjectivity under capitalism, and, through this process, law configures social relations in its image (Althusser, 1971; Fine, 1984: 142; Knox, 2009: 429–433; Pashukanis, 1980): the abstraction of laws from the specific social contexts in which they arise obscures their indeterminacy, their historical contingency, and the power relations underpinning them.

This volume demonstrates several ways in which this form of law has been central to neoliberal thought and policy, not only by providing institutional support for the neoliberal paradigm but also by shaping and modelling this paradigm and the subjectivities required by it, and by reconfiguring the social relations that law increasingly mediates.

Neoliberal legality and the rule of law

Taken together, the chapters identify several ways in which elements of the legal form have been fundamentally constitutive of the principal components of neoliberalism. The first aspect is the ideal of the rule of law, which embodies key characteristics of the legal form, most notably the notion of formal equality – that all are equal before the law.

This notion of the rule of law can be seen in the neoliberal restructuring of the state. In neoliberal thought (echoed in neoliberal rhetoric), the above reorientation of the state away from protecting the public interest and toward facilitating business transactions is framed as a protection of the spontaneous and democratic order that is created through self-interested individual decision-making. State laws and social programmes that pursue social goals such as equality, redistribution, social participation, or social justice are considered to be ad hoc legislation that unfairly applies to some people and not others. Further, they are seen as the undemocratic imposition of some people's interests – or their perception of collective interests – on others by a government that decides whose interests are more important (Hayek, 1944).

This conception of social order relies upon the idea that everyone is (formally) equal – an idea embodied in and structured through the rule of law, which abstracts legal subjects from their historical and political contexts of substantive inequality and frames social relations through the lens of atomised equals. Neoliberal thinkers envisioned a nomocracy: a society governed not by one group's conception of justice or of other people's needs but by abstract, end-independent rules that apply equally to all – in short, a society governed by the rule of law (Hayek, [1978] 1990).

The logic of the rule of law can also be seen in the neoliberal opposition to collective action. This objection frames collective action as an undemocratic attempt to acquire more influence than the parties' individual decision-making would allow, thereby biasing the political process toward those able to organise themselves collectively (Hayek, 1944: 63). The objection raised by neoliberal thinkers is essentially that collective action obstructs the rule of law, which is meant to structure the political process in the neoliberal vision.

This view is applied inconsistently, however, mainly being leveraged in opposition to unions and social movements. In my chapter, I describe how the advocacy of community groups is delegitimised and marginalised in the neoliberal period as the work of 'special interests' speaking only for themselves and not in the public interest, and as stakeholders equal to any other stakeholders. In his chapter, Knox traces how legislative changes have hindered unions' ability to build solidarity and represent the working class as a whole politically, which has transformed unions into this neoliberal image of interest groups that represent only their members' immediate needs. Likewise, Tzouvala describes how the invocation of laws to contain industrial action in Greece has allowed the government to construct a narrative wherein unions unfairly promote particularistic, egotistical interests, whilst the government's neoliberal reforms protect an appropriated conception of the common good. Without collective action, I indicate in my chapter that the neoliberal conception of democracy consists of little more than the rule of law-based notion of 'one citizen, one vote', which enables citizens only to make self-interested decisions between competing political products.

The neoliberal conception of competition between individuals also relies on the perception of equality (creating a 'fair game') and on the related formulation of legal subjects under capitalism 'as autonomous entities, [that are] mutually competitive, self-involved...' (Fine, 1984: 142). In this sense, the rule of law can be seen in neoliberal efforts to incorporate and manage substantive inequalities. For example, the chapters detail how systemically disadvantaged groups are encouraged to identify as equally competitive individuals in the neoliberal period. Veitch details how neoliberal workfare policy encourages the unemployed to see themselves not as the collective product of broader socio-economic processes but as individual competitors willing to accept lower wages. Workfare policy in the UK is oriented toward the personal self-improvement of unemployed individuals so that they can better compete on the labour market. Similarly, Ciupa documents how international indigenous rights instruments construct and manage indigeneity by encouraging indigenous people to see themselves as individuals who are equal to non-indigenous individuals and to express their indigeneity through market participation. In my chapter, I use the example of agrarian reform in Bolivia to illustrate how landless peasants were encouraged to see themselves as individuals who are formally equal to large landowners through the reframing of agrarian reform from a process of state-led redistribution to a process of title allocation, following which land could be redistributed consensually by 'willing buyers' and 'willing sellers' on the market (Akram-Lohdi, 2007: 1438) – essentially a programme to establish the rule of law in land tenure.

Taken together, the chapters suggest that social relations are structured increasingly around the rule of law and the image of legal subjects as competitive individuals. This furthers the neoliberal theoretical project but also its class-based political project by hindering redistributive claims, weakening the collective solidarity of the labour movement and the relationship of the state to the left, and incorporating rather than addressing inequality.

Neoliberal legality and contracts

The authors also showcase diverse aspects of the centrality of contract to neoliberal theory and policy and examine the significance of the juridical nature of contracts to the development of neoliberalism. In contrast to the classical liberal conception of the market as a forum for the exchange of property in the form of commodities, wherein aggregate individual choice determines prices, neoliberal thinkers conceived of the market as a series of contracts (Birch, 2016: 9). Polanyi described neoliberalism as a 'market view of society which equates economics with contractual relationships, and contractual relationships with freedom' (2001: 266).

Like the rule of law, contracts embody the legal form and the assumptions and subjectivities it promulgates. For instance, contracts are understood to be specific/private arrangements made freely by rational, self-determining equals based on self-assessments of their individual utility and without consideration of social consequences. Several chapters demonstrate how these assumptions come to characterise the social relations that are now modelled on, and mediated through, contracts. For instance, Veitch argues that the formulation of welfare benefits as a contract between an unemployed person and the state not only enables but also shapes and legitimises neoliberal policy and ideas: it obscures the authoritarian dimension of neoliberal workfare policy by focusing on the behaviour of the unemployed and not the conditions under which they 'freely' enter into workfare contracts; it hinders their actual escape from poverty by obscuring systemic causes of unemployment; and it depoliticises unemployment by giving it a bureaucratic or juridical front and by adding a moral dimension to unemployment by emphasising the responsibility of unemployed individuals to uphold their contracts.

Similarly, Perrone details the shift in the governance of foreign investment relations since the 1960s from property law (based in domestic law) to contractual rights (based in law at the newly created transnational level). Whilst both property and contract are legal techniques that prevent interference in the private use of resources, property is seen to govern the entire community, and the scope of private property rights accordingly is determined by state laws that can be debated and changed. In contrast, contracts are seen as individual agreements that affect only the parties to those agreements – parties who are considered to have freely entered into those agreements as informed equals. This not only means that favourable contracts with a host state are easier for businesses to obtain than legislation that is subject to democratic debate; it also positions foreign investors as equals to host states, affecting their sovereignty. Perrone argues that negotiating and *contracting* with the state is the strategy of investors in the neoliberal period.

A similar emphasis on contracts is identified throughout the volume. For instance, Knox documents how changes to the regulation of trade unions in the neoliberal period have led to the growing replacement of collective bargaining with individual contracts of employment. Krever specifies that the current focus on law in development policy is a particular type of law defined by property rights, contracts, and economically efficient regulations.

Perrone explains that contracts are functional to neoliberal legality because they allow market actors to govern state behaviour and society more broadly 'through the appearance of mere individual transactions'. Mediating social relations through legal mechanisms like contracts mobilises the orientation of the legal form toward consideration of the facts of individual cases rather than their broader contexts and social significance, or the power relations that underpin them. It reinforces the formal equality of the parties involved and makes social considerations and claims to democratic participation and oversight difficult to pursue.

Neoliberal legality and legal indeterminacy

Legal indeterminacy is a further mechanism through which the legal form shapes and legitimises neoliberalism. The theory of law's indeterminacy rests on the notion that legal argument can justify almost any outcome; that is, for every legal argument there could be an equally legally-valid and compelling counter-argument. As such, legal decisions are not a neutral or automatic process of applying fixed rules to different situations but are the product of factors beyond the content of the law (see Koskenniemi, 2005a, 2005b).

Tzouvala and I demonstrate in our chapters how law's indeterminacy has been mobilised to allow inconsistencies and contradictions of neoliberalism to go unnoticed. Tzouvala explains that legal indeterminacy allows conflicting values and interests to co-exist without the need to resolve their tension. For instance, she describes how '[t]he neoliberal agenda can be realised to a significant degree by *twisting, stretching and creatively interpreting* the ordinary legal framework of a functional liberal Keynesian state' (emphasis hers). Similarly, in my chapter, I document how governments increasingly break and ignore laws, and pass symbolic laws, to avoid implementing their commitments to progressive social change. They mobilise legal indeterminacy, taking advantage of the image of laws as neutral and fixed apolitical facts, in order to avoid political resistance.

Legal indeterminacy allows the under-enforcement of laws not to appear to contradict the neoliberal emphasis on the rule of law, and it allows neoliberal policymakers significant flexibility in their selective transformation of neoliberal theory into class-based policy.

Neoliberal legality and the public/private distinction

The ideological distinction between public and private realms, which the authors indicate is increasingly mobilised during the neoliberal period, is also embodied in law. The boundary between public and private law plays an essential role in conceiving the public and private spheres central to liberal theory and in enabling activity to shift from one to the other.

This boundary is raised in different ways throughout the book and appears to be deployed when convenient in neoliberal thought and policy. Palacios Lleras writes that the liberal idea of state non-intervention in the economy implies a separation between economic and social spheres that is not present in neoliberalism. Knox outlines the re-separation of the political and economic as neoliberal regulation of trade unions prevents unions from performing both a political and economic role, as they did under the British welfare state. In my chapter, I describe a squeezing-out of the public as increasing aspects of social life are considered to be private relations, governed by private law. This, too, additionally furthers neoliberalism as a political project. By shifting social relations, decision-making, and dissent to the private sphere, they are abstracted from their broader political contexts and recast as apolitical relations between individuals. This makes it difficult to articulate redistributive or systemic claims and to develop social solidarities.

Marketisation vs juridification

Several of the book's chapters provide additional detail to the prevalent view that neoliberalism involves an extension of market relations to further aspects of social life (Brown, 2015; Mirowski, 2009). Palacios Lleras, for instance, explores the extension by US policymakers of the logic of capitalist economics to other social spheres, elevating economic efficiency as the template against which other spheres are assessed. Krever, too, describes how legal rules have been evaluated with reference to a calculation of alternative efficiency outcomes in the latest wave of neoliberal development policy.

Yet the chapters also suggest a modified articulation of this trend. By elaborating the constitutive role of law in neoliberal economic and social relations, the book suggests that, as I write in my chapter, the political sphere is increasingly characterised by the same juridical qualities that also constitute the capitalist market. That is, this pattern is in some ways less an economisation, or even a marketisation, of increasing areas of social life, and more of a juridification; it is not (only) the spread of particular economic principles to law because law was already and always constitutive of those economic principles. In light of this, several authors indicate that neoliberal policy has contributed to an unprecedented extension and intensification of capitalist (juridical and economic) rationalities worldwide.

Resistance to neoliberal legality

Understanding the ways in which neoliberalism is conceived and effected through the legal form enforces the symbiosis between the various impulses behind neoliberalism. Neoliberalism as an ideological/theoretical project can be seen as the creation of a particular kind of society and subjectivity rooted in a very limited conception of individuality, democracy, and social life in which public debate and dissent are minimal and contained, collective action is discouraged, and substantive inequalities are ignored or celebrated, as convenient. This method of social organisation is particularly conducive to neoliberalism as a class-based political project, which naturally does not seek to facilitate the increased power of subaltern groups.

The chapters illustrate how, to these ends, the legal form provides a model of social interaction that weakens the relationship between the state and the progressive demands of the political left. It channels dissent toward voting and legalistic, institutional arenas such as human rights – both of which are rooted in the individual advocacy of formal equals. Mediating political decisions through law enables power dynamics amongst individuals to be ignored, limits the possible goals of social change to the institutionalisation of social concerns, and limits the way claims to redress historical and systemic problems can be articulated and understood. When individuals are treated as formally equal to other more powerful parties, their inequality is easily perpetuated.

The authors argue that law's embedded and constitutive role in the formulation and dissemination of neoliberal social relations forecloses or severely limits law as a useful terrain for transformative change to those social relations. In response, Veitch advocates a resurrection of the agonistic element of politics. Knox calls for a use of law only tactically in political resistance, with the ultimate goal of transcending the current legal form, whilst in my chapter I contend that the constitutive role of law necessitates a subversive engagement with law that contains an implicit critique of the legal form. It is here that Hamzić's chapter comes into play. Hamzić discusses the difficulty of imagining alternatives to law in the context of such an expansive and totalising neoliberal legality. However, he argues that this imbues such alternatives with tremendous power where they are found. He thus identifies potential for resistance in alternative regulatory frameworks outside the law, which can represent and spread alternative subjectivities from the bottom up.

The complexity of neoliberal legality

Rather than arguing that neoliberal legality is a fixed formula that is uniformly and seamlessly applied with an automatic and predetermined outcome, the volume also focuses on the tensions that arise as neoliberalism and neoliberal legality develop and expand, and on the interstices between the neoliberal world and what came before or might come after it.

To borrow from Liam McHugh-Russell (2016), the label 'neoliberal' is a lot like that of 'hipster': it is a term thrown around widely and derisively but never fully defined and never actually claimed by those it describes. Despite the detailed historical accounts by Philip Mirowski and others who painstakingly identify the people, networks, and strategies involved in the transformation of neoliberalism from an unpopular theoretical tendency to a globally dominant policy agenda, analysis that employs the term neoliberalism still seems to confront the objection that it is conjuring some kind of centralised force and blaming it for all negative change in the world from 1980 on.

The authors in this volume assist in countering this critique through their description of processes that are not coordinated or controlled but rather messy, complex, and contradictory – and by demonstrating that these qualities are perfectly consistent with the concept of neoliberalism. Neoliberalism is understood in the book as a set of ideas that has been developed and spread in various incarnations by specific people, under particular political circumstances. The chapters reference the networks of neoliberal thinkers and policymakers and their considerable efforts to spread neoliberal thought and policy. For instance, Palacios Lleras describes the diffusion of the semi-autonomous regulatory agency through the networks and status of a new class of lawyer-policy analyst. The chapters also each explore specific mechanisms through which neoliberal ideas have come to shape policies and subjectivities.

Moreover, the chapters acknowledge the diverse incarnations of neoliberalism by laying out neoliberalism's policy trajectories in different contexts. What the chapters describe is not a story about set policy formulas but about the logic or logics shaping and spreading them. The failure to replicate identical institutions and policies around the globe thus is not a sign of the poverty of the concept of neoliberalism but of the adaptability of neoliberal ideas and the strength of the political impetuses propelling them.

The book acknowledges how various (at times competing) currents of thought and policy have converged, contradicted each other, found voice at particular political moments, and shaped what is generalised as neoliberalism. It also demonstrates how neoliberalism has not been applied automatically through one concerted gesture. Krever, for instance, describes the shift in international development policy from an anti-state approach in the 1980s to a utilitarian embrace of the state as a means to facilitate *laissez-faire* business transactions in subsequent decades. This shift can be considered in the context of ongoing tension around the role of the state between schools of neoliberal thought. Moreover, Krever identifies several attempts to reconcile the role of the state in neoliberal development policy within this broader shift, including New Institutional Economics and Law and Economics scholarship. Neoliberal theory has not been seamlessly translated into policy but has been negotiated, contested, and adjusted; it has been interpreted in different ways; and it has interacted with pre-existing ideas about economics and development.

The book further indicates that such negotiations over neoliberal policy have been mediated through existing power relations. For example, in tracing the origins of international human rights mechanisms, Ciupa describes how the struggles in the South for a more just and prosperous post-colonial economic order coincided with the search in the North for a means of maintaining the economic benefits of colonialism without appearing to intervene in the sovereign affairs of the South. Ciupa details how anti-statist, individualist conceptions of rights that are compatible with, and constitutive of, the neoliberal theoretical and political projects eclipsed the collectivist versions advocated in the South. Ciupa's analysis reinforces the point that not everything connected to neoliberalism is uniformly disdained but that neoliberal policy embeds struggle and compromise and can be rather ambiguous.

The chapters also identify the messiness of neoliberalism through discussion of its mix of continuity and novelty. In our chapters, Tzouvala and I address how neoliberal ideas, institutions, and subjectivities have been developed and spread not only through new neoliberal legislation but also through new interpretations of pre-existing laws, which demonstrates that there was no clear break with a pre-neoliberal past and that the development of and transition to neoliberalism most often has been a haphazard process of people with a variety of converging interests using whatever means are at their disposal.

The chapters highlight contradictions in neoliberal thought and policy, such as Tzouvala's observations that neoliberal policymakers have accepted the concept of public good when it is deployed to justify terminating strikes but not when it is used in arguments against privatisations, and that neoliberal opposition to unions as 'labour monopolies' does not extend to corporations as 'enterprise monopolies'.

Importantly, the book does not treat neoliberal legality as uncontested or inevitable. Rather, the chapters draw attention to the implications of the various facets of neoliberal legality that they examine for resistance to neoliberalism.

Finally, in discussing the transition from the welfare state to neoliberalism, the volume considers the welfare state model soberly, acknowledging its advantages and its limitations. For instance, Knox points out that, whilst British trade unions in the Keynesian period were able to represent working class interests beyond individual workplaces, these interests were generally not 'intrinsically antagonistic to the capitalist class or capitalist system'. Yet, because this collective working class subjectivity recognised the common interests and collective economic power of the working class, it could still create conditions for challenges to capitalism.

The book points to the complex array of continuities and ruptures with the welfare state period, taking care not to overstate either the similarities or the differences. Knox cautions that 'it would also be a mistake to argue that neoliberalism simply involves a withdrawal of politics and extension of law…' because law was also involved in the formation of labour subjectivities in the welfare state and prior to it. Likewise, Krever mentions that law has shaped and mediated development in different ways since its origins; law has not simply been added to development in the neoliberal period. Ciupa stresses that the subordination of indigenous peoples through international law was already inscribed in the origins, history, structures, and form of international law. I emphasise in my chapter that the political sphere has always been mediated through law and that the juridical has always been political. Hamzić, too, stresses continuities with the constitutive role of law prior to neoliberalism. The authors acknowledge that juridification is not something neoliberalism has 'done', and they endeavour to specify as much as possible what about its intensification and extensification is specific to neoliberal legality.

There is also variation amongst the approaches of the authors. Some take a wider view and are less concerned with precise actors and more with broad trends. Some are more or less concerned with the role of the state in neoliberal policy or the role of particular states. The volume is interdisciplinary, engaging with legal and socio-legal literature as well as studies in politics, economics, international relations, and sociology. Moreover, the volume not only includes analysis of change to standard legal fields, such as property law and human rights law, but it also captures the broader influence of neoliberal legality in areas such as welfare programmes, international development, social movements, and trade unions. Empirical examples engaged in the text are not region specific but broadly international (e.g. UK, Greece, Bolivia, Pakistan) and are all brought to bear on the overarching theoretical analysis of the volume.

The chapters explicitly and implicitly highlight the juridical nature of neoliberalism: the juridical subjectivities at the heart of neoliberalism; the increased mediation of social relations by law; and the modelling of social relations on legal relations and neoliberal subjects on legal subjects. The volume is not a comprehensive or definitive 'take' on neoliberalism and law, nor does the legal form create neoliberalism on its own. Neoliberalism is not reducible to merely juridical phenomena, but the specificities of the legal form enable law to play a unique and crucial role in this process that extends beyond law's previous mediation of social relations. As I remark in my chapter, it is as though neoliberal theorists and policymakers have discovered the material and symbolic importance of the legal form for capitalist social relations and that mobilising the legal form in certain ways can influence the particular permutation of these relations. If the welfare state period can be understood as a particularly 'political' phase of capitalism, in which it was thought that capitalism should be influenced and moderated by collective political goals implemented through the state, neoliberalism should be understood as a particularly 'juridical' phase of capitalism, in which it is understood (consciously or not) that capitalism should be structured by, and expanded through, the juridical relations of the legal form.

A brief outline of each chapter follows:

Chapter outline

In Chapter 1, 'Law, Development, and Political Closure Under Neoliberalism', Tor Krever situates recurring topics and themes of the volume through an exploration of the turn to law in mainstream development thinking since the 1980s. The chapter demonstrates that the value of law in neoliberal development policy lies in its utility for facilitating market transactions. As such, law's core concerns in the development process have become private property, contracts, and the protection of foreign investors, which subsequent chapters explore in detail. This chapter argues that the legal form reproduces the notion that development is predicated upon individual entrepreneurial activity and to embed the social relations of market competition. This approach to development relies upon a conception of law as the disinterested application of technical principles in the pursuit of efficient outcomes. The chapter argues that this view of law obfuscates both the political character of law and the distributional consequences of development, and it removes development policy decisions from the political domain to the domain of technical expertise. Drawing from development reports and indicators, the chapter argues that this recent focus on law in development has not marked a break from neoliberalism but rather exemplifies key components of a distinctly neoliberal legality.

In Chapter 2, 'Neoliberalism and Economic Sovereignty: Property, Contracts, and Foreign Investment Relations', Nicolás Perrone further explores the neoliberal focus on contract law and foreign investment. He examines how a 'contractualising' shift in the legal techniques used to control and allocate natural resources has been crucial to furthering the neoliberal agenda. Since the 1970s, the proprietary paradigm previously dominant in foreign investment relations has been replaced by investors' pursuit of individual contracts with the state. The chapter argues that this extension of contract law principles to the governance of resources has subordinated state sovereignty and democratic control to the interests of foreign investors through the appearance of individual and consensual agreements between the state and investors as equal parties. The chapter suggests, however, that this extension of contract law to supplant property relations inadvertently opens itself to a parallel extension of legal realist critiques of property, and the chapter explores how such a delegitimising critique might play out.

In Chapter 3, 'Neoliberal Law and Regulation', Andrés Palacios Lleras explores changes to state regulation in the neoliberal period. The chapter identifies a contradictory tendency toward both decreased and *increased* regulation, as the neoliberal privatisation of state enterprises and services has pushed the role of the state from a direct provider of goods and services to a regulator of private providers. The chapter highlights how the coupling of law and economics in the rise of the semi-autonomous regulatory agency has assuaged this tension. These agencies derive legitimacy from their decision-making on the supposedly rational and apolitical basis of law and economics and from their management not by elected officials or bureaucrats but by a new class of lawyer-policy analyst. The chapter traces how the model of the semi-autonomous regulatory agency is dependent upon certain characteristics of the legal form and has been essential to the coherence and management of neoliberal regulatory policy.

In Chapter 4, 'Law, Social Policy, and the Neoliberal State', Kenneth Veitch examines the juridical form and logic of the reframing of UK welfare policy and health care provision in the neoliberal era. The chapter highlights the new contractual form of welfare policy, which uses the rationality of the private law of contract to reframe welfare recipients as rational self-determining agents who freely enter into 'workfare' arrangements as they would any other contract. It illustrates how the contractual legal form depoliticises welfare policy by obscuring the structural factors that create unemployment and the policy choices underlying this approach to resolving it, and by instead focusing on the individual responsibilities and choices of welfare recipients. The chapter demonstrates that the use of the contractual legal form to restructure social policy thus is constitutive of neoliberalism both materially and symbolically, in constructing and instilling the particular subjectivities and social relations necessary for the extension of the neoliberal order.

In Chapter 5, 'Law, Neoliberalism and the Constitution of Political Subjectivity: The Case of Organised Labour', Robert Knox illustrates how law historically has played a key role in shaping and articulating the collective subjectivity of labour, including in the transition to neoliberalism. Knox argues that an essential component of this transition has been the shift from the post-war model of collective *laissez-faire* labour relations – which allowed trade unions to act as organisations of the working class as a whole, to govern workplace life themselves, and to levy their economic power for political goals – to a neoliberal model based on individual, rights-based legislation. The chapter traces how the individual rights-based regulatory approach has relegated trade unions to economic–corporate bodies that represent their members' immediate interests and then separately serve as interest groups which can lobby governments to achieve political objectives. The chapter illustrates how the abstraction, formal equality, and alienation inherent in the liberal legal form have been constitutive of this shift, which has had an individualising, depoliticising, and disempowering effect on working class mobilisation.

In Chapter 6, 'Continuity and Rupture in Restraining the Right to Strike', Ntina Tzouvala draws from the example of Greece to explore the role of law in the neoliberal reconfiguration of the right to strike. The Greek constitutional framework guarantees the right to strike for most workers, which can be overridden only in exceptional circumstances for the public good. Yet invoking such exceptional circumstances to override this right increasingly has become the norm. The chapter outlines the neoliberal view of the right to strike and identifies tensions in neoliberal thought around the invocation of a notion of public good to justify restricting this right. The chapter also demonstrates that this neoliberal reinterpretation of a welfare state-era constitutional provision mobilises the indeterminacy inherent in the liberal legal form. It situates this tactic for curtailing the right to strike in the context of neoliberal attempts to reverse gains won by workers and to reduce their power to win similar victories through collective action in future. The chapter argues that the liberal legal form has been essential to furthering this aspect of the neoliberal project.

In Chapter 7, 'The Promise of Rights: International Indigenous Rights in the Neoliberal Era', Kristin Ciupa examines the rise of international indigenous rights mechanisms in the neoliberal period. Rather than serving as instruments of emancipation, however, the chapter explores not only how indigenous rights are shaped and limited by the neoliberal order, but also how the neoliberal order is constructed and perpetuated through indigenous rights. The chapter traces how the dominant international rights discourse reproduces neoliberal rationalities and assimilates rights bearers into the language and structures of the neoliberal order. It also lays out how international indigenous rights instruments circumscribe the category of indigeneity, incorporating only certain forms of indigeneity that are manageable within the political economic rationality of neoliberalism. The chapter argues that official rights discourses are constitutive of neoliberalism and thus will be limited as a means of improving the structural conditions of indigenous people, but it highlights certain vulnerabilities and spaces where emancipatory potential may still lie.

In Chapter 8, 'Dissent in a Juridified Political Sphere', I discuss how the increased permeation of the logic and language of law identified in previous chapters has restricted the ways in which political debate and dissent are articulated and played out. The chapter distinguishes key mechanisms through which the liberal image of law as an apolitical, ahistorical, equitable, fixed, and self-referential system has been mobilised to reframe social concerns, the state, dissent, and the relationships amongst them. In doing so, the chapter demonstrates how this increased juridification of the political sphere has obscured the political nature of neoliberal policy, depoliticised social concerns, and circumscribed the spaces and conceptual language through which dissent can be articulated. However, it also suggests that this increased juridification may inadvertently open alternative possibilities for dissent that cautiously and consciously exploit and subvert this increased dependence upon legality and the legal form.

In Chapter 9, 'Alegality: Outside and Beyond the Legal Logic of Late Capitalism', Vanja Hamzić also recognises a need to push beyond traditional approaches to resistance in the neoliberal period. Rather than being drawn back into using law in resistance despite its constitutive relationship to neoliberalism, or simply expecting legal change to follow automatically from economic and political change, this chapter suggests the possibility of an alternative approach: resistance through the creation of alternative legalities in the spaces outside or beyond the law. Whilst opposition to law typically has been categorised as *illegal*, the chapter uses the term *alegal* to denote such alternative frameworks. Instances of alegality may not necessarily or immediately be capable of challenging neoliberalism, but in a context where law increasingly mediates and shapes all spheres of social life in a manner constitutive of neoliberalism, the alternative discourses and social relations that are created through these instances of communal, normative life outside official legal frameworks might constitute an important element of counter-neoliberal resistance.

References

Akram-Lodhi, A. Haroon. 2007. 'Land, Markets and Neoliberal Enclosure: An Agrarian Political Economy Perspective.' *Third World Quarterly* 28(8): 1437–1456.

Althusser, Louis. 1971. *Lenin and Philosophy and Other Essays.* New York and London: New Left Books.

Balbus, Isaac D. 1977. 'Commodity Form and Legal Form: An Essay on the "Relative Autonomy" of the Law.' *Law and Society Review* 11(3): 571–588.

Bartholomew, Amy, ed. 2006. *Empire's Law: The American Imperial Project and the 'War to Remake the World'.* London: Pluto Press.

Birch, Kean. 2016. 'Market Vs. Contract? The Implications of Contractual Theories of Corporate Governance to the Analysis of Neoliberalism.' *Ephemera: Theory & Politics in Organization* 16(1): 107–133.

Brown, Wendy. 2015. *Undoing the Demos: Neoliberalism's Stealth Revolution.* New York: Zone Books.

Buchanan, Ruth and Sundhya Pahuja. 2004. 'Legal Imperialism: Empire's Invisible Hand?' In *Empire's New Clothes.* Ed. Paul Passavant and Jodi Dean. New York: Routledge.

Chadwick, Anna. 2016. Discussant comments to the paper 'Neoliberal Legality: Discipline and Dissent' at the workshop 'Why "Neoliberalism?" On Critique and Method'. European University Institute, Florence, Italy, 18 March, 2016.

Cutler, A. Claire. 2003. *Private Power and Global Authority: Transnational Merchant Law in the Global Political Economy.* Cambridge: Cambridge University Press.

Dardot, Pierre and Christian Laval. 2013. *The New Way of the World: On Neoliberal Society.* New York: Verso.

de Sousa Santos, Boaventura and César Rodríguez-Garavito, eds. 2005. *Law and Globalization from Below: Towards a Cosmopolitan Legality.* Cambridge: Cambridge University Press.

Dezalay, Yves and Bryant Garth. 2012. *Lawyers and the Rule of Law in an Era of Globalization.* New York and Abingdon: Routledge.

Duménil, Gérard and Dominique Lévy. 2011. *The Crisis of Neoliberalism.* Cambridge, MA and London: Harvard University Press.

Fine, Bob. 1984. *Democracy and the Rule of Law: Liberal Ideals and Marxist Critiques.* London and Sydney: Pluto Press.

Friedman, Milton. 1962. *Capitalism and Freedom.* Chicago: University of Chicago Press.

Glinavos, Ioannis. 2010. *Neoliberalism and the Law in Post Communist Transition.* New York and Abingdon: Routledge.

Goodale, Mark. 2005. 'Empires of Law: Discipline and Resistance with the Transnational System.' *Social and Legal Studies* 14(4): 553–583.

Harvey, David. 2003. *The New Imperialism.* Oxford: Oxford University Press.

Harvey, David. 2006. 'Neoliberalism as Creative Destruction.' *Geografiska Annaler* 88(2): 145–158.

Hay, Douglas. 1975. *Albion's Fatal Tree: Crime and Society in Eighteenth-Century England.* New York: Pantheon Books.

Hayek, Friedrich. 1944. *The Road to Serfdom.* London and New York: Routledge.

Hayek, Friedrich. [1978] 1990. *New Studies in Philosophy, Politics, Economics and the History of Ideas.* London: Routledge.

Kennedy, Duncan. 2006. 'Three Globalizations of Law and Legal Thought: 1850–2000.' In *The New Law and Economic Development: A Critical Appraisal.* Ed. David Trubek and Alvaro Santos. Cambridge: Cambridge University Press.

Klare, Karl. 1979. 'Law-Making as Praxis.' *Telos* 40: 123–135.

Knox, Robert. 2009. 'Marxism, International Law, and Political Strategy.' *Leiden Journal of International Law* 22: 413–436.

Koskenniemi, Martti. 2005a. 'By Their Acts You Shall Know Them (and Not by Their Legal Theories).' *European Journal of International Law* 15: 839–851.

Koskenniemi, Martti. 2005b. *From Apology to Utopia.* Cambridge: Cambridge University Press.

Lang, Andrew. 2011. *World Trade Law After Neoliberalism.* Oxford: Oxford University Press.

McHugh-Russell, Liam. 2016. Introductory comments to the workshop 'Why "Neoliberalism?" On Critique and Method'. European University Institute, Florence, Italy, 18 March, 2016.

McIntosh, Wayne V. and Laura J. Hatcher. 2010. *Property Rights and Neoliberalism: Cultural Demands and Legal Actions.* Aldershot, UK and Burlington, VT: Ashgate.

McNally, David. 2010. *Global Slump: The Economics and Politics of Crisis and Resistance.* Oakland, CA: PM Press.

Mirowski, Philip. 2009. 'Postface: Defining Neoliberalism.' In *The Road from Mont Pèlerin: The Making of the Neoliberal Thought Collective.* Ed. Philip Mirowski and Dieter Plehwe. Cambridge, MA and London: Harvard University Press. 417–445.

Mirowski, Philip. 2014. *Never Let a Serious Crisis Go to Waste: How Neoliberalism Survived the Financial Meltdown.* New York: Verso.

Palley, Thomas. 2005. 'From Keynesianism to Neoliberalism: Shifting Paradigms in Economics.' In *Neoliberalism: A Critical Reader.* Ed. Alfredo Saad-Filho and Deborah Johnstone. London: Pluto.

Pashukanis, Evgeny. [1929] 1978. *Law and Marxism: A General Theory.* London: Ink Links Ltd.

Pashukanis, Evgeny. 1980. *Pashukanis, Selected Writings on Marxism and Law.* Ed. Piers Beirne and Robert Sharlet. London: Academic Press.

Polanyi, Karl. 2001. *The Great Transformation: The Political and Economic Origins of Our Times.* Boston: Beacon Press.

Rittich, Kerry. 2006. 'The Future of Law and Development: Second-Generation Reforms and the Incorporation of the Social.' In *The New Law and Economic Development: A Critical Appraisal.* Ed. David Trubek and Alvaro Santos. Cambridge: Cambridge University Press.

Thompson, E.P. 1975. *Whigs and Hunters: The Origin of the Black Act.* Harmondsworth, UK: Penguin Books Ltd.

Wacquant, Loic. 2012. 'Three Steps to a Historical Anthropology of Actually Existing Neoliberalism.' *Social Anthropology* 20: 66–79.

Chapter 1

Law, development, and political closure under neoliberalism

Tor Krever[1]

Writing in the *World Bank Research Observer* in 1998, US Court of Appeals judge Richard Posner opined that, when undertaking legal reform, developing countries' priority must be the creation of efficient rules of contract and property.

Property rights and contract enforcement, he claimed, long predate other legal institutions and the latter should be designed to promote the former.[2] Posner's forthright insistence that economic efficiency be the guiding light for jurists and legal reformers stands in sharp contrast with traditional liberal legal paeans to equity and justice, as well as with a traditional indifference to law within development thinking. And yet, in recent decades, it is Posner's view that has increasingly come to dominate thinking about law, both in development circles and the legal academy more generally.

This chapter traces the emergence of this view of law within the field of international development. Mainstream development thinking initially awarded little importance to law. Only with challenges to the neoliberal development paradigm in the late 1980s and early 90s did law and legal institutions attract significant attention. Since then, and especially in the new century, law has taken centre stage in development thinking, embraced explicitly as an engine of development. Rule of law departments have sprouted in all major international financial institutions, bilateral aid agencies, and non-governmental development organisations, and scholars and practitioners now regularly advocate legal reform in developing countries as a means to

1 PhD candidate in Law, London School of Economics and Political Science and Visiting Research Fellow at the Centre for Social Studies, University of Coimbra. This chapter builds upon work originally published in volume 52 of the *Harvard International Law Journal*.

2 Richard A. Posner, 'Creating a Legal Framework for Economic Development', 13(1) *The World Bank Observer* (1998) 1, 2. The co-constitutive relationship between law and capitalist development has, of course, long been recognised within the Marxist tradition. Pashukanis, for instance, famously described the juridification of social life under capitalism, arguing that the legal form is generated by commodity exchange. E. Pashukanis, *Law and Marxism: A General Theory* (Ink Links, 1978).

sustainable economic growth. For many mainstream commentators, the new attention awarded to the law marks a break from an earlier neoliberal development project epitomised by the so-called 'Washington Consensus'.

Yet, this chapter argues, the view of law that has come to dominate development thinking is specifically that advanced by Posner, one that in fact reproduces many of neoliberalism's core assumptions. On this view, law is understood as a market-oriented instrument for furthering the economic, political, and social ends of the neoliberal project. Private property and contract, individual entrepreneurialism, and protection of foreign investors are elevated as the core concerns of the law. In short, the chapter argues, the legal turn in development theory marks not the displacement of neoliberalism by law but the embrace of a distinctly neoliberal legality.

The growing hegemony of neoliberal legality is not without consequence. The neoliberal understanding of law, the chapter argues, seeks to depoliticise law and foreclose it as a terrain for political struggle. So too the development policies in which neoliberal legality is today awarded centrality. The primacy awarded legal protections for capital, for instance, becomes not a political choice but the technical requirement of the rule of law – a move, the chapter suggests, with important implications for efforts to resist neoliberalism.

From law and development to structural adjustment

In the wake of post-war decolonisation, many developing countries pursued trade and industrial policies based on import substitution industrialisation and high tariff barriers. The state, many development economists agreed, could play a constructive role in determining the allocation of resources and investment in the economy so as to promote economic growth.[3] In line with this view, some legal experts, starting in the 1960s and predominantly in the US, believed law could be used as a tool to empower the state and facilitate its exercise of macroeconomic control.[4] This early Law and Development movement, supported by the Ford Foundation and the US Agency for International Development (USAID), undertook law reform projects – which in practice amounted to the transplant of US legal institutions – primarily in Latin America and Africa.[5]

3 See Raúl Prebisch, *The Economic Development of Latin America and its Principal Problems* (UN Department of Economic Affairs, 1950).

4 Daniel Berkowitz, Katharina Pistor, and Jean-Francois Richard, 'The Transplant Effect', 51 *American Journal of Comparative Law* (2003) 163, 163.

5 See David M. Trubek and Marc Galanter, 'Scholars in Self-Estrangement: Some Reflections on the Crisis in Law and Development Studies in the United States', *Wisconsin Law Review* (1974) 1062. See also Elliot M. Burg, 'Law and Development: A Review of the Literature & a Critique of "Scholars in Self-Estrangement"', 25 *American Journal of*

The movement was short-lived and by the mid-1970s its leading figures had become disillusioned.[6] Many had discovered that societies and institutions in developing countries were resistant to formal legal transplantation, while the transplants themselves often had unpredictable or even counterproductive effects.[7] But even at its height, the movement made little impress on the major development actors such as the Bretton Woods institutions and other major international financial institutions (IFIs). The World Bank, for instance, showed little interest in legal reform, its focus on broad economic planning and the development of infrastructure, especially power, transport, and telecommunications.[8] 'We have never had a lawyer included on a mission because of his legal knowledge', the Bank explained in 1962.[9]

By the mid-1970s, Western development policy, especially that of the World Bank and IMF, had begun to shift decisively to the neoliberal, macroeconomic reforms that would soon become synonymous with structural adjustment lending.

Neoliberalism, of course, had earlier roots than structural adjustment. An early exposition of its major tenets, drawing on the Austrian-Libertarian tradition, was formulated by the members of the Mont Pèlerin society, a 'thought collective' founded in 1947 which would prove particularly influential in the spread of neoliberal ideas.[10] As a political-economic programme, and supporting ideology, neoliberalism holds that the liberation of individual entrepreneurial activity is necessary, or at the very least is the best means, to promote economic welfare and human well-being. To this end, its adherents advocate free markets, the liberalisation of trade and finance, and a limited role for the state in the economic and social organisation of society.[11]

The southern cone of Latin America in the 1970s – in particular Pinochet's Chile – offered an early testing ground. The experiment proved

---

Comparative Law (1977) 492, 496–7; John Henry Merryman, 'Comparative Law and Social Change: On the Origins, Style, Decline & Revival of the Law and Development Movement', 25 *American Journal of Comparative Law* (1977) 457, 458.

6 A now famous critique of the Law and Development movement was published in 1974 by two of its former leading figures: see Trubek and Galanter (1974).

7 Trubek and Galanter (1974) 1063–64, 1076.

8 Devesh Kapur, John P. Lewis, and Richard Webb, 'The Bank of the 1950s', in Devesh Kapur, John P. Lewis, and Richard Webb (eds), The World Bank: Its First Half Century, vol. 1 (Brookings Institution, 1997) 85, 109–10.

9 Alexander Wiener, 'Law and Economic Development', 40 University of Detroit Law Journal (1962–63) 510, 512, quoting letter from Doris R. Eliason, Office of Information, IBRD, to Alexander L. Wiener, Jr., 15 March 1962.

10 Early members of the collective included Friedrich von Hayek, Karl Popper, Ludwig von Mises, and Milton Friedman. See Philip Mirowski and Dieter Plehwe (eds), *The Road from Mont Pèlerin: The Making of the Neoliberal Thought Collective* (Harvard University Press, 2009); Bernhard Walpen, *Die offenen Feinde und ihre Gesellschaft: Eine hegemonietheoretische Studie zur Mont Pèlerin Society* (VSA-Verlag, 2004).

11 David Harvey, A Brief History of Neoliberalism (Oxford University Press, 2005) 2–4.

highly lucrative to ruling elites and foreign investors, with a now familiar concomitant explosion of social inequality: growing wealth for the rich accompanied by the retrenchment of the welfare state and immiseration of the working class. Indeed, the iniquities produced by neoliberal policies support the contention discussed throughout this volume that neoliberalism should be understood not simply as a collection of economic policies, but as a political class project.[12]

By the end of the decade, neoliberal ideas had made significant incursions into the major development institutions. Led by the World Bank, with its formidable resources as both lender and research institute, mainstream development thinking took a distinct turn to focus on neoliberal market-stimulating (and anti-state) reforms.[13]

The neoliberal development agenda that emerged was to become a familiar set of policies known, following John Williamson's coinage, as the 'Washington Consensus'.[14] The policies Williamson identified included maintaining small budget deficits, broadening the tax base, ending state subsidies, allowing the market to set interest rates, liberalising trade and foreign investment, privatising state-owned enterprises, abolishing impediments to foreign direct investment, and guaranteeing secure property rights.[15] The role of the state was to be limited to one of supporting private economic activity; in short, Bank policy from the late 1970s held that development would follow 'from rolling back the state and placing faith in the market'.[16]

What of law's role in development? While certainly no longer understood as a tool to empower the state, as it was by the Law and Development movement, it was also not entirely absent from the neoliberal conception of development. The neoliberal view conceived of the economy as a market where individuals would use resources efficiently in reaction to price signals. Markets in developing countries were no different from those found in developed countries, and both would require the same

12 Harvey (2005) 19; Leo Panitch and Sam Gindin, 'Superintending Global Capital', 35 New Left Review (2005) 101, 110.

13 See World Bank, Accelerated Development in Sub-Saharan Africa: An Agenda for Action (World Bank, 1981); William Easterly, 'What Did Structural Adjustment Adjust? The Association of Policies and Growth with Repeated IMF and World Bank Adjustment Loans', 76 Journal of Development Economics (2005) 1, 2–3.

14 John Williamson, 'What Washington Means by Policy Reform', in John Williamson (ed.), Latin American Adjustment: How Much has Happened (Institute for International Economics, 1990) 7, 7.

15 Williamson (1990) 8–17.

16 Graham Harrison, The World Bank and Africa: The Construction of Governance States (Routledge, 2004) 18; World Bank, World Development Report 1987: Barriers to Adjustment and Growth in the World Economy, Industrialization and Foreign Trade, World Development Indicators (World Bank, 1987) 38.

'universal' legal foundations.[17] But such legal considerations were merely implicit in economic theorising, and concrete legal reforms, it followed, were entertained only as the necessary concomitants to economic policy. A reduction of trade tariffs, for instance, might require amendment of supporting legislation and regulations.[18] Law itself, though, was not an explicit feature of the neoliberal development model.

Challenges to neoliberalism

By the late 1990s, neoliberalism's hegemony was quickly approaching universality: almost all governments, regardless of political orientation, adhered to its tenets. And with the turn of the century, Perry Anderson could write of 'the virtually uncontested consolidation, and universal diffusion, of neoliberalism'.[19] However, its application to development policy and prescription by the IFIs had not gone unchallenged. Already in the 1980s and early 1990s, structural adjustment came under widespread attack. Failure to achieve promised growth,[20] increasing inequality both within and between countries,[21] and dissent by influential donors such as Japan,[22] put advocates of Washington Consensus policies on the defensive.

The ill effects of neoliberal policies in developing countries have been extensively rehearsed elsewhere. But in short, neoliberalism has tended to concentrate wealth in an increasingly small and privileged stratum in core and periphery alike, with a concomitant growth of socioeconomic inequality and human misery.[23] It was not mere coincidence that increasing inequality and the advance of neoliberal policies were coeval. Neoliberal restructuring is 'widely recognised as being characterized by profoundly uneven development, including increased poverty and

17 David Kennedy, 'The "Rule of Law", Political Choices, and Development Common Sense', in David M. Trubek and Alvaro Santos (eds), The New Law and Economic Development: A Critical Appraisal (Cambridge University Press, 2006) 95, 129.

18 It is indicative that the authors of a history of the World Bank's intellectual role from its inception until the early 1990s make no mention of legal reforms or the Bank's theorising on law and legal institutions in development. Although their focus is on the Bank's contributions to economics, they observe that the Bank has also been influential in the fields of 'political science, demography, statistics and sociology. . . .' Law does not rate a mention. Nicholas Stern and Francisco Ferreira, 'The World Bank as "Intellectual Actor"', in Kapur et al. (eds) (1997) vol. 2, 523, 524.

19 Perry Anderson, 'Renewals', 1 New Left Review (2000) 1, 6.

20 B. Milanovic, 'The Two Faces of Globalization: Against Globalization as We Know It', 31(4) World Development (2003) 667.

21 United Nations Development Programme, Human Development Report 1992 (Oxford University Press, 1992) 34.

22 Robert Wade, 'Japan, The World Bank, and the Art of Paradigm Maintenance: The East Asian Miracle in Political Perspective', I/217 New Left Review (1996) 3.

23 William I. Robinson, Promoting Polyarchy: Globalization, US Intervention, and Hegemony (Cambridge University Press, 1996) 339.

inequality at the global level'.[24] Indeed, one prominent commentator attributes 'the disastrous results brought to most of Africa, Latin America, and Eastern Europe' directly to 'two decades of unabashedly free market policies'.[25]

The opening of developing countries' political economies to the free movement of products and financial flows from the North was combined with a transformation of states' domestic social relations.[26] In one commentator's words,

> [n]eoliberal structural adjustment professed a fundamental re-articulation of social relations.... This was to be achieved through a process of social engineering by which the abstract disciplines inherent to capitalist social relations could be imposed in an increasingly direct fashion upon both state and society.[27]

As economies were opened to transnational capital and state controls swept away, Susan Marks observes,

> asymmetries in the distribution of material and cultural resources bec[a]me magnified. The hardships of [neoliberal] restructuring precludes the implementation of social and economic policies – agrarian reform, industrial planning, expanded programmes of education and training, etc. – which might help to correct this.'[28]

The result, Robert Wade argues, was not only slower growth, but an assortment of social ills. As he put it, neoliberal reforms 'prohibit the use of protection or subsidies as part of any industrial strategy to stimulate new activities beyond those that might occur in free-market conditions' and '[t]his is a recipe for slower growth, higher poverty, higher unemployment and higher crime'.[29]

The neoliberal development model came under further attack with the failure of neoliberal policies in post-Soviet Eastern Europe. With the collapse of the Soviet Bloc, the intellectual heirs of Friedrich von Hayek and

24 Marcus Taylor, 'Responding to Neoliberalism in Crisis: Discipline and Empowerment in the World Bank's New Development Agenda', in Paul Zarembka and Susanne Soederberg (eds), Neoliberalism in Crisis, Accumulation, and Rosa Luxemburg's Legacy (Emerald, 2004) 3, 13.

25 Milanovic (2003) 679.

26 See Harvey (2005) 5–38.

27 Taylor (2004) 10.

28 Susan Marks, The Riddle of All Constitutions (Oxford University Press, 2000) 58.

29 Robert Wade, 'The Ringmaster of Doha', 25 New Left Review (2004) 146, 152. See also Jeff Faux and Larry Mishel, 'Inequality and the Global Economy', in Will Hutton and Anthony Giddens (eds), On the Edge: Living with Global Capitalism (Jonathan Cape, 2000) 93.

Milton Friedman rushed to apply their 'shock therapy' or 'Big Bang' reforms.[30] In Russia, for instance, shock therapy reforms 'deregulated most prices and launched a mass privatization program'.[31] Between the dissolution of the Soviet Union in December 1991 and July 1994, some 14,000 medium and large state enterprises amounting to 70 per cent of Russian industry were privatised. Further privatisations followed between 1995 and 1997.[32]

In the wake of rapid liberalisation and privatisation, neoliberal economists believed a market economy would develop quite naturally. In Jeffrey Sachs's words, 'markets spring up as soon as central planning bureaucrats vacate the field'.[33] When no such development occurred, neoliberalism's champions, inside both the IFIs and the academy, sought to explain the dismal failure without undermining the neoliberal model itself. As Joseph Stiglitz observed in 1999,

> those who advocated shock therapy and rapid privatization argue that the problem was not too much shock and too little therapy, but that there was too little shock.... Other defenders of the recommended reform programs argue that the failures were not in the design of the reforms, but in their implementation.[34]

The problem, in short, some observers suggested, was an *institutional* failure.[35] This critique was developed most extensively by theorists of the New Institutional Economics (NIE),[36] rooted in the work of Ronald Coase. Coase's seminal work on the 'nature of the firm' and the 'problem of social cost' had highlighted the importance of transaction costs for economic analysis.[37] The costs of exchange, Coase showed, were dependent on various institutions in society – a 'complicated set of interrelationships' overlooked by neoclassical economic theory.[38]

30 See Peter Gowan, The Global Gamble (Verso, 1999) 187–242.

31 Karla Hoff and Joseph E. Stiglitz, 'After the Big Bang? Obstacles to the Emergence of the Rule of Law in Post-Communist Societies', National Bureau of Economic Research, Paper No. 9282 (2002) 7.

32 Ibid. 7–8.

33 Jeffrey Sachs, Poland's Jump to the Market Economy (MIT Press, 1993) xiii.

34 See Joseph E. Stiglitz, 'Whither Reform? Ten Years of the Transition', Address at the World Bank Annual Bank Conference on Development Economics, 28–30 April 1999.

35 Neoliberalism was, of course, as Harvey and others have noted, quite successful as a class project.

36 The prefix 'new' distinguished this school from an earlier current of economic thought associated with Thorstein Veblen, Gunner Myrdal, and John Commons.

37 Ronald Coase, 'The Nature of the Firm', 4 Economica (1937) 386; Ronald Coase, 'The Problem of Social Cost', 3 Journal of Law and Economics (1960) 1.

38 Ronald Coase, 'The New Institutional Economics', 88(2) The American Economic Review (1998) 72.

Building on Coase's insights, Douglas North also argued that the neoclassical model of economics ultimately rested on institutional foundations, institutions which needed to be made central to any convincing theory of economic change.[39] Institutions, North explained, 'are the humanly devised constraints that structure political, economic and social interaction. They consist of both informal constraints (sanctions, taboos, customs, traditions, and codes of conduct), and formal rules (constitutions, laws, property rights)'.[40]

The central focus in North's work was a theory of property rights. Property rights, above all institutions, establish individual and group incentives of economic behaviour and exchange, North and his fellow NIE theorists explained. An absence of clearly defined and consistently enforced property rights leads to high transaction costs and, on North's analysis of economic history, is a key contributing factor to poor economic performance and growth.[41]

In sharp contrast with the neoclassical model of individuals engaged in free exchange under a system of *laissez-faire* markets, the NIE invoked an explicit, if still minimal, role for the state. While the primacy of markets remained, such markets were in reality underpinned by a collection of institutions, many of which were maintained by the state. On the NIE view, it is the state that specifies and enforces the 'rules of the game'. In short, the state provides the necessary institutions and legal infrastructure to ensure the protection of property rights.[42]

Good governance and the turn to law

The NIE was championed by the World Bank and other mainstream development actors precisely when the neoliberal model of development was under strongest challenge. Starting in the early 1990s, the Bank was quick to point to the importance of institutions – and, foremost, stable property rights – in explaining the failures of SAPs and shock therapy. If the latter had not led to a functioning market economy, it was due not to any failing in the policies of privatisation and liberalisation, but rather to the absence of a secure institutional environment.

Under the rubric of 'good governance', policymakers and academics increasingly spoke and wrote of the importance of institutions. By 1994, the Bank was arguing that sustainable development required 'a predictable and

39 See, e.g., Douglas C. North and Robert P. Thomas, The Rise of the Western World: A New Economic History (Cambridge University Press, 1973); Douglas C. North, Structure and Change in Economic History (Norton, 1981); Douglas C. North, Institutions, Institutional Change and Economic Performance (Cambridge University Press, 1990).

40 Douglas C. North, 'Institutions', 5 Journal of Economic Perspectives (1991) 97, 97.

41 See North (1990) 33; North (1973).

42 North (1981) 3.

transparent framework of rules and institutions for the conduct of private and public business'.[43]

'History and recent experience', then-Bank president James Wolfensohn explained in 1999, have 'taught us that development is not *just* about getting the right economic and technical inputs. It is also about the underlying, institutional environment: the rules and customs that determine how these inputs are used'.[44]

In contrast to an earlier conviction that the state was the source of all developmental problems, the state was now 'the key institution to ensure that the market functions properly'.[45] But if at first blush this seemed at odds with earlier neoliberal convictions, it was in fact entirely of-a-piece with neoliberalism: the state, if not inherently venal, still existed solely to facilitate 'private businesses and individuals'. In Wolfensohn's words, the successful developmental state will 'set rules underpinning private transactions' and 'enforce the rule of law to underpin market transactions'.[46]

If (market-facilitating) institutions were now at the fore of development thinking, law and *legal* institutions were awarded primacy. As Wolfensohn wrote in a memorandum to the Bank's board, management, and staff in 1999:

> A government must ensure that it has an effective system of property, contract, labor, bankruptcy, commercial codes, personal rights laws and other elements of a comprehensive legal system that is effectively, impartially and clearly administered by a well-functioning, impartial and honest judicial and legal system.[47]

Having attributed the failure of SAPs and shock therapy to the lack of a suitable institutional environment, the IFIs now increasingly invoked the rule of law, and legal institutions more generally, to further deflect criticism of neoliberal policies. This was particularly apparent in the aftermath of the Asian Financial Crisis of 1997. Critical observers identified the rapid and unrestrained financial liberalisation and deregulation of economies under World Bank guidance as an important antecedent to the crisis.[48]

43 World Bank, Governance: the World Bank's Experience (World Bank, 1994) vii.

44 Ibid (emphasis added).

45 Harrison (2004) 19–20.

46 Ibid.

47 W.P. Ofosu-Amaah, 'Legal and Judicial Reform in Developing Countries: Reflections on World Bank Experience', 8 Law & Business Review of the Americas (2002) 556, quoting Memorandum from James D. Wolfensohn to the Board, Management, and Staff of the World Bank, 'A Proposal for a Comprehensive Development Framework: A Discussion Draft', 21 January 1999.

48 See Ha-Joon Chang, 'The Hazard of Moral Hazard: Untangling the Asian Crisis', 28 World Development (2000) 775, as well as various articles in 22 Cambridge Journal of Economics (1998).

When the crisis hit, however, the Bank quickly denied any connection; if a lesson was to be drawn, it was of the importance of a strong rule of law. In its 2002 report, the Bank's Legal Vice Presidency noted:

> One of the critical lessons from the East Asian financial crisis and the collapse of some of the Eastern European transition economies in the 1990s was that, *without the rule of law, economic growth ... can be neither sustainable nor equitable.*[49]

Similarly, in its 2004 report, the Vice Presidency insisted that '[t]he Asian financial crisis ... vividly illustrated that economic growth without the firm foundation of effective laws and legal institutions was vulnerable and unsustainable'.[50]

Neoliberal legality

What exactly did the World Bank and other development thinkers mean by their invocation of law as a necessary foundation for economic growth? Which legal institutions, specifically, did they understand as central to sustainable development? The emerging consensus about law's role in development was summarised succinctly by Posner in his *World Bank Research Observer* article: protection of private property and enforcement of contract as law's *raison d'être.* 'Legal reform is an important part of the modernization process of poor countries', he explained, 'but the focus of such reform should be on creating substantive and procedurally efficient rules of contract and property'. Other concerns of liberal lawyers – 'a first-class judiciary or an extensive system of civil liberties' – could wait.[51]

Posner had developed this view along with his fellow theorists in the Law and Economics movement (discussed further in Chapter 5). Like the economists who embraced law within a 'new institutional' approach to development, the Law and Economics scholars began with the same assumption, articulated perhaps most clearly by Gary Becker, that all systematic behaviour is rational and economic. North and other representatives of the NIE had argued not only that the economy rests on an institutional foundation, but also that the development and structure of those institutions should be understood as the efficient response to rational individuals' concern with information and transaction costs. Already, then, in the NIE was the view that the assumptions and methodology

49 World Bank, Legal and Judicial Reform: Observations, Experiences and Approach of the Legal Vice Presidency (World Bank, 2002) 1 (emphasis added).

50 World Bank Legal Vice Presidency, Initiatives in Legal and Judicial Reform (World Bank, 2004) 2.

51 Posner (1998) 9.

of *economic analysis* could be generalised and extended to treat institutional problems *beyond* the market economy.[52]

From this starting point, it was an easy step to also analyse non-market phenomena as if they were the consequence of market transactions carried out by optimising individuals. In the realm of politics this took the form of public choice theory, which posits the idea that politics and political actors can be reduced to, and modelled based on, assumptions of self interest, exchange, and individualism.[53] Ultimately, the extension of an economic analysis to non-economic social intercourse and treatment of the social 'as if it were or could be akin to perfectly working markets'[54] enables proponents of this view the opportunity to explain a broad range of non-market transactions using economic theory. In this world view, which is discussed throughout this book, economics can be used to explain the entire spectrum of non-market individual behaviour including marriage, education, suicide, and the environment.

And of course law. Coase, in his 1960 article, 'The Problem of Social Cost', had already elevated efficiency as a guiding concern for legal analysis.[55] But like others in the wake of the NIE, the Law and Economics scholars took this further, building upon the methodological starting point that all human behaviour can be explained as the product of individual agents making rational, utility-maximising decisions, based on a stable set of preferences. Legal rules, on this view, are evaluated with reference solely to a calculation of alternative efficiency outcomes. On this approach, the role of law is the facilitation of utility-maximising exchange and optimal market allocation; law consists not in socially constitutive norms but as a mere concomitant to market forces.[56] Low transaction costs, secure property rights, enforceable contracts, and economically efficient regulations become the sole criteria for evaluating the law.

52 Fine and Milonakis describe the extension of economic rationality from the market economy to all areas of social life as a manifestation of 'economics imperialism'. Ben Fine and Dimitris Milonakis, From Economics Imperialism to Freakonomics: The Shifting Boundaries between Economics and Other Social Sciences (Routledge, 2009). On economics imperialism, see also Uskali Mäki, 'Symposium on Explanations and Social Ontology 2: Explanatory Ecumenism and Economics Imperialism', 18 Economics and Philosophy (2002) 235.

53 See, e.g., James Buchanan, 'Politics without Romance: A Sketch of Positive Public Choice Theory and Its Normative Implications', in James Buchanan and Robert Tollison (eds), The Theory of Public Choice – II (University of Michigan Press, 1984) 11; Richard McKenzie and Gordon Tullock, The New World of Economics: Explorations into the Human Experience (R.D. Irwin, 1978).

54 Fine and Milonakis (2009) 12.

55 Coase (1960).

56 I have written about this reductionism in Tor Krever, 'Calling Power to Reason?', 62 New Left Review (2010) 141.

In the context of development thinking, IFI policymakers have adopted this preoccupation with 'the inviolability of private property and the entrenchment of universally-accepted contractarian market regulations'.[57] 'Where private property rights are not protected', Wolfensohn explained already in 1997, 'and where contracts are not enforced predictably, or where judicial enforcement is unreliable, the private sector does not believe that the state will enforce the rules of the game' and '[i]nvestment suffers because entrepreneurs choose not to commit resources in highly uncertain and volatile environments'.[58] Law, it quickly became clear, was essential merely insofar as it creates 'the incentive structure to which economic agents respond' and facilitates the private sector's 'ability to function'.[59]

More recently, the World Bank's Legal Vice Presidency similarly explained that legal institutions 'engender investment and jobs' by providing an 'environment conducive to economic activities'.[60] For instance, secure property rights and enforceable contracts – inevitably the first legal institutions cited – enable individuals to 'take opportunities in business, commerce and other activities'.[61] In providing the rule of law, the state may thus 'empower private individuals to contribute to economic development by confidently engaging in business, investments and other transactions'.[62] An independent and credible judiciary is similarly important for its market-enhancing role, able to ensure enforcement of private contracts and restrain government arbitrariness.[63] As Ibrahim Shihata, World Bank Vice President and General Counsel, observed, 'experience has clearly demonstrated the quintessential role of law in development and, especially, the need for the rule of law and for well-functioning judicial institutions'. Why? The rule of law, he explained, 'creates certainty and predictability; it leads to lower transaction costs, greater access to capital, and the establishment of level playing fields'. Moreover, Shihata opined, 'worldwide experience confirms the importance to rapid and sustainable development of the clarification and protection of property rights, the

57 Harrison (2004) 122; see also Alain Supiot, Homo Juridicus: On the Anthropological Function of the Law (Verso, 2007) 78–109.

58 James D. Wolfensohn, Foreword to World Bank, World Development Report 1997: The State in a Changing World (World Bank, 1997) 36.

59 Ibid. 32.

60 World Bank (2002) 3.

61 Ibid. 2.

62 Ibid.

63 The law's market-facilitating role was foreshadowed in Bank reports in the 1990s. See, e.g., World Bank, Governance and Development (World Bank, 1992) 37, which argued for the importance of contract enforcement 'for conducting efficient private economic activities'.

enforcement of contractual obligations, and the enactment and application of rigorous regulatory regimes'.[64]

Contemporary mainstream development thinking is now dominated by talk of legal institutions. Law now provides a vocabulary for policymaking, but in the new development vernacular, law's role in the developmental process remains narrowly conceived, undergirding the same assumptions as earlier forms of neoliberal thinking: individual entrepreneurship remains the engine of growth; the role of the state must be limited to facilitating the operation of a system of *laissez faire* markets. As Wydick explains, 'to provide an incentive for exchange, people have to be confident in the contractual promises of their reciprocating partners'.[65] Without such confidence, transactions will not happen. Thus, legal institutions such as 'contract law, property rights, and civil courts inspire confidence by ensuring that partners on the other side of a transaction keep their promises'.[66]

The growth of justice-sector 'reform' projects to bring developing countries' laws and legal institutions in line with 'international standards' has given rise to a veritable industry over the past two decades. The neoliberal view of law's relationship with development informs many such projects, with many concerned primarily with securing private property and entrenching contractarian market relations. Only few contain 'access to justice' components.[67]

Efforts to produce quantitative indicators measuring the quality of national legislation and legal institutions – scholarly or otherwise – are also characteristic. For example, the World Bank Institute's Worldwide Governance Indicators (WGIs), updated annually under the title *Governance Matters*,[68] collect data on over 200 jurisdictions measuring six dimensions of governance since 1996. Data are aggregated to create measures of six dimensions of governance, including the 'rule of law'. This measure seeks to capture

64 Ibrahim F.I. Shihata, 'Judicial Reform in Developing Countries and the Role of the World Bank', in Malcolm Rowat, Waleed H. Malik, and Maria Dakolias (eds), Judicial Reform in Latin America and the Caribbean (World Bank, 1995) 13, 13.

65 B. Wydick, Games in Economic Development (Cambridge University Press, 2008) 149.

66 Ibid.

67 A 2007 study reported that of some 555 World Bank-supported law reform projects, the majority were focused on the development of legal institutions for a market economy, with only 40 including 'access to justice' components. Victoria Harris, 'Consolidating Ideology in Law? Legal and Judicial Reform Programmes at the World Bank', Bretton Woods Project, 25 July 2007, available at www.brettonwoodsproject.org/art-554671.

68 See, e.g., D. Kaufmann, A. Kraay and P. Zoido-Lobatón, 'Governance Matters', World Bank Policy Research Working Paper No. 2196 (1999); D. Kaufmann, A. Kraay and M. Mastruzzi, 'Governance Matters VIII: Aggregate and Individual Governance Indicators 1996–2008', World Bank Policy Research Working Paper No. 4978 (2009).

> perceptions of the extent to which agents have confidence in and abide by the rules of society, and in particular the quality of contract enforcement, property rights, the police, and the courts, as well as the likelihood of crime and violence.[69]

In reality, however, the WGIs simply reproduce the neoliberal vision of law, gauging primarily perceptions of the efficacy of business-facilitating legal institutions. Alternative conceptions of the rule of law might have privileged institutional features providing for equality before the law, the uniform application of laws to all individuals irrespective of commercial status, the existence of clear, consistent, and publicly promulgated legal rules, or any of the other institutions commonly associated with liberal legal thought. Alternatively, they might have approximated a 'thick' conception of the rule of law, concerned with institutions protecting political liberties and human rights, ensuring democracy, or entrenching political moral concepts of justice and fairness. Such conceptions are of course, in their own ways, equally problematic. But the point is that the WGIs, like the new developmental discourse generally, reproduce a distinctively neoliberal legality: the rule of law consists in those legal institutions which provide the predictability required for private commerce and market-based business activity, while acting as a constraint on a predatory, property-appropriating state.

Like the WGIs, the Bank's annual *Doing Business* reports similarly compile 'objective measures' of laws and regulations across countries.[70] The specific features of the legal system that the project seeks to assess include, for instance, the ease of starting a business, employing workers, enforcing a contract, obtaining credit, and protecting investors.[71] The vision of law reflected in these indicators is again one which privileges (private) individual business activity as the animating concern of law and legal regulation: high scores for security of private property and facilitation of business activity, low scores for labour protection or other 'inefficiencies'.[72]

69 Kaufmann et al. (2009) 4.

70 World Bank, Doing Business 2013: Smarter Regulations for Small and Medium-Size Enterprises (World Bank, 2013) v. The original 2004 report included data on only five areas of law in 133 countries.

71 For example, Doing Business 2010 included the following areas: (1) starting a business, (2) obtaining licences, (3) employing workers, (4) enforcing a contract, (5) obtaining credit, (6) closing a business, (7) registering property, (8) protecting investors, (9) paying taxes, and (10) trading across borders. The most recent report, Doing Business 2013, includes: (1) starting a business, (2) dealing with construction permits, (3) getting electricity, (4) registering property, (5) getting credit, (6) protecting investors, (7) paying taxes, (8) trading across borders, (9) enforcing contracts, (10) resolving insolvency, and (11) employing workers. See World Bank, Doing Business 2010: Reforming Through Difficult Times (World Bank, 2009).

72 For a detailed discussion of legal indicators in development thinking, see Tor Krever, 'Quantifying Law: Legal Indicator Projects and the Reproduction of Neoliberal Common Sense', 34(2) Third World Quarterly (2013) 131.

In short, the neoliberal view of law understands it as merely a platform for individual productivity, facilitative of the private sector and the market. It follows that if the turn to law in mainstream development thinking appeared at first blush a break from earlier neoliberal policymaking, in reality it reflects much greater continuity.

The free market and individual entrepreneurialism remain the privileged agents of growth. In embracing law as a priority for development and promoting legal reform, policymakers have seized on a particular conception of law, neoliberal legality. And its diffusion under IFI tutelage amounts to what Boaventura de Sousa Santos has termed 'neoliberal legal globalization'.[73]

The new legal development policymakers adopt the vernacular of the NIE and Law and Economics movements in lieu of the explicit binary state-market dichotomy of neoclassical theory, but policy prescriptions such as liberalisation and privatisation remain unchanged, even bolstered. Even while opining about the importance of the law in supporting markets, the World Bank's Legal Vice Presidency celebrates the era of SAP-led policies: 'The first generation of "neoliberal" programs ... helped move the global economy to the much more open and dynamic stage we see today.'[74] Some such programmes were admittedly unsuccessful due to the failure to establish the requisite legal support: 'Privatization without having in place a legal and regulatory framework beforehand resulted in the opaque transfer of ownership, corruption, and dissipation of assets.'[75] But the programme itself – privatisation or otherwise – remains unquestioned. The core policy proposals of the Washington consensus – trade liberalisation, privatisation, financial liberalisation, strict inflation control, etc. – remain central to the agenda. Below the surface of rhetorical flourishes, neoliberalism remains hostile towards government: the integration of world markets is necessarily tied to the atrophying of the state; an unfettered global market will lead to economic growth; and government or state interference in that market will be inherently counterproductive and inhibit the workings of the market.

Neoliberalism and political closure

The grafting of law on late development theory has had significant implications not only for economic theory but also for legal theorising. Under the neoliberal view, the law's value – for economic development, but also more generally – lies in its ability to provide a stable investment

73 Boaventura de Sousa Santos, Toward a New Legal Common Sense: Law, Globalization and Emancipation (LexisNexis, 2002) 314.

74 World Bank (2002) 17.

75 Ibid. 4.

environment and the predictability necessary for markets to operate. Such a view orients representations and conceptions of the law to its effect on the market-based business activity of individual economic agents.

When understood in the narrow terms of neoliberal legality, the promotion of legal reform and the rule of law as a central component of development policy is attractive to neoliberals precisely because it helps reproduce and embed social relations of the free market and a belief that development is predicated on individual entrepreneurial activity. But neoliberal legality should be of concern to critics of neoliberalism not only because of its ideological serviceability. It not only undergirds continued neoliberal assumptions about development, but it also risks obfuscating the role that law has played in historical development experiences. As discussed in Chapter 8, by uncritically rehearsing a functionalist, market-facilitating view of law, its champions naturalise those legal institutions and forms distinctive to modern Western society, hiding their contingent character and mystifying the social relations from which they arise. Neoliberal legality encourages a process-driven deployment of law as an objective, non-controversial technique – the disinterested application of technical principles to facilitate an efficient outcome with law as a neutral platform for individual productivity.

As elaborated throughout this volume, such an approach deflects attention from the political character of the law and its significant distributional consequences, foreclosing the law as a site of political contestation. Policy-making – about, say, legislation or regulation or the inviolability of property rights – shifts from the political domain, the site of deliberation and choice, to the domain of technical expertise. Political questions about justice, equity, and distribution become mere technical questions; they become the subject of institutional and bureaucratic practice and 'sink into the background'.[76] Neoliberal legal institutions and arrangements become naturalised, no longer understood as socially produced but rather fixed and immutable, technical necessities or, as one World Bank official revealingly puts it, the 'basic requirement … for a modern state'.[77] Alternative institutions or social arrangements are pushed beyond our line of sight or even our imagination.

The result, to paraphrase Susan Marks, is that we take the legal world for granted and treat it as an 'objective domain' rather than one shaped

76 David Kennedy, 'Challenging Expert Rule: The Politics of Global Governance', 27 Sydney Law Review (2005) 14. Honor Brabazon, 'Juridification and its Discontents: How Neoliberal Legality has Reframed Dissent and How Some Social Movements Are Responding', Understanding Neoliberal Legality Conference: Perspectives on the Use of Law By, For, and Against the Neoliberal Project, University of Oxford, UK, 21 June 2013.

77 Ibrahim F.I. Shihata, The World Bank in a Changing World: Selected Essays (M. Nijhoff, 1991) 85.

through political struggle.[78] Law is not the product of political and ideological contest – such as the conflict between customary norms and the extension of capitalist property relations in pre-industrial Britain.[79] Nor on this view can legal arrangements such as the labour regulations central to the contemporary welfare state be understood as a historically contingent balance between competing political interests – the product of struggle and negotiation between capital and labour. Rather, they are simply inefficiencies, impediments to a technically mandated and universally applicable rule of law, the adoption of which is not a decision grounded in political choice, but a neutral, technical imperative.

Political participation and domestic contestation in legal policy, needless to say, is thus narrowed or even foreclosed. National legislation is replaced by 'technical' norms – 'indicators of healthy management as defined by experts in international economic and financial institutions' – while government by locally accountable, elected representatives gives way to 'governance' by appointed experts, who answer to unseen masters.[80] Indeed, one commentator sees in neoliberal legality the dissolution of the state *tout court*: the market is advanced as 'the *Grundnorm* of every national regulatory order; a meta-juridical principle that must be imposed on every aspect of social life in every country, leading eventually to the withering-away of the state'.[81]

Conclusion

Following the financial crash of 2008, many pronounced the end of neoliberalism. Others proclaimed a new era of government intervention in, and regulation of, the economy. Still others, however, were less sanguine. In a recent intervention, Pierre Dardot and Christian Laval argue that '[f]ar from impairing neoliberal policies, the crisis led to their dramatic *reinforcement*, in the shape of austerity plans put in place by states that were increasingly active in promoting the logic of competition in financial markets'.[82] Dardot and Laval note the seeming paradox between the 'relative discredit surrounding the ideology of laissez-faire today' and the fact that neoliberalism prevails

> more than ever as a normative system possessed of a certain efficiency – that is, the capacity to direct from within the actual practice of

78 Marks (2000) 22.

79 See E.P. Thompson, Customs in Common (New Press, 1992); Peter Linebaugh, The London Hanged: Crime and Civil Society in the Eighteenth Century (Penguin, 1991).

80 Krever (2010) 145 citing Supiot (2007).

81 Alain Supiot, 'Law and Labour', 39 New Left Review (2006) 109, 115.

82 Pierre Dardot and Christian Laval, The New Way of the World: On Neoliberal Society, trans. Gregory Elliott (Verso, 2013) 1 (emphasis in original).

governments, enterprises and, in addition to them, millions of people who are not necessarily conscious of the fact.[83]

For Dardot and Laval, the paradox is resolved with the recognition that neoliberalism is not simply a negative ideology, one that advances a programmatic attack on regulation and state institutions. Rather, '[i]t is also *productive* of certain kinds of social relations, certain ways of living, certain subjectivities', enjoining all to engage in generalised competition and 'align[ing] social relations with the model of the market'.[84] The further global diffusion of neoliberal legality through the field of development is one example of neoliberalism's reproduction as a productive system – a 'rationality' in Dardot and Laval's words. Even as the neoliberalism of structural adjustment, with its state-market dichotomy, is challenged, neoliberal legality is entrenching itself further, reproducing, if not the ideology of *laissez faire*, the very same norms of generalised competition and utility maximisation and the individualisation of social relations that undergirded neoliberalism's earlier ideological incarnations. Thanks to neoliberal legality, neoliberalism is alive and well, its perceived legitimacy – and even necessity – given new life.

References

Anderson, Perry. 'Renewals', 1 *New Left Review* (2000) 1, 6.

Berkowitz, Daniel, Katharina Pistor, and Jean-Francois Richard, 'The Transplant Effect', 51 *American Journal of Comparative Law* (2003) 163, 163.

Brabazon, Honor. 'Juridification and its Discontents: How Neoliberal Legality has Reframed Dissent and How Some Social Movements Are Responding', Understanding Neoliberal Legality Conference: Perspectives on the Use of Law By, For, and Against the Neoliberal Project, University of Oxford, UK, 21 June 2013.

Buchanan, James. 'Politics without Romance: A Sketch of Positive Public Choice Theory and Its Normative Implications', in James Buchanan and Robert Tollison (eds), *The Theory of Public Choice – II* (University of Michigan Press, 1984) 11.

Burg, Elliot M. 'Law and Development: A Review of the Literature & a Critique of "Scholars in Self-Estrangement"' 25 *American Journal of Comparative Law* (1977) 492, 496–7.

Chang, Ha-Joon. 'The Hazard of Moral Hazard: Untangling the Asian Crisis', 28 *World Development* (2000) 775.

Coase, Ronald. 'The Nature of the Firm', 4 *Economica* (1937).

Coase, Ronald. 'The Problem of Social Cost', 3 *Journal of Law and Economics* (1960).

Coase, Ronald. 'The New Institutional Economics', 88(2) *The American Economic Review* (1998) 72.

83 Ibid. 2–3.
84 Ibid. 3 (emphasis in original).

Dardot, Pierre and Christian Laval. *The New Way of the World: On Neoliberal Society*, trans. Gregory Elliott (Verso, 2013) 1.

de Sousa Santos, Boaventura. *Toward a New Legal Common Sense: Law, Globalization and Emancipation* (LexisNexis, 2002) 314.

Easterly, William. 'What Did Structural Adjustment Adjust? The Association of Policies and Growth with Repeated IMF and World Bank Adjustment Loans', 76 *Journal of Development Economics* (2005) 1, 2–3.

Faux, Jeff and Larry Mishel. 'Inequality and the Global Economy', in Will Hutton and Anthony Giddens (eds), *On the Edge: Living with Global Capitalism* (Jonathan Cape, 2000) 93.

Fine, Ben and Dimitris Milonakis. *From Economics Imperialism to Freakonomics: The Shifting Boundaries between Economics and Other Social Sciences* (Routledge, 2009).

Gowan, Peter. *The Global Gamble* (Verso, 1999) 187–242.

Harris, Victoria. 'Consolidating Ideology in Law? Legal and Judicial Reform Programmes at the World Bank', *Bretton Woods Project*, 25 July 2007, available at www.brettonwoodsproject.org/art-554671.

Harrison, Graham. *The World Bank and Africa: the Construction of Governance States* (Routledge, 2004) 18.

Harvey, David. *A Brief History of Neoliberalism* (Oxford University Press, 2005) 2–4.

Hoff, Karla and Joseph E. Stiglitz. 'After the Big Bang? Obstacles to the Emergence of the Rule of Law in Post-Communist Societies', National Bureau of Economic Research, Paper No. 9282 (2002) 7.

Kapur, Devesh, John P. Lewis, and Richard Webb. 'The Bank of the 1950s', in Devesh Kapur, John P. Lewis and Richard Webb (eds), *The World Bank: Its First Half Century*, vol. 1 (Brookings Institution, 1997) 85, 109–10.

Kaufmann, D., A. Kraay, and P. Zoido-Lobatón, 'Governance Matters', World Bank Policy Research Working Paper No. 2196 (1999).

Kaufmann, D., A. Kraay, and M. Mastruzzi. 'Governance Matters VIII: Aggregate and Individual Governance Indicators 1996–2008', World Bank Policy Research Working Paper No. 4978 (2009).

Kennedy, David. 'Challenging Expert Rule: The Politics of Global Governance', 27 *Sydney Law Review* (2005) 14.

Kennedy, David. 'The "Rule of Law", Political Choices, and Development Common Sense', in David M. Trubek and Alvaro Santos (eds), *The New Law and Economic Development: A Critical Appraisal* (Cambridge University Press, 2006) 95, 129.

Krever, Tor. 'Calling Power to Reason?', 62 *New Left Review* (2010) 141.

Krever, Tor. 'Quantifying Law: Legal Indicator Projects and the Reproduction of Neoliberal Common Sense', 34(2) *Third World Quarterly* (2013) 131.

Linebaugh, Peter. *The London Hanged: Crime and Civil Society in the Eighteenth Century* (Penguin, 1991).

Mäki, Uskali. 'Symposium on Explanations and Social Ontology 2: Explanatory Ecumenism and Economics Imperialism', 18 *Economics and Philosophy* (2002) 235.

Marks, Susan. *The Riddle of All Constitutions* (Oxford University Press, 2000) 58.

McKenzie, Richard and Gordon Tullock. *The New World of Economics: Explorations into the Human Experience* (R.D. Irwin, 1978).

Merryman, John Henry. 'Comparative Law and Social Change: On the Origins, Style, Decline & Revival of the Law and Development Movement', 25 *American Journal of Comparative Law* (1977) 457, 458.
Milanovic, B. 'The Two Faces of Globalization: Against Globalization as We Know It', 31(4) *World Development* (2003) 667.
Mirowski, Philip and Dieter Plehwe (eds), *The Road from Mont Pèlerin: The Making of the Neoliberal Thought Collective* (Harvard University Press, 2009).
North, Douglas C. *Structure and Change in Economic History* (Norton, 1981).
North, Douglas C. *Institutions, Institutional Change and Economic Performance* (Cambridge University Press, 1990).
North, Douglas C. 'Institutions', 5 *Journal of Economic Perspectives* (1991) 97, 97.
North, Douglas C. and Robert P. Thomas, *The Rise of the Western World: A New Economic History* (Cambridge University Press, 1973).
Ofosu-Amaah, W.P. 'Legal and Judicial Reform in Developing Countries: Reflections on World Bank Experience', 8 *Law & Business Review of the Americas* (2002) 556, quoting Memorandum from James D. Wolfensohn to the Board, Management, and Staff of the World Bank, 'A Proposal for a Comprehensive Development Framework: A Discussion Draft', 21 January 1999.
Panitch, Leo and Sam Gindin. 'Superintending Global Capital', 35 *New Left Review* (2005) 101, 110.
Pashukanis, E. *Law and Marxism: A General Theory* (Ink Links, 1978).
Posner, Richard A. 'Creating a Legal Framework for Economic Development', 13(1) *The World Bank Observer* (1998) 1, 2.
Prebisch, Raúl. *The Economic Development of Latin America and its Principal Problems* (UN Department of Economic Affairs, 1950).
Robinson, William I. *Promoting Polyarchy: Globalization, US Intervention, and Hegemony* (Cambridge University Press, 1996) 339.
Sachs, Jeffrey. *Poland's Jump to the Market Economy* (MIT Press, 1993) xiii.
Shihata, Ibrahim F.I. *The World Bank in a Changing World: Selected Essays* (M. Nijhoff, 1991) 85.
Shihata, Ibrahim F.I. 'Judicial Reform in Developing Countries and the Role of the World Bank', in Malcolm Rowat, Waleed H. Malik, and Maria Dakolias (eds), *Judicial Reform in Latin America and the Caribbean* (World Bank, 1995) 13, 13.
Stern, Nicholas and Francisco Ferreira, 'The World Bank as "Intellectual Actor"', in Kapur *et al.* (eds) (1997) vol. 2, 523, 524.
Stiglitz, Joseph E. 'Whither Reform? Ten Years of the Transition', Address at the World Bank Annual Bank Conference on Development Economics, 28–30 April 1999.
Supiot, Alain. 'Law and Labour', 39 *New Left Review* (2006) 109, 115.
Supiot, Alain. *Homo Juridicus: On the Anthropological Function of the Law* (Verso, 2007) 78–109.
Taylor, Marcus. 'Responding to Neoliberalism in Crisis: Discipline and Empowerment in the World Bank's New Development Agenda', in Paul Zarembka and Susanne Soederberg (eds), *Neoliberalism in Crisis, Accumulation, and Rosa Luxemburg's Legacy* (Emerald, 2004) 3, 13.
Thompson, E.P. *Customs in Common* (New Press, 1992).
Trubek, David M. and Marc Galanter. 'Scholars in Self-Estrangement: Some

Reflections on the Crisis in Law and Development Studies in the United States', *Wisconsin Law Review* (1974) 1062.

United Nations Development Programme. *Human Development Report 1992* (Oxford University Press, 1992) 34.

Wade, Robert. 'Japan, The World Bank, and the Art of Paradigm Maintenance: The East Asian Miracle in Political Perspective', I/217 *New Left Review* (1996) 3.

Wade, Robert. 'The Ringmaster of Doha', 25 *New Left Review* (2004) 146, 152.

Walpen, Bernhard. *Die offenen Feinde und ihre Gesellschaft: Eine hegemonietheoretische Studie zur Mont Pèlerin Society* (VSA-Verlag, 2004).

Wiener, Alexander. 'Law and Economic Development', 40 *University of Detroit Law Journal* (1962–63) 510, 512, quoting letter from Doris R. Eliason, Office of Information, IBRD, to Alexander L. Wiener, Jr., 15 March 1962.

Williamson, John. 'What Washington Means by Policy Reform', in John Williamson (ed.), *Latin American Adjustment: How Much has Happened* (Institute for International Economics, 1990) 7, 7.

Wolfensohn, James D. Foreword to World Bank, *World Development Report 1997: The State in a Changing World* (World Bank, 1997) 36.

World Bank. *Accelerated Development in Sub-Saharan Africa: An Agenda for Action* (World Bank, 1981).

World Bank. *World Development Report 1987: Barriers to Adjustment and Growth in the World Economy, Industrialization and Foreign Trade, World Development Indicators* (World Bank, 1987) 38.

World Bank. *Governance and Development* (World Bank, 1992).

World Bank. *Governance: the World Bank's Experience* (World Bank, 1994).

World Bank. *Legal and Judicial Reform: Observations, Experiences and Approach of the Legal Vice Presidency* (World Bank, 2002) 1.

World Bank. *Doing Business 2010: Reforming Through Difficult Times* (World Bank, 2009).

World Bank. *Doing Business 2013: Smarter Regulations for Small and Medium-Size Enterprises* (World Bank, 2013).

World Bank Legal Vice Presidency. *Initiatives in Legal and Judicial Reform* (World Bank, 2004) 2.

Wydick, B. *Games in Economic Development* (Cambridge University Press, 2008) 149.

Chapter 2

Neoliberalism and economic sovereignty

Property, contracts, and foreign investment relations

Nicolás M. Perrone

Introduction

The law constitutes our societies in many ways. Broadly speaking, it articulates core purposes, including material purposes, and defines the means to achieve these purposes.[1] Neoliberal legality can be understood as the laws that articulate the purposes of wealth maximisation and internal social order, and more importantly, that provide only certain means to achieve these goals. These means are legal techniques based on the bilateralisation of relations and microeconomic rationality, two core disciplines of a neoliberal governmentality.[2] Given that the idea of governmentality is tightly related to the control and use of resources, any legal account of a neoliberal governmentality also needs to consider the particular legal techniques that actors use to control resources. The objective of this contribution is to explore the proprietary and contractual techniques that serve to allocate control over resources in the context of neoliberal legality, using foreign investment relations as a case study. This chapter seeks to examine how the dominant legal techniques make possible 'the impossibility of the existence of an economic sovereign'.[3]

The distinction between private and public law is as persistent in the study of the law as it is inadequate to capture the interconnectedness of the legal order. One of these basic interconnections is between private property and sovereignty. As Cohen has shown, stronger private property rights mean less sovereignty and vice versa.[4] The contribution of legal realism in the 1920s and 1930s was not only to show this correlation, but also to suggest that the relationship between private and public authority

1 Annelise Riles, 'Property as Legal Knowledge: Means and Ends', 10 The Journal of the Royal Anthropological Institute (2004): 775–95.

2 Michel Foucault, The Birth of Biopolitics: Lectures at the Collège de France, 1978–1979 (Chippenham, UK: Palgrave Macmillan, 2010).

3 Ibid., at 283.

4 Morris Cohen, 'Property and Sovereignty', 13(8) Cornell Law Quarterly (1927–1928): 8–30.

can be adjusted by regulation, paving the way for state intervention in the economy during the post-war period. The concrete legal basis for a larger public role in the control and use of resources ranged from grand theories, such as the social function of property, to the adjustment of private institutions, like contracts, to the needs of the administration.

This kind of intervention, as Foucault suggests in his work, was incompatible with the neoliberal order that emerged during the 1970s, in which states appeared incapable of carrying out large planning or coordination functions. This premise had important implications for the legal techniques to control and use resources. It was necessary not only to allocate resources to private actors – in fact most industrial resources remained in private hands in the post-war period – but also to ensure that future state activity would be functional to the individual coordination of economic activities. In the neoliberal economic ideal this coordination is not simply a question of increasing corporate ownership to the detriment of state sovereignty, but of facilitating the coordination of an endless number of economic actors. In this context, contracts became the pre-eminent legal technique for neoliberal and neoinstitutional economists,[5] and hierarchies gradually dissolved in large chains of contractual relations, of which global value chains are a paradigmatic example.[6]

This shift from property to contractual techniques of resource control had transformative social implications. The idea of property was tightly connected to the need for individual calculability in the nineteenth century. Property was the means to fulfil this need.[7] Legal realism managed to put property in crisis by showing the indeterminacy and relational character of this legal technique. This implied that there can be many different properties, and that given the important social implications of property this concept cannot be self-referenced.[8] But these two conclusions are at odds with fundamental neoliberal principles, which state that actors should be blind to the social consequences of their actions, and that the coordination of economic activity should be based on market transactions only.[9]

More specifically, the idea of contract can disarticulate state sovereignty in a powerful way. While property is the product of the law, and states can manipulate the law, contracts are the outcome of consent. This means that

5 Oliver Williamson, The Economic Institutions of Capitalism: Firms, Markets, Relational Contracting (London: Collier Macmillan, 1985).

6 Luc Boltanski and Eve Chiapello, The New Spirit of Capitalism (New York: Verso, 2005).

7 Max Weber, 'Parliament and Government in Germany under a New Political Order', in Peter Lassman (Ed.), Weber: Political Writings (Cambridge: Cambridge University Press, 1994), pp. 147–8.

8 Stefano Rodotà, El terrible derecho: estudios sobre la propiedad privada (Madrid: Civitas, 1986).

9 Michel Foucault, above n 2, at 12, 279.

whenever states grant control over resources through contractual techniques, they could be relinquishing sovereign power depending on the interpretation of these contractual commitments. States can contract out sovereignty in ways unthinkable under a property-sovereign paradigm. In this way, contractual techniques can be relevant means for a neoliberal governmentality, promoting private economic coordination and the bilateralisation of economic relations at the same time.

The main argument of this chapter is that the use of contractual legal techniques to define the control and use of resources contributes to the impossibility of an economic sovereign. Contracts and contractualisation, as opposed to property, have historically served to conceal unequal bargaining power and social interconnectedness.[10] The contractualisation of crucial private-public relations reduces the relevance of the social in legal reasoning.

This chapter is organised as follows. The first section examines the use of property and contractual techniques to allocate control over resources. The second section explores the shift from a property to a contractual paradigm using foreign investment relations as a case study. This field is important for my argument because it shows not only the evolution from property to contracts but also the emergence of a particular interpretation of contracts. The final section aims to show that the legal realist critique of property can be extended to contracts that serve to allocate control over resources. This chapter concludes by highlighting a plural understanding of contracts. This could be a first step to push the debate about contracts in a progressive way, as has been done with property, focusing on ideas such as equity and the social function of resources.

Private property, contract, and the control of resources

In the traditional view, private property represents a means to preserve individual freedom: 'A man's house is his castle', said Sir Coke.[11] Private property is in this context a legal technique that serves to prevent the state and other individuals from intervening with the private use of resources. This conception of property, however, was severely criticised by legal realists, who showed that one person's freedom very often represented another person's coercion.[12] Since the 1930s, then, many scholars have

10 Ute Gerhard, Trudie Knijn, and Jane Lewis, 'Contractualization', in Barbara Hobson, Jane Lewis, and Birte Siim, Contested Concepts in Gender and Social Politics (Northampton, MA: Edward Elgar), at 110–11.

11 Cited in Joseph Singer, 'How Property Norms Construct the Externalities of Ownership', in Gregory Alexander and Eduardo Peñalver (Eds), Property and Community (New York: Oxford University Press, 2010), at 59.

12 Robert Hale, 'Coercion and Distribution in a Supposedly Non-Coercive State', 38 Political Science Quarterly (1923): 470–94.

recharacterised property as a relational concept in which the owner is seen together with all other individuals and the state.[13] This conception of property can be further divided between those rights that refer to a static and to a dynamic use of resources. As Rodotà explains, dynamic property is essentially a right to participate in the organisation of economic activities or, in the words of Foucault, in the art of government.[14]

The private individuals who participate in the organisation of resources – who hereinafter I will refer to as investors – see their rights as a means to control resources and ensure profit.[15] This form of control and calculability is quite different from the typical notion of ownership. The traditional premise that property rights serve to exclude others from using resources may not be enough for investors to assert private control against state regulatory interventions. An investor in public utilities may obtain a concession in the water sector, but this entitlement may not be enough to ensure the expected profitability of the business. Some of the issues that may remain out of her control may include the quality of the water and the tariffs. Similarly, another investor in the maquila sector may own the factory and the technology, but his business may still depend on the stability of the taxes to obtain a profit.

These investors can try to resist regulatory change by asserting their private property rights against the state before the courts. They can claim that measures changing the conditions for operating the water concession or the maquila affect their investment-backed expectations. But unless the courts and tribunals adopt a very strong definition of property, the investors may find it difficult to prevail.[16] When planning their business, one could argue, investors should have taken into consideration state regulatory powers. States cannot block the private authority to decide on the use of resources, but they can regulate private property reasonably by narrowing or expanding the potential uses.[17] This premise may sound clear, but it is difficult for courts to determine when state regulation is or is not reasonable. Many property scholars in the United States, in practice, see the field of regulatory takings as a muddle.[18]

13 See, for instance, Bruce Ackerman, Private Property and the Constitution (New Haven, CT and London: Yale University Press), at 27.

14 Stefano Rodotà, above n 8, at 145–56.

15 Richard Swedberg, 'Max Weber's Contribution to the Economic Sociology of Law', 2 Annual Review of Law and Social Science (2006): 61–81.

16 See the discussion of Lucas v South Carolina Coastal Council in Jeremy Waldron, The Rule of Law and the Measure of Property (Cambridge: Cambridge University Press, 2012).

17 Larissa Katz, 'Red Tape and Gridlock', 23(1) Canadian Journal of Law and Jurisprudence (2010): 113–14.

18 Carol Rose, 'Mahon Reconstructed: Why the Takings Issue is Still a Muddle', 57 Southern California Law Review (1984): 561–99.

This is just one of the several expressions of the indeterminacy of private property. The struggle for the control of resources, in particular between investors and states, rarely ends with allocation. As private activity and state regulation become more sophisticated, these legal disputes have overshadowed typical private law cases on property.[19] The main reason for this litigation is that, as opposed to allocation, the scope of private property rights is debatable or even debated. Private property rights are not self-defining.[20] The liberal state shows in this respect an inherent tension or internal contradiction regarding private property. It was conceived to protect private property, but its creation and the sovereign powers granted the state came with a cost for property defenders: the death of natural law and the birth of civil law.[21] Thinking about property as an artefact of the law and state sovereignty entitles states to reshape the scope of ownership to quite large extents, without affecting the private allocation of the rights. It is possible for states to respect private allocation of resources while reshaping market dynamics through state intervention.

Neoliberalism is a response to the possibility of state control of resources, while neoliberal legality represents the means to limit state manipulation of property and fulfil investors' need for calculability. Neoliberalism criticises state authority due to its inefficiency and moral inappropriateness.[22] The neoliberal policies implemented in the 1980s and 1990s were a mixture of privatisations, in both the developed and the developing world, and of a widespread political transformation. The main premise behind this transformation was that economic growth is the best social policy, and that corporations, particularly large multinational corporations (MNCs), are the most efficient actors for growth. Neoliberal reform, in short, redefined the state in market terms ensuring that the remaining public functions are exercised in manners compatible with investor expectations.[23]

The legal dimension of neoliberalism facilitates these goals by promoting legal techniques that block, minimise, or make state intervention excessively expensive. Property and contracts, despite their obvious differences, are legal techniques that can deal with the governance of resources. From a traditional perspective, they look quite different because property rights are pieces of legislation that bind the entire community, while

19 See Charles Donahue Jr, 'The Future of the Concept of Property Predicted from its Past', in Roland Pennock and John Chapman (Eds), Nomos 22: Property (New York: New York University Press, 1980), at 46–55.

20 Joseph Singer, 'Sovereignty and Property', 6(1) Northwestern University Law Review (1991), at 48.

21 Stefano Rodotà, above n 8, at 101–2.

22 Ronald Coase, 'The Problem of Social Cost', 3 Journal of Law and Economics (1960): 1–44; Michel Foucault, above n 2, at 101–21.

23 Ibid., at 131, 172.

contracts are individual agreements whose effects are limited to the parties of the deal.[24] However, when contracts are employed to modify the scope of private property, they have effects well beyond the parties to the agreement. They are no longer the typical *inter-partes* agreements that have few if any implications for other members of the community.[25] On the contrary, these deals are highly political and affect everybody in a community, starting from (but not ending with) the state's authority. The strategy of investors in the neoliberal period is to negotiate and contract with the state specific negative duties in relation to their private ownership.[26] These contractual commitments allow investors to clarify and expand the normal bundle of rights in property in areas such as taxation or environmental regulation.[27]

In his work, Zumbansen describes this use of contracts under neoliberalism as a shift from government to governance. A goal of contractual governance is to liberate investment-state relations from investor-unfriendly regulation.[28] Contracts become a fundamental piece of neoliberal legality or, at least, the means to impose a microeconomic rationale on human relations. A basic premise of neoliberal governmentality is that investors need to be blind to the social consequences of their actions. Contracts are functional to this goal because they are not supposed to create social consequences. The idea of contract assumes that all the relevant information is in the transaction. This is a fundamental premise for any microeconomic rationale of governance in which contracts are just means for coordinating individual actions.

The use of contractual techniques to provide investors with calculability disrupts the idea of government and sovereignty in two fundamental ways. First, it can be much easier for investors to obtain a contract rather than to force the modification of legislation. Passing new environmental legislation may create larger social resistance than signing an agreement to settle an environmental dispute. Second, contractual rules, as opposed to property, are not meant to change through public or democratic mechanisms. The fundamental principle of contracts is *pacta sunt servanda*. Although

24 H.L.A. Hart, 'Are There Any Natural Rights?', 64(2) Philosophical Review (1955), at 185–6; Jeremy Waldron, The Right to Private Property (Oxford: Clarendon Press, 1988), at 106–26.

25 Gregory Alexander and Eduardo Peñalver, An Introduction to Property Theory (Cambridge: Cambridge University Press, 2012), at 2.

26 See International Institute for Sustainable Development, 'Lifting the Lid on Foreign Investment Contracts: The Real Deal for Sustainable Development', 1 Sustainable Markets (2005), at 1–7; Andrea Shemberg, 'Stabilization Clauses and Human Rights', International Finance Corporation and the United Nations Special Representative to the Secretary General on Business and Human Rights (2008), at 17–31.

27 Gregory Alexander and Eduardo Peñalver, above n 25, at 75–6.

28 See Peer Zumbansen, 'The Law of Society: Governance Through Contract', 14(2) Indiana Journal of Global Legal Studies (2007) at 193, 203.

this principle can be subject to different readings, a strict interpretation of *pacta sunt servanda* can disarticulate the authority that a civil conception of property grants to states. This makes possible in the legal field the core of the neoliberal project, which – in the words of Foucault – is a state under the supervision of the market and market transactions.[29]

Putting states under the supervision of markets: the case of foreign investment relations

The control of resources is a question of domestic law according to principles of public and private international law. This presently undisputed premise, at least formally, was a subject of debate when the dominant justifications for private property were found in natural law. Natural property predated the state and clearly exceeded its boundaries. The order emerging from the Westphalian model changed this, consolidating the idea of territorial sovereignty together with the domestic authority to pass laws to govern any resources, in particular, private property laws. The regulation of resources became, as a result, a civil and domestic matter.[30] Despite the strong idea of sovereignty, some disciplines on property protection, based on the natural law ideas of Vitoria and Grotius, continued to be very relevant in the international sphere.[31] The protection of property remained in many ways one of the main variables explaining the evolution of public international law, and, arguably, the erosion of an absolute idea of sovereignty.[32]

Customary international law does not impose property rules on the domestic legal orders. The premise is instead that there are some minimum standards of treatment that states need to respect when regulating foreign-owned private property.[33] These minimum standards have two dimensions. The first, or the minimum standard *stricto sensu*, was consolidated in the mid-1930s in an arbitration between a citizen of the United States and Mexico. This standard prohibits host states from behaving in an egregious, outrageous, shocking, or otherwise extraordinary manner.[34] The second dimension imposes three limitations on any expropriation of foreign investor acquired rights. Expropriations have to be for a public

29 Michel Foucault, above n 2, at 116.

30 Ernst Rabel, The Conflict of Laws: A Comparative Study, Volume 4 (Ann Arbor: University of Michigan Law School), at 7–8, 30.

31 F. García Amador, The Changing Law of International Claims (New York: Oceana Publications, 1984), at 46.

32 Jacob Viner, International Economics: Studies (Glencoe, IL: Free Press, 1951), at 218.

33 Edwin Borchard, 'Minimum Standard of the Treatment of Aliens', 38(4) Michigan Law Review (1940): 445–61.

34 L.F.H. Neer and Pauline Neer (U.S.A.) v. United Mexican States, 15 October 1926, Reports of International Arbitral Awards, Volume IV, at 60–6.

purpose, must not be discriminatory, and require the payment of adequate compensation.

Most of these standards are quite vague and ambiguous and therefore tribunals needed to interpret notions such as egregious and adequate compensation. International customary laws show, on the other hand, that the scope of foreign investor rights is a question of domestic law. The doctrine of acquired rights refers to domestic law as the default rule, and this reference to the law – as opposed to agreements or dealings – shows the importance of the proprietary paradigm in foreign investment relations at least until the 1950s–1960s.[35]

For foreign investors, in other words, international customary law posed similar problems as property in the domestic order. It granted protection against host state misbehaviour, biased domestic tribunals, and inadequate compensations, but it could not ensure foreign investor calculability. Leaving aside the procedural obstacles to launching international claims, these individuals still had to deal with the relevance of domestic laws for the scope of their rights. As explained earlier, host states can use their regulatory authority to intervene in the control of the resources allocated to foreign investors, narrowing or expanding the scope of foreign investor rights. International customary law did not promote absolute property rights, or, at least, it abandoned this idea together with the courts of most countries after the economic crisis of 1930.[36]

A paradigmatic decision in this regard was rendered in 1937 in the *Oscar Chinn* case, where the Permanent Court of International Justice affirmed that:

> The Court, though not failing to recognize the change that had come over Mr. Chinn's financial position, a change which is said to have led him to wind up his transport and shipbuilding businesses, is unable to see in his original position – which was characterized by the possession of customers and the possibility of making a profit – anything in the nature of a genuine vested right. Favourable business conditions and goodwill are transient circumstances, subject to inevitable changes; the interests of transport undertakings may well have suffered as a result of the general trade depression and the measures taken to combat it.[37]

35 F. García-Amador, 'International Responsibility: Fourth Report', International Law Commission, A/CN.4/119, 1959, at 9; Bin Cheng, 'The Rationale of Compensation for Expropriation', Transactions of the Grotius Society, Problems of Public and Private International Law 44, Transactions for the Year 1958–1959 (1958), at 283.

36 Andreas Zimmermann, Karin Oellers-Frahm, Christian Tomuschat, and Christian J. Tams, The Statute of the International Court of Justice: A Commentary (New York: Oxford University Press, 2006), at 68.

37 The Oscar Chinn Case (Britain v. Belgium), PCIJ, 1937, (Ser. A/B), No. 70, at 88.

The interpretation of acquired rights did not produce a large doctrinal debate until the decolonisation process. In that context, the former colonial powers claimed that, by virtue of international law, newly independent states were limited to modifying domestic property laws, which they inherited precisely from the former colonial empires.[38] For these states, sovereignty exists within international law, including the limitations to state authority to abrogate acquired rights. The newly independent nations responded with a large and coordinated attempt regarding the content of international law, struggling for their economic sovereignty as well as their right to manage their natural resources freely. These efforts were certainly not in vain. The General Assembly passed two fundamental resolutions, which for most of the literature constituted the basis of a new, although short-lived, international economic order.[39]

A broader look at this period, however, shows that parallel developments were undermining most of the efforts of the newly independent countries. These developments had much less to do with public international law principles and more with private legal techniques, in particular contracts and the idea of transnational law.[40] The claim of economic sovereignty had, as an important pillar, the social implications at stake. Sovereignty is about the people who live in each country; it is about self-determination and their ways of life. Public international law, in other words, was discussing the question at a macro-level, in which powerful ideas like sovereignty and decolonisation were confronting other international law principles. The strategy of foreign investors, who had similar interests to former colonial powers, was to oppose economic sovereignty with different ideas, essentially those of contracts: *pacta sunt servanda* and equality. The legal claim changed dramatically as a result, shifting from the respect of acquired rights according to domestic law to the enforcement of contractual rights emerging from freely entered agreements.

At first, this argument was at least debatable because it remained unclear whether state breaches of contracts could constitute a breach of international law. This was, for instance, the position of the International Court of Justice in the Anglo Iranian Oil Co. Case in 1952. To the extent that domestic law governed state contracts, these agreements were subject to changes in the same way as private property. The focus on domestic laws blurred the fundamental importance of the *pacta sunt servanda* principle. If the host state changed the laws applicable to the contract in order to justify its non-compliance, it could be said that the *pacta sunt servanda*

38 Antony Anghie, Imperialism, Sovereignty and the Making of International Law (New York: Cambridge University Press, 2004), at 213–14.

39 Ibid., at 211.

40 Ibid., at 223.

principle remained unaffected.[41] This view was additionally supported by the flexible interpretation of this principle by domestic courts, which was dominant during the post-war period as a result of Keynesian policies.[42]

As Anghie brilliantly describes, despite these antecedents, the status of foreign investor contractual rights suffered a fundamental transformation in the 1960s and 1970s. Foreign investors began challenging the breach of state contracts in international as opposed to domestic law. The thesis that eventually prevailed in a series of arbitrations involving Arab nations was that oil concessions were economic development contracts and, as such, were subject to international and transnational law. For these arbitral tribunals, these contracts were internationalised because of their developmental purpose. It was not only contracts, then, but also a particular interpretation of contracts based on ideas such as transnational law, that became the means to allocate control over domestic resources to foreign investors.[43]

Along these lines, a number of arbitral tribunals established that foreign investor rights are not susceptible to amendment by domestic law. In this view, contracts, such as concessions, grant rights to foreign investors that states cannot extinguish at a later stage.[44] Annihilating contractual rights through new laws or regulations constitutes confiscatory measures comparable to the full abrogation of property rights. The main justification for this position was that the use of state sovereign authority to modify the terms of the contracts is a form of arbitrary behaviour.[45] This interpretation of concessions, however, overlooked the post-colonial scenario, ignoring the conditions in which these contracts were signed, the unequal bargaining powers, and the imperial past.

For Anghie, this shows the continuation of colonial legal patterns in international law well after the decolonisation process.[46] The principle of sovereignty was disarticulated by the internationalisation of contracts signed between newly independent governments and foreign investors. This interpretation, however, was promoted for the periphery only. Developed countries, on the contrary, rejected the application of this doctrine to their own nations. This attitude was as hypocritical as the present

41 Fritz Mann, 'State Contracts and State Responsibility', 54 American Journal of International Law (1960), at 580–1. See also R.Y. Jennings, 'State Contracts in International Law', 37 British Yearbook of International Law (1961), at 161, 176–7.

42 Georges Langrod, 'Administrative Contracts: A Comparative Study', 4(3) The American Journal of Comparative Law (1955): 325–64; Alan Mewett, 'The Theory of Government Contracts', 5 McGill Law Journal (1958): 222–46.

43 Antony Anghie, above n 38, at 235–44.

44 Stephen Schwebel, 'On Whether the Breach by a State of a Contract with an Alien is a Breach of International Law', in Justice in International Law (Cambridge: Cambridge University Press, 1994), at 426–429; R.Y. Jennings, above n 41, at 168, 177.

45 Ibid.

46 Anthony Anghie, above n 38, at 243–4.

position of some countries of the European Union, such as France and Germany, who are resisting investment arbitration in the negotiation of a free trade agreement with the United States. Like 40 years ago, the reason is that well-developed legal systems do not need to outsource the protection of foreign investors.[47]

The undisputable post-colonial origin of this interpretation of state contracts does not mean that this use of contracts has no relation with the emerging neoliberal legality in the 1970s. On the contrary, it may well be the origin of particular legal techniques that later consolidated and spread to other fields. The developments of the 1990s and 2000s support the argument that similar contractual techniques spread as a tool to disarticulate other forms of authority, including, for instance, family authority.[48] The shift in the interpretation of state contracts is particularly relevant because this was a crucial issue in the neoliberal and neoinstitutional agenda.[49] It was very prominent in foreign investment debates, where academics were concentrating on the difficulties that MNCs were facing in developing nations, such as expropriations, renegotiations, and increasing regulation.[50] In the field of international investment law, concretely, the need for an efficient mechanism to enforce state contracts became a top issue.[51] And by the 1990s, the focus of international investment law had changed completely towards concentrating on individual transactions – e.g. foreign investor and host state actions – as opposed to focusing on a holistic picture.

The outcome of this change was the consolidation of the international investment regime. This regime presently consists of a network of more than 3,000 bilateral and regional treaties for the protection of foreign investment.[52] Despite a few differences among them, the literature agrees that these treaties constitute a regime with common 'principles, norms, rules and decision making procedures'.[53] The main element of this regime is investment arbitration. Investment treaties empower foreign investors to sue host states directly before an international arbitral tribunal, without exhausting local remedies or requesting the espousal of their home states. The task of investment arbitrators is to consider whether the host state

47 Nicolás Perrone, 'The Governance of Foreign Investment at a Crossroad: Is an Overlapping Consensus the Way Forward?', 15(1), Global Jurist (2015): 1–28.

48 Ute Gerhard et al., above n 10, at 113.

49 Oliver Williamson, above n 5, at 52.

50 See Raymond Vernon, Sovereignty at Bay: The Multinational Spread of U.S. Enterprises (London: Longman, 1971), at 46; Jeswald Salacuse, The Law of Investment Treaties (New York: Oxford University Press, 2010) at 78–9.

51 See Jan Paulsson, 'Arbitration Without Privity', 10(2) ICSID Review (1995): 232–57.

52 UNCTAD, World Investment Report 2013: Global Value Chains: Investment and Trade for Development (New York and Geneva: United Nations, 2013), at xix.

53 Jeswald Salacuse, 'The Emerging Global Regime for Investment', 51 Harvard International Law Journal (2010), at 431.

breached the standards of protection incorporated in the applicable treaty, such as indirect expropriation, fair and equitable treatment, and arbitrary treatment.[54] However, the arbitrariness of a state measure cannot be determined in the abstract. For any decision on state responsibility, the interpretation of property and contractual rights is key. Otherwise, as Allot suggests, we may fall into a 'dangerous fiction'.[55]

Most investment law literature has looked at the IIR from the perspective of global administrative or constitutional law, focusing principally on state behaviour. This literature, at least in general, has overlooked the implications of this regime for the interpretation of foreign investor rights.[56] A look at the investment awards, however, shows a process of contractualisation that has increased the importance of the *pacta sunt servanda* principle in the reasoning of investment arbitrators. Investment tribunals, for instance, highlight the importance of the principle of good faith, which is essentially a contract law principle.[57] Contracts need to be interpreted and executed in good faith, but good faith is not a source of obligations.[58]

A very important consequence of the contractualisation of foreign investor relations is the replacement of the acquired rights doctrine by the legitimate expectations doctrine.[59] While acquired rights were traditionally seen as emerging from legislation, the legitimate expectations doctrine focuses on facts,[60] i.e. the dealings between foreign investors and host states, in particular, before and at the moment of establishment.[61] This

54 TECMED v. Mexico, ICSID Case No. ARB (AF)/00/2, Award, 29 May 2003, para. 119–20.

55 Philip Allott, 'State Responsibility and the Unmaking of International Law', 29(1) Harvard International Law Journal (1988), at 7.

56 Nicolás Perrone, 'The International Investment Regime and Foreign Investors' Rights: Another View of a Popular Story', 11(3) Manchester Journal of International Economic Law (2014): 397–420.

57 Waguih Elie George Siag v. Egypt, ICSID Case No. ARB/05/15, Award, 1 June 2009, para. 450; Total v. Argentina, ICSID Case No. ARB/04/01, Decision on Liability, 27 December 2010, para. 128; El Paso v. Argentina, ICSID Case No. ARB/03/15, Award, 31 October 2011, para. 348.

58 See Border and Transborder Armed Actions Case (Nicaragua v. Honduras), Jurisdiction and Admissibility, Judgment, 20 December 1988, ICJ Rep 69, para. 105; Nuclear Tests Case (Australia v. France), 1974, ICJ Reports, para. 46.

59 Emmanuelle Gaillard, 'Chronique des sentences arbitrales – Centre International pour le Règlement des Différends Relatifs aux Investissements (CIRDI)', Revue trimestrielle Lexis Nexis Juris Classeur (2008), at 332–4.

60 Spyridon Roussalis v. Romania, ICSID Case No. ARB/06/1, Award, 7 December 2011, para. 318; Joseph Charles Lemire v. Ukraine, ICSID Case No. ARB/06/18, Decision on Jurisdiction and Liability, 14 January 2010, para. 284; Siag and Vecchi v. Egypt, ICSID Case No ARB/05/15, Award, 1 June 2009, para. 450.

61 Christoph Schreuer and Ursula Kriebaum, 'At What Time Must Legitimate Expectations Exist?', in Jacques Werner and Arif Ali (Eds), A Liber Amicorum: Thomas Wälde (London: CMP Publishing Ltd, 2009), at 265–76, 269.

emphasis on the moment of establishment is inspired by a contractualised view of foreign investment relations, in which the initial intention and position of the parties matters the most. The *TECMED* v. *Mexico* tribunal was the first to apply the doctrine of legitimate expectations explicitly in an investment arbitration. These arbitrators considered their duty to be to assess the exercise of state action against 'the deprivation of economic rights and the legitimate expectations of [those] who suffered such deprivation'.[62] The investment treaty, 'in light of the good faith principle established by international law, requires the Contracting Parties to provide to international investments treatment that does not affect the basic expectations that were taken into account by the foreign investor to make the investment'.[63]

The legitimate expectations doctrine is a step further towards the contractualisation of foreign investment relations. Not only does equality become a common denominator of these relations, to the detriment of sovereignty, but host states are also now bound by obligations and duties they may not have explicitly accepted. Legitimate expectations are based on the reliance theory of contracts that focuses not on the promise of the counterparty, but on the expectations of the party pursuing the claim, i.e. foreign investors.[64] These expectations can emerge from explicit as well as from implicit representations. The justification for this approach is eminently economic: this interpretation aims at maximising wealth.

But in terms of sovereignty, the result is a net loss. There is much less freedom from contract.[65] It is not a coincidence, in this regard, that the IIR has been in crisis since it attracted the attention of the international community in the early 2000s. Developing and most recently developed countries do not want to be bound by these rules, although they want MNCs based in their territories to benefit from this regime.

An analysis of the evolution of international investment law shows, in short, that foreign investment relations were governed in the first part of the twentieth century by legal techniques more respectful of sovereignty, e.g. the acquired rights doctrine. After the 1960s, however, the idea of contract began gaining more and more importance. This was possible thanks to a different interpretation of contractual rights, in which state contracts were removed from their domestic legal orders and elevated to a newly created transnational level. There, foreign investors and host states are equals, and the applicable law is a mix of international law and general principles of private law. This shift to contractual governance in foreign

62 TECMED v. Mexico, ICSID Case No. ARB (AF)/00/2, Award, 29 May 2003, para 122.
63 Ibid., para. 154.
64 Andrew Gold, 'A Property Theory of Contract', 103(1) Northwestern University Law Review (2009), at 19–24.
65 Randy Barnett, 'The Sound of Silence: Default Rules and Contractual Consent', 78 Virginia Law Review (1992), at 828.

investment relations fits in to the larger picture of the neoliberal era. Legitimate expectations and the reliance theory are products of the move from government to governance. All of this shows a legal reasoning where rights are means for wealth maximisation, as promoted by investors, while sovereignty and autonomy are sacrificed.

A heuristic tool to understand neoliberal legality: property, contract, and the impossibility of an economic sovereign

The previous sections show that property and contract can be seen as two legal techniques, i.e. an interface, to govern resources. Beyond the *numerus clausus* rule, there is nothing impeding individuals from making particular arrangements about resources. Legal realists were extremely successful in criticising dominant views of property in the early twentieth century. This critique, however, was not so successful regarding contracts, arguably because of the assumed limited scope of the effects of this legal technique.[66] While we can formally distinguish between property and contract by looking at the effects, this criterion may be more elusive than we think.

A way to illustrate this is by comparing the way law and economics distinguish between property and contracts, relying on efficiency, with a relational approach to the same question. In law and economics, investors and the state choose proprietary arrangements when they are looking for standardisation. They rely on the law when they prefer circulation to a more detailed scope of the rights (i.e. the *numerus clausus* rule). But when it comes to specifying the rights over the resources, investors prefer to rely on contractual techniques.[67] The use of contractual techniques – particularly according to international law – allows investors to acquire the necessary calculability, but disregards any effects this may produce on third parties. The advantage of contracts is that negative effects on third parties are rarely taken into consideration. The remediation agreement signed by Ecuador and Chevron/Texaco regarding the Lago Agrio region is a good example of this.[68]

Following this argument, it would be possible to extend the realist critique to a large number of contracts, in particular, those that serve to govern resources. Contracts are functional to neoliberal legality precisely because they serve to govern the entire society through the appearance of mere individual transactions. This grants market actors the possibility of supervising state behaviour in manners that are unimaginable under a

66 See Charles Donahue Jr, above n 19, at 46; Peer Zumbansen, above n 28, at 207.

67 Thomas Merrill and Henry Smith, 'The Property/Contract Interface', 101(4) Columbia Law Review (2001), at 778–9.

68 See Chevron v. Ecuador, UNCITRAL, PCA Case No. 2009-23, First Partial Award on Track I, 17 September 2013.

property-sovereign paradigm. The correlation described by Cohen between sovereignty and property does not vanish when we use contracts to govern resources. When market actors are put on an equal footing with states, the resulting contracts are correlatives of sovereignty: more contractual rights imply a diminution of sovereignty and vice versa. But the implications are more systemic because the main principle of contracts according to international law is a strict *pacta sunt servanda*. This helps to free contractual governance and market coordination from state intervention and democratic decision-making.

This analytical reflection corroborates Foucault's claim about the impossibility of an economic sovereign under neoliberalism. The neoliberal legality formula is to disarticulate, commodify, and marketise sovereignty. The property-contract interface seems to be, in this respect, an adequate heuristic tool to identify and deconstruct neoliberal legality. Traditional property techniques remain important in the legal order, but they are limited to static rights that circulate in the market. They apply, for instance, to consumable goods. Contractual techniques, on the other hand, have become crucial to governing the relations between investors and the rest of the population, including states.

Conclusions

To say that some contractual techniques – e.g. those found in international law – make possible the impossibility of an economic sovereign is not to say that contracts are a means to neoliberalism. Alternative views of contracts can be means for different purposes. For the legal realists who challenged the dominant understanding of property in the early twentieth century, the problem was not property as such but the view of property favoured by classical legal thinking. The issue was not doctrinal. A different view of property, such as the progressive property or the social function view, implies a transformation of the entire legal order and, as a result, of a basic social pillar.[69] When it is clear that contracts are means for governing and shaping people's lives, the idea of contracts as one's free decision becomes obsolete too. Or, to put it differently, once we understand that a particular view of contracts is constitutive of neoliberalism, it is easier to advocate alternatives aimed at reshaping our society. This requires rethinking basic contractual categories, and taking seriously the possibilities of talking about an equitable conception of contracts or the social functions of resources and contracts.[70]

69 See Gregory Alexander, Eduardo Peñalver, Joseph Singer, and Laura Underkuffler, 'A Statement of Progressive Property', 94 Cornell Law Review (2009): 743–4.

70 See Robert Wai, 'Transnational Private Law and Private Ordering in a Contested Global Society', 46 Harvard International Law Journal (2005): 471–88.

References

Ackerman, Bruce. *Private Property and the Constitution* (New Haven and London: Yale University Press), at 27.

Alexander, Gregory and Eduardo Peñalver. *An Introduction to Property Theory* (Cambridge: Cambridge University Press, 2012), at 2.

Alexander, Gregory, Eduardo Peñalver, Joseph Singer, and Laura Underkuffler. 'A Statement of Progressive Property', 94 *Cornell Law Review* (2009): 743–4.

Allott, Philip. 'State Responsibility and the Unmaking of International Law', 29(1) *Harvard International Law Journal* (1988), at 7.

Anghie, Antony. *Imperialism, Sovereignty and the Making of International Law* (New York: Cambridge University Press, 2004), at 213–14.

Barnett, Randy. 'The Sound of Silence: Default Rules and Contractual Consent', 78 *Virginia Law Review* (1992), at 828.

Boltanski, Luc and Eve Chiapello. *The New Spirit of Capitalism* (New York: Verso, 2005).

Borchard, Edwin. 'Minimum Standard of the Treatment of Aliens', 38(4) *Michigan Law Review* (1940): 445–61.

Border and Transborder Armed Actions Case (*Nicaragua* v. *Honduras*), Jurisdiction and Admissibility, Judgment, 20 December 1988, ICJ Rep 69, para. 105.

Cheng, Bin. 'The Rationale of Compensation for Expropriation', *Transactions of the Grotius Society*, Problems of Public and Private International Law 44, Transactions for the Year 1958–59 (1958), at 283.

Chevron v. *Ecuador*. UNCITRAL, PCA Case No. 2009-23, First Partial Award on Track I, 17 September 2013.

Coase, Ronald. 'The Problem of Social Cost', 3 *Journal of Law and Economics* (1960): 1–44.

Cohen, Morris. 'Property and Sovereignty', 13(8) *Cornell Law Quarterly* (1927–1928): 8–30.

Donahue, Charles Jr. 'The Future of the Concept of Property Predicted from its Past', in Roland Pennock and John Chapman (Eds), *Nomos 22: Property* (New York: New York University Press, 1980), at 46–55.

El Paso v. *Argentina*. ICSID Case No. ARB/03/15, Award, 31 October 2011, para. 348.

Foucault, Michel. *The Birth of Biopolitics: Lectures at the Collège de France, 1978 – 1979* (Chippenham, UK: Palgrave Macmillan, 2010).

Gaillard, Emmanuelle. 'Chronique des sentences arbitrales – Centre International pour le Règlement des Différends Relatifs aux Investissements (CIRDI)', *Revue trimestrielle Lexis Nexis Juris Classeur* (2008), at 332–4.

García-Amador, F. 'International Responsibility: Fourth Report', International Law Commission, A/CN.4/119, 1959, at 9.

García-Amador, F. *The Changing Law of International Claims* (New York: Oceana Publications, 1984), at 46.

Gerhard, Ute, Trudie Knijn, and Jane Lewis. 'Contractualization', in Barbara Hobson, Jane Lewis, and Birte Siim (Eds), *Contested Concepts in Gender and Social Politics* (Northampton, MA: Edward Elgar), at 110–11.

Gold, Andrew. 'A Property Theory of Contract', 103(1) *Northwestern University Law Review* (2009), at 19–24.

Hale, Robert. 'Coercion and Distribution in a Supposedly Non-Coercive State', 38 *Political Science Quarterly* (1923): 470–94.

Hart, H.L.A. 'Are There Any Natural Rights?', 64(2) *Philosophical Review* (1955), at 185–6.

International Institute for Sustainable Development. 'Lifting the Lid on Foreign Investment Contracts: The Real Deal for Sustainable Development', 1 *Sustainable Markets* (2005), at 1–7.

Jennings, R.Y. 'State Contracts in International Law', 37 *British Yearbook of International Law* (1961), at 161, 176–7.

Joseph Charles Lemire v. *Ukraine*. ICSID Case No. ARB/06/18, Decision on Jurisdiction and Liability, 14 January 2010, para. 284.

Katz, Larissa. 'Red Tape and Gridlock', 23(1) *Canadian Journal of Law and Jurisprudence* (2010): 113–14.

Langrod, Georges. 'Administrative Contracts: A Comparative Study', 4(3) *The American Journal of Comparative Law* (1955): 325–64.

L. F. H. Neer and Pauline Neer (U.S.A.) v. *United Mexican States*. 15 October 1926, Reports of International Arbitral Awards, Volume IV, at 60–6.

Mann, Fritz. 'State Contracts and State Responsibility', 54 *American Journal of International Law* (1960), at 580–1.

Merrill, Thomas and Henry Smith. 'The Property/Contract Interface', 101(4) *Columbia Law Review* (2001), at 778–9.

Mewett, Alan. 'The Theory of Government Contracts', 5 *McGill Law Journal* (1958): 222–46.

Nuclear Tests Case (*Australia* v. *France*). 1974, ICJ Reports, para. 46.

The Oscar Chinn Case (*Britain* v. *Belgium*). PCIJ, 1937 (Ser. A/B), No. 70, at 88.

Paulsson, Jan. 'Arbitration without Privity', 10(2) *ICSID Review* (1995): 232–57.

Perrone, Nicolás. 'The International Investment Regime and Foreign Investors' Rights: Another View of a Popular Story', 11(3) *Manchester Journal of International Economic Law* (2014): 397–420.

Perrone, Nicolás. 'The Governance of Foreign Investment at a Crossroad: Is an Overlapping Consensus the Way Forward?', 15(1), *Global Jurist* (2015): 1–28.

Rabel, Ernst. *The Conflict of Laws: A Comparative Study*, Volume 4 (Ann Arbor: University of Michigan Law School), at 7–8, 30.

Riles, Annelise. 'Property as Legal Knowledge: Means and Ends', 10 *The Journal of the Royal Anthropological Institute* (2004): 775–95.

Rodotà, Stefano. *El terrible derecho: estudios sobre la propiedad privada* (Madrid: Civitas, 1986).

Rose, Carol. 'Mahon Reconstructed: Why the Takings Issue is Still a Muddle', 57 *Southern California Law Review* (1984): 561–99.

Salacuse, Jeswald. 'The Emerging Global Regime for Investment', 51 *Harvard International Law Journal* (2010), at 431.

Salacuse, Jeswald. *The Law of Investment Treaties* (New York: Oxford University Press, 2010) at 78–9.

Schreuer, Christoph and Ursula Kriebaum. 'At What Time Must Legitimate Expectations Exist?' in Jacques Werner and Arif Ali (Eds), *A Liber Amicorum: Thomas Wälde* (London: CMP Publishing Ltd, 2009), at 265–76, 269.

Schwebel, Stephen. 'On Whether the Breach by a State of a Contract with an Alien is a Breach of International Law', in *Justice in International Law* (Cambridge: Cambridge University Press, 1994), at 426–9.

Shemberg, Andrea. 'Stabilization Clauses and Human Rights', International

Finance Corporation and the United Nations Special Representative to the Secretary General on Business and Human Rights (2008), at 17–31.

Siag and Vecchi v. *Egypt*. ICSID Case No ARB/05/15, Award, 1 June 2009, para. 450.

Singer, Joseph. 'Sovereignty and Property', 6(1) *Northwestern University Law Review* (1991), at 48.

Singer, Joseph. 'How Property Norms Construct the Externalities of Ownership', in Gregory Alexander and Eduardo Peñalver (Eds), *Property and Community* (New York: Oxford University Press, 2010), at 59.

Spyridon Roussalis v. *Romania*. ICSID Case No. ARB/06/1, Award, 7 December 2011, para. 318.

Swedberg, Richard. 'Max Weber's Contribution to the Economic Sociology of Law', 2 *Annual Review of Law and Social Science* (2006): 61–81.

TECMED v. *Mexico*. ICSID Case No. ARB (AF)/00/2, Award, 29 May 2003, para. 119–20.

Total v. *Argentina*. ICSID Case No. ARB/04/01, Decision on Liability, 27 December 2010, para. 128.

UNCTAD. *World Investment Report 2013: Global Value Chains: Investment and Trade for Development* (New York and Geneva: United Nations, 2013), at xix.

Vernon, Raymond. *Sovereignty at Bay: The Multinational Spread of U.S. Enterprises* (London: Longman, 1971), at 46.

Viner, Jacob. *International Economics: Studies* (Glencoe, IL: Free Press, 1951), at 218.

Waguih Elie George Siag v. *Egypt*. ICSID Case No. ARB/05/15, Award, 1 June 2009, para. 450.

Wai, Robert. 'Transnational Private Law and Private Ordering in a Contested Global Society', 46 *Harvard International Law Journal* (2005): 471–88.

Waldron, Jeremy. *The Right to Private Property* (Oxford: Clarendon Press, 1988), at 106–26.

Waldron, Jeremy. *The Rule of Law and the Measure of Property* (Cambridge: Cambridge University Press, 2012).

Weber, Max. 'Parliament and Government in Germany under a New Political Order', in Peter Lassman (Ed.), *Weber: Political Writings* (Cambridge: Cambridge University Press, 1994), at 147–8.

Williamson, Oliver. *The Economic Institutions of Capitalism: Firms, Markets, Relational Contracting* (London: Collier Macmillan, 1985).

Zimmermann, Andreas, Karin Oellers-Frahm, Christian Tomuschat, and Christian J. Tams. *The Statute of the International Court of Justice: A Commentary* (New York: Oxford University Press, 2006), at 68.

Zumbansen, Peer. 'The Law of Society: Governance Through Contract', 14(2) *Indiana Journal of Global Legal Studies* (2007) at 193, 203.

Chapter 3

Neoliberal law and regulation

Andrés Palacios Lleras[1]

Introduction

After 35 years of neoliberal policy, as scholars and citizens we are familiar with neoliberalism, yet we seldom consider its legal dimensions. In part, this is because when we characterize neoliberalism as a series of ideas and policies (as we often do) we do not address the legal rules and institutions in which they are embedded. By bringing to the forefront the relations between neoliberalism, law and regulation I wish to highlight the considerable influence – sometimes taken for granted – that neoliberalism has exercised over regulatory law. In doing so, I contend that neoliberalism has been a driving force behind some of the most important developments in contemporary legal and regulatory theory. At the same time, however, I also highlight ways that the nature and logic of the liberal legal form have allowed law to be easily coupled with neoliberal economic rationality through the concept of 'law and economics' that I argue has reframed regulatory law in the neoliberal period. Thus, while neoliberalism has changed regulatory law, so too have legal forms shaped the development and expansion of neoliberalism.

This chapter charts the origins and evolution of the interrelation between neoliberal ideas, law and regulation. It addresses the origins of neoliberal ideas, how they were adapted into legal and regulatory discourses, and how they have changed over time as they travel across the globe. The second section offers a description of the origins and transformation of neoliberal ideas about law and regulation. The third section then explains the use of economic analysis in the framing and interpretation of legal rules, which has become a distinctive feature of contemporary neoliberal ideas about law and regulation. The next section then briefly addresses the global diffusion of neoliberal ideas and institutions. In particular, it deals with the diffusion of institutions and theories. The final

1 PhD Candidate, UCL Faculty of Laws.

section offers some tentative conclusions about the future of neoliberal law and regulation.

Definitions, origins and developments

Neoliberalism is a particularly hard term to define because it has stood for different things over time. Moreover, there is hardly an agreement among social scientists regarding what it stands for today. For our purposes, neoliberalism is a doctrine that views free markets as essential for preserving freedom, and that views such markets as the result of active political choices aiming to protect and preserve freedom. In doing so, it challenges the classical liberal notion that markets result from the spontaneous activities of individuals devoid of legal rules or other institutions, and instead it argues that states have an active duty to promote free markets – envisioned as institutional arrangements – through which individual freedom is preserved and promoted. Because of this characteristic, neoliberalism provides an account of more than just how markets work or the nature of regulation; it aims to reconceive how political, economic and legal relations should take place in a society founded upon individual liberty.[2] Given the complexity of neoliberal ideas, a detailed account of all its elements exceeds the purpose of this chapter. Therefore, we will focus on how neoliberalism assesses the role of governments regarding economic activity.

In the lectures that would eventually become *The Birth of Biopolitics*,[3] Michel Foucault argues that neoliberalism represents a departure from a core tenet of classical liberalism, which was the (ideal) separation between State and society aptly summarized in the maxim *laisser faire, laisser passer*. Classical liberalism viewed the deployment of economic activity (and most areas of social activity in general) as outside the State's realm of intervention; the idea that the State 'intervenes' in the economic sphere of social activities suggests that the former is to a large extent independent from the latter. The 'invisible hand' that guides markets towards the optimal allocation of social goods is, in the classical liberal perspective, opposed to the evident and very present hand of the State, which exercises its sovereignty through commands. Neoliberalism replaces this classical liberal view with a different notion of the involvement of the State wherein economic activities could not be simply left to their own devices. Foucault traces the origins of this new view to the scholars belonging to the Freiburg School, also referred to as 'Ordoliberals'. They claimed that one

2 See also Harvey, David. A Brief History of Neoliberalism. Oxford University Press (2005), p. 2.

3 Foucault, Michel. The Birth of Biopolitics: Lectures At The Collège de France, 1978–1979. Palgrave Macmillan Ed. (2008).

of the fundamental causes of the Nazi regime was the close alliance between political and economic powers in Germany. If left unchecked, economic powers would eventually align and influence each other unduly, thus threatening individual liberty and the general welfare of the population at large. The Ordoliberal solution was to make individual freedom a core principle of the entire legal system, thus giving the protection of property rights and of competition a privileged position in a new legal order. Neither markets nor property rights could be viewed as resulting from a 'natural order'; instead, their functioning should be regulated in order to ensure that economic actors do not obtain enough power to suppress or control entire economic processes at the expense of individual freedom, both political and economic. Hence, by extending the role of law to the control of economic processes via the protection of property rights and competition, the 'invisible hand' was replaced in this view by the much more active 'sustaining hand' of a new legal order.[4] This distinctively positivist view (in a jurisprudential sense) of competition and property rights gave rise to a *neo*-liberal way of conceiving the role of the State and of law in general.

It is important to consider briefly the success of this first variant of neoliberal ideas in the post-war European context. Ordoliberalism became influential first in Germany and later across Europe because its adherents had always opposed Nazism, an act of defiance that won them legitimacy in the eyes of the Occupation regime after WWII. Eventually, the core tenets of Ordoliberal thought became highly influential throughout Europe and contributed to the theoretical underpinnings of the European Union.[5]

Although not an Ordoliberal himself, F.A. Hayek also offered a view of neoliberalism in which legal rules have a prominent role. Hayek knew personally some of the members of this movement, and became a key character in the globalization of neoliberal ideas.[6] While not aiming to do justice to the complexity of his views, I believe that two related sets of ideas are key for understanding his views about the relationships between markets and the role of law in the promotion and protection of freedom – a sort of 'classical' neoliberal synthesis.[7]

4 Ibid., chapter 5.

5 Gerber, David J. Law and Competition in Twentieth-Century Europe: Protecting Prometheus. Oxford University Press (2001), chapters VIII and XIX.

6 For a testimony of his influence in the US, see Coase, Ronald. Law and Economics at Chicago, 36 Jnl. of Law & Econ. 239, 246 (1993). Regarding Latin America (and specially Chile) consider Fiss, Owen M. The Autonomy of Law. 26 Yale J. Int'l L. 517 (2001).

7 It is important to consider that Hayek's economic theory and political and legal theory are intertwined, and hence they should be considered together. See Beaulier, Scott A., Boettke, Peter J. and Coyne, Christopher J. Knowledge, Economics, and Coordination: Understanding Hayek's Legal Theory. 1 NYU Jnl. of Law and Lbty. 209 (2005).

The first idea has to do with government rationality and capability. Hayek claimed that individuals possess important rational skills but a limited and dispersed knowledge of the world. Hence, the expectation that society could be organized based on a rational design established beforehand is unattainable.[8] In his view, patterns of social organization result from the interactions of individuals via the free and spontaneous exercise of their rights, not from a pre-ordained plan. In particular, prices allow individuals to convey their limited and dispersed knowledge and coordinate their efforts in ways that are impossible for a system that centralizes knowledge and decision-making.[9]

The second idea is about the political and legal structure required to encourage and protect spontaneous and free decision-making by individuals. For Hayek, 'the rule of law' consists of a series of traits that any legal system should comply with in order to protect such a 'spontaneous order', including generality, universality and certainty.[10] Conversely, individual liberty is threatened when states issue *ad-hoc* regulation applicable only to a few, for in doing so individual rights are sacrificed in the name of a pre-ordained plan crafted after a common goal.[11] However, the process through which the spontaneous order takes place requires active intervention, not just a passive stance or a legal vacuum. As Hayek stated,

> a condition of liberty in which all are allowed to use their knowledge for their purposes, restrained only by rules of just conduct of universal application, is likely to produce for them the best conditions for achieving their aims; and that such a system is likely to be *achieved and maintained* only if all authority, including that of the majority of the people, is limited in the exercise of coercive power by general principles to which the community has committed itself.[12]

Hayek's views about government and markets were appealing beyond academia, for example in industry policy circles, where he found support for the development of institutions like the Mont Pèlerin Society. This contributed to increasing his prominence in academic circles outside Europe and especially in the United States. For example, Frank Knight, a

8 Hayek, F.A. Individualism: True or False. In: Individualism and Economic Order. University of Chicago Press. 1st. Edition (1948). Third Impression (1958), pp. 4 and 5, 9 and 10.

9 Hayek, F.A. The Use of Knowledge in Society. In: Individualism and Economic Order. University of Chicago Press. 1st. Edition (1948). Third Impression (1958).

10 Hayek, F.A. The Constitution of Liberty. University of Chicago Press (1960) (hereinafter, Constitution), pp. 152–154 (referring to the general character of laws and the universality of their application) and 208 (referring to certainty).

11 Hayek, Constitution, op. cit., pp. 227–228.

12 Hayek, F.A. Law, Legislation and Liberty. Vol. I. Rules and Order. University of Chicago Press (1973), p. 55 (italics not included in the original text).

professor at the University of Chicago, was one of the founding members of the aforementioned society.[13] His views became highly influential among the first generation of scholars belonging to the law and economics movement at the University of Chicago.[14] The American reception of Hayek's ideas contributed to shaping a new form of neoliberal law and regulation. While exhibiting ideas also apparent in Ordoliberalism and in Hayek's distinctive views about the organization of the State, this new form of neoliberal law and regulation had a different focus. To begin with, it expanded the logic of economic analysis to social spheres that were until then considered non-economic, like family and crime.[15] In doing so, it challenged the classical liberal epistemological separation of the economic and the social as two distinct social orders.[16] So, while Ordoliberals pursued the idea of constructing a political and legal order around markets as expressions of human freedom, the US neoliberal views redefined the social sphere as another economic domain. This perspective distinguishes this view of neoliberalism from others. Economic rationality becomes the regulative principle for justifying and limiting regulatory activity, and it does so by using economic rationality as a template for redesigning activities – like healthcare or education – in ways in which direct state activity is replaced by markets. From this perspective, the economy is no longer conceived as a separate domain characterized by its own internal logic, but becomes the template against which all activities are assessed in terms of the allocation of limited resources to competing goals under the aegis of efficiency. In turn, state intervention in markets via regulation is internally challenged by the economic rationality that supposedly guides it, to the extent that this rationality becomes its regulative principle.[17] We can see evidence of this new form of understanding neoliberal law and regulation in a paper published in 1978 by Elizabeth Landes and Richard Posner asserting the following:

> [a]lthough economists have studied extensively the efforts of government to regulate the economy, public regulation of social and personal life has largely escaped economic attention. With the rapid development of the economic analysis of nonmarket behavior, the

13 See, in general, Jones, Daniel Stedman. Masters of the Universe: Hayek, Friedman, and the Birth of Neoliberal Politics. Princeton University Press (2012).

14 See Teles, Steven M. The Rise of the Conservative Legal Movement: The Battle for Control of the Law. Princeton University Press (2008), pp. 91–96.

15 Foucault, op.cit., pp. 219–221. Foucault considers several pieces regarding family and crime, some of which are closely associated with law and economics. See footnotes 10 and 11, 17 and 18. For example, he refers to Gary Becker's article Crime and Punishment: An Economic Approach. 76 Jnl. of Pol. Econ. 196 (1968).

16 Ibid., pp. 243–246.

17 Ibid., p. 246.

> conceptual tools necessary for the economic study of social (as distinct from narrowly economic) regulation are now at hand. Nor is there any basis for a presumption that government does a good job of regulating nonmarket behavior; if anything, the negative presumption created by numerous studies of economic regulation should carry over to the nonmarket sphere. An example of nonmarket regulation that may be no less perverse than the widely criticized governmental efforts to regulate imports, transportation, new drugs, bank entry, and other market activities is the regulation of child adoptions – the subject of this paper.[18]

The US variant of the relation between neoliberalism, law and regulation has important similarities and differences with the ideas brought forward by German Ordoliberals and F.A. Hayek. Perhaps the single most important similarity is that they all share the premise that individual freedom follows from an explicit political choice (as opposed to being a 'natural' trait of individuals as classical liberal theories contend). Therefore, the protection of this individual freedom is founded upon an adequate legal order and the active participation of the State. Among the differences, we note that the US variant distinctively relies upon cost/benefit analysis of rules and regulations – independently of the behaviour they address – to assess their adequacy. As an example, consider again Landes's and Posner's claim; even child adoption regulation is a governmental activity that can and should be viewed from an economic perspective in order to improve how it takes place. In turn, cost/benefit analysis is a form of utilitarian reasoning that is at odds with the deontological approaches to individual freedom typically found in both Ordoliberalism and the ideas of F.A. Hayek. This is so because cost/benefit analysis may limit individual freedom in the name of a common good ('efficiency') in ways that are inconsistent with taking individuals as ends in themselves.[19] From a distinctive legal perspective, awareness about this inconsistency opens up possibilities and alternatives to neoliberal views about law and regulation.

The US variant of neoliberal law and regulation has been highly influential across the globe since the late 1980s. In part, this has been so because, by combining legal and economic analysis, it appeals to expectations about the rationality of law and regulation at the core of the Rule of Law. On one hand, it offers a coherent rationale that justifies the rights and duties that comprise legal regimes in a formally logical manner, or, in

18 Landes, Elisabeth M. and Posner, Richard A. The Economics of the Baby Shortage. 7 Jnl. of Lgl. Stds. 323 (1978).

19 See in general Coleman, Jules L. Economics and the Law: A Critical Review of the Foundations of the Economic Approach to Law. Ethics, 649 (1984).

other words, an 'internal point of view' about such regimes. In this sense, this variant provides a template for describing and justifying what different regimes are about – their goals and substantive rules – by taking into consideration the economic relevance of legal rules. On the other, it can also justify the enforcement of these rules through rational procedures involving decision-making institutions like courts and administrative agencies. Both aspects – the substantive and the procedural – are tightly knit; substantive principles guide the decision-making institutions, which in turn work in such a way as to distil new, more appropriate rules. At the same time, its influence also results from the dominant position of the US in the world resulting originally from the outcome of WWII and reinforced by the fall of the Berlin Wall in 1989.[20] In either case, it is an example of a 'globalized localism'.[21]

Neoliberalism and the role of economics in jurisprudence

The idea that legal rules should promote a goal like the general welfare is not part of neoliberal accounts of the law.[22] What makes the US variant of neoliberal law and regulation distinctive is the idea that economics provides the elements to measure the adequacy of the law. In its original context, this trait was associated with two distinctively legal issues: the efficiency of legal rules, and the allocation of decision-making authority.

The origins of the inroads of economic analysis in law can be traced to discussions about the economic role of the common law rules pertaining to contract, property and tort.[23] A thesis that gained traction by the late 1970s is that these rules allocated scarce resources efficiently, thus contributing to welfare maximization.[24] This positive claim about the common law became discredited because of several examples at hand that proved it otherwise, and because of the general difficulties in actually proving such a claim for the totality of the common law.[25] These criticisms contributed

20 Mattei, Ugo. A Theory of Imperial Law: A Study on US Hegemony and the Latin Resistance. 3 Global Jurist Frontiers (2003).

21 Regarding the concept of globalized localism, see De Sousa Santos, Boaventura. Toward a New Common Sense: Law, Science and Politics in the Paradigmatic Transition. Routledge (1995), p. 263.

22 Consider, for example, Rudolf von Ihering's classic book, Law as a Means to an End. Vol. 5. Boston Book Company (1914).

23 Most L&E scholars would hardly recognize themselves as neoliberals, in spite of the fact that they regularly acknowledge the impact that scholars like Gary Becker, Richard Posner and F.A. Hayek had in the development of this field of law.

24 See for example Priest, George L. The Common Law Process and the Selection of Efficient Rules. 6 J. Legal Stud. 6 65 (1977).

25 For a summary and thorough analysis of these criticisms, see Kelman, Mark. A Guide To Critical Legal Studies. Harvard University Press (1987), pp. 114–117.

to toning down the *positive* claims that law and economics scholars made, but had little effect on more normative approaches that argued that legal rules *should* maximize efficiency. In turn, normative approaches have also met with considerable resistance for it is far from clear that maximizing social welfare can be a goal comparable to fairness or equality, or that we could have a way of comparing individual utility functions in order to assess how well the law performs.[26] Even so, normative theory in the area of law and economics has made considerable inroads in academia in the United States, although to a lesser extent elsewhere.[27]

Just as the common law rules pertaining to property, contracts and torts were deemed to be somewhat efficient, regulation – the rules emanating from Congress and administrative agencies – was under considerable attack. During the late 1960s and 1970s challenges to regulation using economic efficiency arguments became highly influential in academic and policy circles, leading eventually to shifts in different areas.[28] Consider for example the Landes and Posner article mentioned before on child adoption; the discussion it presents only makes sense if we assume that resource allocation by the State – in this case, the rights and duties of child-rearing – should be a matter of economic efficiency. For our purposes, the key insights it offers are mainly two. First, the established regulation is inefficient and therefore unnecessarily burdensome, for it aims to achieve particular goals without considering the expenses incurred in order to do so. A more efficient regulation would enable economic actors to internalize to the fullest the costs and benefits of the activities they chose to achieve in their own terms – much like markets do. Second, the burdensome nature of regulation was not gratuitous. It evidenced that regulations benefited certain social actors more than others, and (most of the time) at the expense of consumers; the political process was skewed against actors unable to organize themselves in defence of their interests. Moreover, underlying regulatory proposals is also the intent of 'capturing' the State so that it works in ways that are congenial to the interests of the regulated actors, thus skewing the State's apparatus in favour of the interests of certain actors.[29] Since the State could be 'captured', regulation reflected *and* furthered the influence of these groups. The expression 'deregulation', which makes sense in the context of this discussion, alludes primarily to the

26 See, in general, Coleman, Jules L. The Grounds of Welfare. 112 Yale Law Journal 1511 (2003).

27 See Garoupa, Nuno and Thomas S. Ulen. The Market for Legal Innovation: Law and Economics in Europe and the United States. 59 Ala. L. Rev. 1555 (2007).

28 See Teles, op. cit.

29 See for example the seminar paper by Stigler, George J. The Theory of Economic Regulation. 2 Bell Journal of Economics and Management Science. 3 (1971). Also Posner, Richard A. Theories of Economic Regulation. 5 Bell Journal of Economics and Management Science 335 (1974).

idea of freeing actors from the economic burdens of regulation, but also includes ending unmerited benefits awarded by it.[30]

The preceding discussion about the use of economic rationality to determine the efficiency of legal rules, or lack of efficiency, has also prompted debates about the interpretation of legal rules. Taking place in the context of the US legal system, where judges are often outspoken about their decisions, this debate evidences the use of cost/benefit analysis in decision-making. Richard Posner, for example, has argued that judges interpreting legal rules are not constrained by the language of the rules they apply, and that they have a utility function they aim to maximize.[31] Other authors argue that it would be better if judges aimed to interpret legal rules in a straightforward, literal way, because doing so would minimize the error costs produced by the entire legal system, and not just the errors associated with their own tasks.[32] This discussion has also complemented more general considerations about the allocation of decision-making authority among the branches of government from an economic perspective.[33] Some of these general considerations are narrowed down when discussing, among other topics, the proper scope of the judicial review that courts should exercise vis-à-vis administrative agencies.[34]

Independently of what side we may take in these debates, they evidence the extent to which neoliberal ideas have pervaded traditional jurisprudential debates in the United States (and elsewhere). Moreover, they suggest two important points worth considering. First, using economic analysis to interpret legal rules is not straightforward as it originally appears because it invites new considerations in order to make definitive assessments. Questions regarding who should be the correct interpreter/applier of such rules also become relevant, and make it more difficult to reach general conclusions. Second, they also suggest that economic analysis is not capable by itself of making the law more determinate. Moreover, law-and-economics has become so broad that almost every claim based on it can be met with a counter-claim also based on similar premises; the key issue is to understand why some claims are accepted and others

30 Regarding the impact of Stigler's and Posner's arguments, see Peltzman, Sam, Michael E. Levine and Roger G. Noll. The Economic Theory of Regulation After a Decade of Deregulation. 1989 Brookings Papers on Economic Activity. Microeconomics 1 (1989).

31 Posner, Richard A. What Do Judges and Justices Maximize? (The Same Thing Everybody Else Does). Sup. Court Econ. Rev. 1 (1993).

32 See, for example, Sunstein, Cass R. and Adrian Vermeule. Interpretation and Institutions. 101 Mich. L. Rev. 885 (2002–2003). Vermeule, Adrian. Judging Under Uncertainty: An Institutional Theory of Legal Interpretation. Harvard University Press (2006).

33 See for example, Cooter, Robert. The Strategic Constitution. Princeton University Press (2002).

34 See for example Miles, Thomas J. and Cass R. Sunstein. The New Legal Realism. 75 U. Chi. L. Rev. 831 (2008).

discarded.[35] This is an insight made by Critical Legal Studies scholars on different occasions, and which shows that neoliberal approaches to legal issues lead to familiar conundrums.[36]

The globalization of neoliberal law and regulation

The globalization of neoliberal ideas about law and regulation takes place through the diffusion of regulation based on liberalizing certain economic sectors to foster market-like transactions. Particular examples of this can be seen in the adoption of regulatory regimes in Eastern Europe after the fall of communism in 1989, and in the development of the so-called 'Washington Consensus' in Latin America after the debt crisis of the 1980s. Particular instances of regulation that we identify as distinctively neoliberal, such as the privatization of State-owned enterprises, transport sectors and public utilities, had their heyday between the late 1980s and the late 1990s. The diffusion of regulations like the ones considered above have several dimensions; among the most obvious are the changes that take place in administrative law as the State assumes a new role as a regulator instead of being a direct provider of goods and services. Consider, for example, the privatization of State-owned enterprises; this usually involves turning a public good into a private asset and, at the same time, turning the State from a provider to a regulator.

A particular institution that has been widely diffused during periods of neoliberal change is the semi-autonomous regulatory agency. Administrative agencies existed before the dawn of neoliberalism, although they did not have much political or legal autonomy, and functioned according to the precepts of the 'developmental' regulatory paradigm overtaken by neoliberalism. The new agencies, in contrast, are semi-autonomous; the officials working in them usually combine political connections with academic credentials, their appointments are insulated from ordinary politics, and have their own budgets. In spite of this, these agencies have been central to the development of neoliberal ideas.[37] The ubiquitous presence of these agencies can be found in a diversity of legal fields – ranging from securities regulation to competition law, public utilities, corporate law and environmental law – to the extent that they now are one of the most

35 For a law and economics answer, consider Sunstein, Cass R. On Academic Fads and Fashions. 99 Mich. L. Rev. 99 1251 (2000–2001).

36 See Kelman, op. cit. Also Kennedy, Duncan. Law and Economics from the Perspective of Critical Legal Studies, in P. Newman (ed.). The New Palgrave Dictionary of Economics and the Law. Macmillan (1998), p. 465.

37 See, in general, Levi-Faur, David. The Global Diffusion of Regulatory Capitalism. 598 Annals of the American Academy of Political and Social Science 12 (2005). For a history of federal regulation, see Rabin, Robert L. Federal Regulation in Historical Perspective. 38 Stan. L. Rev. 1189 (1986).

important elements of executive branches of governments around the world.

The diffusion of these agencies is consistent with neoliberal thought. First, these agencies contribute to a division of labour within the State itself. They are supposed to be staffed by experts on particular economic sectors, and therefore the agencies themselves gather a set of skills not found in other governmental institutions. This enables representative bodies (congress, parliament, etc.) to delegate decision-making to these agencies, and to exercise oversight over them when it is not clear that they have acted within their boundaries. Courts also contribute to raising the accountability of these agencies by exercising judicial review over the legality of their decisions.[38] Second, the delegation of certain decision-making processes to a group of experts is seen to minimize the dangers associated with the ordinary political process, like regulatory capture. This is so because the formal autonomy, or detachment, of these agencies from the political process is seen to prevent them from being captured by particular actors and their interests.[39] Certainly, removing instances of decision-making from the political process may seem undemocratic – unless democracy is conceived as being about protecting the private entitlements of individuals. If this is the case, then limiting the possibility of affecting such entitlements via harmful regulation is compatible with democracy. Third, and perhaps more importantly, the rational basis on which the decisions of these agencies rely is considered to be science, not politics. Similarly to classical liberal accounts of law, where courts were bound by the logical application of pre-established principles in a deductive fashion, neoliberal regulation is bound by the application of economics as a 'science'.[40] By relying on the (arguably) scientific character of economics, regulation comes across as independent from particular interests and devoid of any value judgements. This, in turn, makes it more appropriate than other alternatives or perspectives for conceiving regulation and devising how it should be enforced.[41] The particular appeal of economics has reinforced the diffusion of law and economics as a complement to general neoliberal theories about regulation. Moreover, neoliberal institutions travel with complementary theories that justify their adoption and explain how they are supposed to work.

38 See in general Cooter, op. cit., chapter 6.

39 See for example Spulber, Daniel F. and David Besanko. Delegation, Commitment, and the Regulatory Mandate. 8 Jnl. of Law, Econ. & Org. 126 (1992).

40 Regarding the similarities between nineteenth century legal formalism and some variants of law and economics, see Grey, Thomas C. Langdell's Orthodoxy. 45 U. Pitt. L. Rev. 1, 51–52 (1983–1984).

41 For an illustrative discussion, see Blaug, Mark. Economic Theory in Retrospect. Cambridge University Press (1997), chapter 17.

The diffusion of the semi-autonomous regulatory agency has political implications that critics of neoliberalism have pointed out, but that have had little echo in mainstream legal circles. In particular, it has contributed to the development of a new class of lawyer/policy analyst that is able to combine policy analysis based on economics with more traditional legal analysis – a variant of the so-called 'technocrat'. The development of this new legal intelligentsia has both global and local dimensions. At the global level, it has contributed to the strengthening of elite policy networks where individuals with similar skill-sets and backgrounds share their experiences and mutually reinforce the social value of their knowledge.[42] Also, organizations like the Organisation for Economic Co-operation and Development (OECD), the United Nations Conference for Trade and Development (UNCTAD), the World Bank and the International Monetary Fund (IMF) play important roles in the conformation of these networks; they are at times gatekeepers, repositories of neoliberal perspectives, and supporters of 'policy entrepreneurs'. In turn, at the local level, lawyer/policy analysts tend to find themselves ahead of neoliberal policy changes, and are either directly involved in making the changes themselves or are able to benefit from the new business conditions that result from the changes. In developing countries, lawyer/policy analysts usually obtain their skill-set from their studies abroad, and are therefore seen as pioneers when they return home. Also, this new legal intelligentsia has gradually supplanted professionals who lacked both the skill-set and the connections necessary for participating in the politics involved in policy change.[43] The elitist nature of these networks – which ultimately depends more on access to elite education, social standing and the like – makes it particularly hard to believe that their operation and reproduction are in any way connected with broader claims of social justice or fairness.

As this section suggests, the global diffusion of neoliberal ideas about law and regulation – including the diffusion of semi-autonomous administrative agencies – is a complex phenomenon that has broader implications for the ways in which we conceive the State and its interaction with markets. These implications concern the structure of the State, the ways in which its different branches and agents interact, how we are able to rationalize and justify these interactions, and who takes part in these changes. In doing so, the ideas here presented show that the distinctive legal institutions of neoliberalism present issues that are particularly hard to justify and which invite further consideration.

42 See in general Slaughter, Anne-Marie. A New World Order. Princeton University Press (2004), chapter 6 (notably, also including judges as prominent members of 'government networks').

43 See for example Dezalay, Yves and Bryant G. Garth. The Internationalization of Palace Wars: Lawyers, Economists, and the Contest to Transform Latin American States. University of Chicago Press (2002).

Conclusions – the possibility of neoliberal legalities

One of the results of the diffusion of neoliberal ideas about law and regulation is that some of them turned out differently in practice than expected. From a legal perspective, this is referred to as 'the transplant effect': the reception of a rule into a new context often leads to unexpected results, as social existence is more complex than transplant models allow and the transplanted rule will interact with a unique and complex local context in each case;[44] in some instances the result is a huge success, while in others it can be a complete failure. The evidence about the wholesale success (or lack thereof) of legal transplants, especially of those associated with neoliberalism, is a matter of debate.[45] In any case, the global diffusion of neoliberalism has led to the establishment of different political, legal and economic orders that, notwithstanding the traits they share, exhibit considerable differences and, more importantly, produce different outcomes. In other words, it opens the possibility of considering different varieties of neoliberal law and regulation.[46]

The 'transplant effect' offers hope to critics of neoliberalism, as well as to its supporters, although in smaller doses. Critics can point to this effect in order to argue the futility of transplanting the legal institutions associated with neoliberal ideas about law and regulation. They can argue, for example, that these ideas are facile, one-size-fits-all recipes that are so ambitious that they can hardly be useful for bringing about significant institutional changes. Not only does the later variant of neoliberalism have a questionable basis; it is also unattainable as a large-scale recipe for policy change. In turn, supporters of neoliberalism can view in the 'transplant effect' an opportunity to complement it – neoliberalism – with more sophisticated theories of institutional translation and development. In this view, the failure to replicate neoliberal institutions across different jurisdictions does not lay in the content of neoliberalism, but rather in the mechanisms used for its diffusion. If we understand the process of diffusion better, supporters of neoliberal principles would argue, then alternative institutional arrangements based on grounded notions of fairness and social justice that supersede neoliberal institutions could be conceived. In any case, the 'transplant effect' simply shows that neoliberalism as a global trend can be diluted or changed, but does not necessarily suggest that it can be prevented or reversed.

44 See in general Berkowitz, Daniel, Katharina Pistor and Jean-Francois Richard. The Transplant Effect. 51 Am. J. Comp. L. 163 (2003).

45 See Davis, Kevin E. and Michael J. Trebilcock. The Relationship Between Law and Development: Optimists Versus Skeptics. 56 Am. J. Comp. L. 895 (2008).

46 This may strengthen the argument discussed in other chapters that neoliberalism should be seen as a phase of capitalism. See in general Hall, Peter A. and David Soskice (eds) Varieties of Capitalism: The Institutional Foundations of Comparative Advantage. Oxford University Press (2001).

Throughout this chapter we have argued that neoliberalism has shaped the development of elements commonly found in contemporary visions of legality in many important ways. In particular, it contributed to the development of the semi-autonomous regulatory agency as well as to the development of law and economics as a *parole* for talking about regulation – both of which in turn have been integral to the development and functioning of neoliberalism. Neoliberalism shares some common elements with theories of law in classical liberal thought (for example, its reliance on 'science' and its supposedly rational structure) and, perhaps, aims to achieve the same goals of classical liberal legality. These elements continue to be present in discourses about the Rule of Law, and as such provide the normative foundation for the development of neoliberal forms of legality. However, neoliberal legality is also quite different from the legality envisioned in classical liberal theory (as we have argued) in that it posits the State as an active supporter of markets and economic activities (via regulation). In doing so, however, neoliberal doctrines have adapted to different legal traditions and contexts, sometimes reaching unexpected results; these variations invite us to look at the limits of neoliberal reforms, as well as to potential alternatives.

References

Beaulier, Scott A., Boettke, Peter J. and Coyne, Christopher J. Knowledge, Economics, and Coordination: Understanding Hayek's Legal Theory. 1 *NYU Jnl. of Law and Lbty.* 209 (2005).

Becker, Gary. Crime and Punishment: An Economic Approach. 76 *Jnl. of Pol. Econ.* 196 (1968).

Berkowitz, Daniel, Katharina Pistor and Jean-Francois Richard. The Transplant Effect. 51 *Am. J. Comp. L.* 163 (2003).

Blaug, Mark. *Economic Theory in Retrospect.* Cambridge University Press (1997).

Coase, Ronald. Law and Economics at Chicago. 36 *Jnl. of Law & Econ.* 239, 246 (1993).

Coleman, Jules L. Economics and the Law: A Critical Review of the Foundations of the Economic Approach to Law. *Ethics* 649 (1984).

Coleman, Jules L. The Grounds of Welfare. 112 *Yale Law Journal* 1511 (2003).

Cooter, Robert. *The Strategic Constitution.* Princeton University Press (2002).

Davis, Kevin E. and Michael J. Trebilcock. The Relationship Between Law And Development: Optimists Versus Skeptics. 56 *Am. J. Comp. L.* 895 (2008).

De Sousa Santos, Boaventura. *Toward a New Common Sense: Law, Science and Politics in the Paradigmatic Transition.* Routledge (1995).

Dezalay, Yves and Bryant G. Garth. *The Internationalization of Palace Wars: Lawyers, Economists, and the Contest to Transform Latin American States.* University of Chicago Press (2002).

Fiss, Owen M. The Autonomy of Law. 26 *Yale J. Int'l L.* 517 (2001).

Foucault, Michel. *The Birth of Biopolitics: Lectures at the Collège de France, 1978–1979.* Palgrave Macmillan Ed. (2008).

Garoupa, Nuno and Thomas S. Ulen. The Market for Legal Innovation: Law and Economics in Europe and the United States. 59 *Ala. L. Rev.* 1555 (2007).

Gerber, David J. *Law and Competition in Twentieth-Century Europe: Protecting Prometheus.* Oxford University Press (2001).

Grey, Thomas C. Langdell's Orthodoxy. 45 *U. Pitt. L. Rev.* 1, 51–52 (1983–1984).

Hall, Peter A. and David Soskice (eds) *Varieties of Capitalism: The Institutional Foundations of Comparative Advantage.* Oxford University Press (2001).

Harvey, David. *A Brief History of Neoliberalism.* Oxford University Press (2005).

Hayek, F.A. Individualism: True or False. In: *Individualism and Economic Order.* University of Chicago Press. 1st Edition (1948). Third Impression (1958).

Hayek, F.A. The Use of Knowledge in Society. In: *Individualism and Economic Order.* University of Chicago Press. 1st Edition (1948). Third Impression (1958).

Hayek, F.A. *The Constitution of Liberty.* University of Chicago Press (1960).

Hayek, F.A. *Law, Legislation and Liberty. Vol. I. Rules and Order.* University of Chicago Press (1973).

Jones, Daniel Stedman. *Masters of the Universe: Hayek, Friedman, and the Birth of Neoliberal Politics.* Princeton University Press (2012).

Kelman, Mark. *A Guide to Critical Legal Studies.* Harvard University Press (1987).

Kennedy, Duncan. Law and Economics from the Perspective of Critical Legal Studies, in P. Newman (ed.), *The New Palgrave Dictionary of Economics and the Law.* Macmillan (1998).

Landes, Elisabeth M. and Posner, Richard A. The Economics of the Baby Shortage. 7 *Jnl. of Lgl. Stds.* 323 (1978).

Levi-Faur, David. The Global Diffusion of Regulatory Capitalism. 598 *Annals of the American Academy of Political and Social Science* 12 (2005).

Mattei, Ugo. A Theory of Imperial Law: A Study on US Hegemony and the Latin Resistance. 3 *Global Jurist Frontiers* (2003).

Miles, Thomas J. and Cass R. Sunstein. The New Legal Realism. 75 *U. Chi. L. Rev.* 831 (2008).

Peltzman, Sam, Michael E. Levine and Roger G. Noll. The Economic Theory of Regulation After a Decade of Deregulation. 1989 *Brookings Papers on Economic Activity. Microeconomics* 1 (1989).

Posner, Richard A. Theories of Economic Regulation. 5 *Bell Journal of Economics and Management Science* 335 (1974).

Posner, Richard A. What Do Judges and Justices Maximize? (The Same Thing Everybody Else Does). *Sup. Court Econ. Rev.* 1 (1993).

Priest, George L. The Common Law Process and the Selection of Efficient Rules. 6 *J. Legal Stud.* 6 65 (1977).

Rabin, Robert L. Federal Regulation in Historical Perspective. 38 *Stan. L. Rev.* 1189 (1986).

Slaughter, Anne-Marie. *A New World Order.* Princeton University Press (2004).

Spulber, Daniel F. and David Besanko. Delegation, Commitment, and the Regulatory Mandate. 8 *Jnl. of Law, Econ. & Org.* 126 (1992).

Stigler, George J. The Theory of Economic Regulation. 2 *Bell Journal of Economics and Management Science* 3 (1971).

Sunstein, Cass R. On Academic Fads and Fashions. 99 *Mich. L. Rev.* 99 1251 (2000–2001).

Sunstein, Cass R. and Adrian Vermeule. Interpretation and Institutions. 101 *Mich. L. Rev.* 885 (2002–2003).

Teles, Steven M. *The Rise of the Conservative Legal Movement: The Battle for Control of the Law.* Princeton University Press (2008).

Vermeule, Adrian. *Judging Under Uncertainty: An Institutional Theory of Legal Interpretation.* Harvard University Press (2006).

Von Ihering, Rudolf. *Law as a Means to an End.* Vol. 5. Boston Book Company (1914).

Chapter 4

Law, social policy, and the neoliberal state

Kenneth Veitch[1]

This chapter explores the relationship between law and neoliberalism in the context of contemporary social policy. Among the many areas to be affected by the emergence of neoliberalism as the guiding philosophy of today's politics, welfare has been one of the most prominent and controversial. The nature of the changes within the sphere of welfare that have accompanied the shift to a neoliberal politics have been charted extensively. Increasing privatisation and marketisation of social services; the importance attached to the empowerment of those who use social services by extending their range of choices and opportunities to provide feedback on their experiences; the rise in the importance of league tables within the National Health Service in the UK – these are just some of the features characteristic of the application of neoliberalism within the spheres of welfare and social services. While these have been the subject of a voluminous critical literature in the fields of politics, sociology, social policy, and economics, academic lawyers have tended to concentrate on the implications of such developments for the law within their particular legal subdisciplines, such as health care law and housing law. There has been comparatively little work undertaken by lawyers exploring what these types of developments in welfare and social services might reveal more generally about the manner in which law shapes, and is shaped by, neoliberalism and the neoliberal state. This chapter offers some preliminary reflections on this wider issue.

The chapter has three objectives. First, it aims to identify the types of law and legal categories to be found in two areas of contemporary social policy – unemployment and health care. Second, it explores the form and underlying logic of those laws and legal categories and seeks to explain how these contribute, in a constitutive way, to the development and maintenance of neoliberalism and the neoliberal state. Finally, the chapter aims to place the foregoing analysis in the context of literature that comprehends neoliberalism as a political project that involves a central role for

1 Sussex Law School, University of Sussex, UK.

the state and a range of institutional means that are devised and deployed to further the goals of neoliberalism.

'Crafting the neoliberal state'

One of the myths surrounding neoliberalism is that it envisages a minimal role for the state. This myth, peddled by advocates and critics of neoliberalism alike, confuses the arguments about laissez-faire and the minimal state advanced by adherents of classical liberalism in the nineteenth century with the more nuanced views on the state propounded by theorists of neoliberalism. Of course, the goal of proponents of neoliberalism is to create a society founded upon the market – a market order – but this is not incompatible with a strong state; indeed, it demands a strong, active state to construct the necessary conditions for the establishment and maintenance of that market order. Thus, *inter alia*, the state must create markets where they do not already exist and ensure their continued operation; guarantee property rights; and ensure the absence of monopolies. But it needs to do more than this to ensure that societies function on the basis of markets. The state must also shape social relations accordingly and construct a specific worldview that enables the market to define the manner in which societies operate in practice. As Loïc Wacquant has noted: '[W]hat is "neo" about neoliberalism [is] the reengineering and redeployment of the state as the core agency that sets the rules and fabricates the subjectivities, social relations and collective representations suited to realising markets'.[2]

Wacquant's analysis of neoliberalism is helpful for two reasons. First, in emphasising the importance of the state, he identifies neoliberalism as a political, as opposed to an economic, project. In other words, while the establishment of a market order is the goal of neoliberalism, this is accomplished through politics, rather than the product of neoclassical economics. Second, he points to the need to develop 'a "thick" sociological conception' of neoliberalism that identifies both the institutional means deployed by the state to establish, maintain, and impose the market order on society, and the types of consequences this has for citizenship. For Wacquant, those institutional means are not confined to the rules of the marketplace, but also include the criminal justice system – especially the prison, the 'disciplinary' social policy of workfare, and the 'trope of individual responsibility'. Whether or not one agrees with the relevance of the particular institutional means or 'logics' he identifies, this manner of conceptualising neoliberalism and what he calls the crafting of the neoliberal state succeeds in highlighting the importance

2 L. Wacquant, 'Three Steps to a Historical Anthropology of Actually Existing Neoliberalism' (2012) 20(1) Social Anthropology 66–79, p. 66.

of concrete state institutional mechanisms in shaping the material components of those phenomena (e.g. the construction of new markets) and their symbolic components ('the capacity that the state has to trace salient social demarcations and produce social reality through its work of inculcation of efficient categories and classifications'[3]). If we wish to understand market societies, we need to attend to the different ways and means through which the state constructs these.

How does law fit within this analysis of neoliberalism and the crafting of the neoliberal state? While Wacquant himself includes (presumably the criminal) courts as part of the penal wing of the neoliberal state that he explores in his recent work, there is little discussion of the role that these, or law and legal categories more generally, play in neoliberalism and the construction of the neoliberal state. And yet for the pioneers of neoliberalism law was to play a foundational role in the development and implementation of the neoliberal vision. Two dimensions of this can be identified. First, for neoliberals, markets are creatures of law. Their existence demands, and depends on, the presence of a legal framework suited to this end. In Marxist terms, though contrary to traditional Marxist teachings, law, in this vision, is not a part of the superstructure determined by the economic base; rather, law is an inherent aspect of the base – law founds the market order, rather than being determined by it. This has consequences for common assumptions surrounding the nature of economic entities and their regulation. Thus, the property bought and sold on the market, the contracts through which the sale and purchase are made, and the companies involved in selling and buying the property are all, in the first instance, legal entities, rather than, as is commonly assumed, objects that exist outside of the law and are only subsequently regulated, or not, by the law. As Walter Lippmann, whose eponymous Colloquium is often cited as constituting the beginnings of neoliberalism, wrote:

> Only by recognizing that legal rights are declared and enforced by the state is it possible to make a rational examination of the value of any particular legal right. The latter-day liberals did not see this. They fell into a deep and confusing error when they failed to see that property, contracts, corporations, as well as governments, electorates, and courts, are creatures of law, and have no existence except as bundles of enforceable rights and duties.[4]

3 L. Wacquant, Punishing the Poor: The Neoliberal Government of Social Insecurity (Durham and London: Duke University Press, 2009), p. xvi.

4 W. Lippmann, An Enquiry into the Principles of the Good Society, quoted in P. Dardot and C. Laval, The New Way of the World: On Neoliberal Society (London: Verso, 2013), p. 59.

Second, for neoliberals law must take the form of a set of formal abstract general rules that apply equally to everyone's conduct. This is necessary because the market order is based on the idea that individuals are free to pursue their different objectives via the market. The alternative – social law – defeats this purpose as it involves the creation of rules designed to further a particular, predetermined end such as the redistribution of wealth between classes. Here, law would prescribe individual conduct rather than respect liberty of action. The market order, then, is what Hayek refers to as a nomocracy (governed by law), as opposed to a teleocracy (governed by an end or ends). It is what he called a 'private law society' where the formal abstract general rules – the 'rules of just conduct' – that constitute the market order are synonymous with 'the essential content of all contemporary systems of private law, ["]freedom of contract, the inviolability of property, and the duty to compensate for damage due to his fault["]'.[5] In his influential book *The Road to Serfdom*, Hayek was already setting out this vision of law in the course of his argument that competition – the defining norm of neoliberalism and what Hayek called 'the principle of social organisation' – required a rigorous legal framework for its successful and beneficial operation. It was a crucial part of what he endorsed as the state's 'planning for competition', as opposed to 'planning against competition', which involved the 'central direction of all economic activity according to a single plan, laying down how the resources of society should be "consciously directed" to serve particular ends in a definite way'.[6]

The foregoing discussion identifies themes that provide a useful context for the analysis of the relationship between law, social policy, and the neoliberal state in the remainder of the chapter. What types of law and legal categories do we encounter in the design and implementation of social policy in the two areas explored here – unemployment and health care? What forms and logics structure those laws and legal categories? And how do those forms and logics function both materially and symbolically to shape the neoliberal vision and help craft the neoliberal state? These are the types of questions with which the chapter engages.

Unemployment and workfare

Workfare schemes – which operate on the basis that access to welfare benefits is conditional on undertaking work or work-related activities –

5 F.A. Hayek, Law, Legislation and Liberty: A New Statement of the Liberal Principles of Justice and Political Economy (London and New York: Routledge, 2013), p. 206, referring to Leon Duguit as described by J. Walter Jones, Historical Introduction to the Theory of Law (Oxford: Oxford University Press, 1940), p. 114.

6 F.A. Hayek, The Road to Serfdom (London: Routledge, 1944), p. 26.

have become important mechanisms through which increasing numbers of governments manage unemployment and the unemployed. While the justification advanced by governments for such schemes is that engagement in work is the surest means of escaping poverty, critical commentators have identified a number of other reasons for their existence. One of these sees a transformation in the nature of social policy from one that protected those in need from the deleterious social and economic consequences of capitalism to one that is driven primarily by economic policy and the needs of capitalism.[7] This latter characterisation describes the impact on social policy of the requirement of states to reduce their social spending in order to remain economically competitive within the global economy. One way of doing this is to ensure the unemployed are ultimately removed from the welfare rolls and (re-)engage in the flexible and casualised labour market characteristic of our contemporary era.

While acknowledging the link between workfare and capital, others are less willing to view economics as the determinant of this social policy. For them, workfare is as much about a shift from a protective to a disciplinary form of social policy focused on transforming the ways in which individuals behave, as it is about the economy. The unemployed must be trained to accept the low wages of the labour in which workfare recipients mostly find themselves; they must learn that they are individually responsible for their predicaments – whether these are positive or negative; and they must conceive of themselves as competitors and life as a competition. Whatever one's views of the merits of those different ways of conceptualising workfare, what is clear is that the features identified by both are indelibly characteristic of neoliberalism and the neoliberal state.

The form through which workfare operates is contract. Initially called the Jobseekers' Agreement, after the passing of the Welfare Reform Act 2012, this is now known as the 'claimant commitment'. Essentially, benefit claimants must sign a contract that details the type of work being sought and the steps to be taken in looking for work and in improving one's chances of securing work. While the philosophy of conditionality has underpinned unemployment legislation for many years,[8] the use of contract as the form of workfare is novel.

There are a number of ways in which the use of contract in this context feeds in to, and furthers, the neoliberal project. First, while not a legal contract per se, the workfare contract aligns the management of the social and economic problem of unemployment to the type of liberal political rationality underpinning the classical private law of contract – which, as we

7 See, for e.g., B. Jessop, The Future of the Capitalist State (Cambridge: Polity, 2002).

8 Though it was never invoked in practice in the UK in the way in which it has been since the mid-1990s. Until then, access to unemployment benefits was basically viewed as a social right.

saw earlier, neoliberal theorists such as Hayek view as a key legal institution framing the neoliberal vision. This rationality stresses notions of individual liberty, individual responsibility and fault, and the voluntary consent of the individual. The rational, self-determining agent, who makes autonomous choices about whether to enter into agreements based upon self-assessments of individual utility, underpins this rationality. As such, the workfare contract does not, in theory at least, compel welfare beneficiaries to sign up to it; rather it emphasises the importance of consent, negotiation, and reciprocity in the construction of the agreement. The idea of contract as a binding agreement freely made in the marketplace between formally equal contracting parties (*pacta sunt servanda*) lies at the heart of workfare. That this liberal rationality pertains in the context of workfare is evidenced by the sanctions that flow from a breach of the contract. Failure to comply with the duties therein results in the progressive withholding of a claimant's benefits, whatever the consequences,[9] indicating that individual fault expressed in the failure to keep one's promises lies at the root of this contract.

Second, this liberal construction of the workfare contract feeds into the neoliberal form of social relations and subjectivities being shaped by the state. Thus, the focus on individual responsibility and self-reliance corresponds to the idea behind the so-called social investment state in which the state invests in individuals' human capital through education and training, rather than providing them with economic benefits. Individuals actively work on themselves and create individual plans of action with a view to being in a position to compete in the labour market. They are no longer passive recipients of welfare but active entrepreneurs acting on their own initiative and able to carve out opportunities for themselves in the market.

Third, related to, but beyond, the formation of subjectivities, the mechanism of contract enables the state to produce in reality powerful classifications of the unemployed. In the present context, the liberal political rationality underlying the workfare contract, with its emphasis on individual responsibility, voluntary consent, and the honouring of promises, lends the politics of unemployment a moral dimension that structures the manner in which society perceives this phenomenon. This is especially clear in the context of the government's sanctions regime, which provides for the progressive withdrawal of economic benefits from claimants who fail to discharge their contractual duties. This enables the resurrection of the old classification of the poor into the 'deserving' and the 'undeserving'. Those who fail to fulfil their obligations are not only deprived of the

9 For an indication of the types of consequences flowing from such a breach, see A. Gentleman, '"No one should die penniless and alone": the victims of Britain's harsh welfare sanctions', The Guardian, 3 August 2014 (www.theguardian.com/society/2014/aug/03/victims-britains-harsh-welfare-sanctions).

material resources by which to live, thereby exacerbating their poverty; importantly, they are also deemed to be undeserving – a morally loaded term often synonymous with characterisations of those individuals as, *inter alia*, lazy, work-shy, and benefit fraudsters. This cleavage illustrates the symbolic dimension of the state's deployment of contract within the context of workfare, which takes the form of maintaining and deepening the social divides between morally upstanding citizens and the immoral who fail to live up to the norms associated with workfare. The state's use of contract as an institutional mechanism by which to manage unemployment therefore succeeds, in Wacquant's words, in 'produc[ing] social reality through its work of inculcation of efficient categories and classifications'.[10]

Finally, the foregoing symbolic effects of the workfare contract contribute to the legitimation of neoliberalism and the neoliberal state by working to obscure a number of controversial features surrounding the management of unemployment. Here are a few. First, at the level of the making of the contract itself, they divert attention from the fact that it is highly questionable whether the workfare contract is a contract at all. Peter Vincent-Jones, for instance, has argued that it is difficult to call the Jobseekers' Agreement a contract as it complies poorly with a number of common contract norms, including reciprocity (the idea that both parties benefit from the contract through the mutual exchange of acts or promises), consent (the notion that parties voluntarily enter into agreements rather than being coerced to do so), and choice or freedom of contract (the idea that parties are free to determine the nature of their contractual obligations). He argues that the latter, for example, is largely a myth as genuine options are frequently not offered to jobseekers in practice. Similarly, consent is more theoretical than real as welfare recipients have little alternative but to accept the terms of the Agreement – at least if they wish to have access to basic material resources.[11] As a result, Vincent-Jones has noted the coercive, as opposed to voluntary, nature of the so-called contracts in the field of social policy.[12] Their imposition by the state for concrete policy ends dilutes the component of individual autonomous choice

10 Wacquant, op. cit., note 3.

11 See P. Vincent-Jones, The New Public Contracting: Regulation, Responsiveness, Relationality (Oxford: Oxford University Press, 2006), ch. 9, and P. Vincent-Jones, 'Contractual Governance: Institutional and Organizational Analysis' (2000) 20(3) Oxford Journal of Legal Studies 317–51. Further sceptical analysis of the workfare 'contract' along these lines can be found in M. Freedland and D. King, 'Contractual Governance and Illiberal Contracts: Some Problems of Contractualism as an Instrument of Behaviour Management by Agencies of Government' (2003) 27(3) Cambridge Journal of Economics 465–77.

12 See Vincent-Jones, The New Public Contracting, ibid.

characteristic of freedom of contract.[13] Here, we encounter one of the 'institutional logics' – *disciplinary* social policy – Wacquant identifies as being characteristic of the re-engineering of the state that defines neoliberalism. The precise effect of the deployment of contract here is to obscure this authoritarian dimension of the neoliberal state as its underlying liberal political rationality succeeds in directing one's focus towards the behaviour of unemployed individuals and the degree to which they abide by their 'freely' made obligations.

The second, hidden issue is the trajectory of those on workfare. Empirical analyses on this point identify key structural factors – such as class, poor education, and the low-paid and precarious nature of the labour market – that impede the permanent and successful re-integration into society of many of those on workfare, but cannot be addressed via the workfare contract.[14] What is secured through the assimilation characteristic of workfare is not necessarily an escape from poverty and the heightened possibility of de-socialisation that poverty engenders, but its entrenchment and ongoing production as a result of low-skilled and poorly paid labour. Discipline here is not confined to the signing of the workfare contract; it extends to the insertion of the unemployed into the casualised and insecure forms of labour that characterise the flexible labour markets that, as we saw earlier, are a product of neoliberal economic policies. The point here is not only that the workfare contract does not address those structural factors; the symbolic effects it produces also mean that those factors remain entirely absent from the state's politics, and policies, of unemployment.

The final, related, point revolves around this reference to the politics of unemployment. It is suggested that there is something of a paradox here. Thus, while neoliberalism is best understood as a political project, one of its concrete effects, discussed throughout this volume, is to depoliticise issues. In the current context, this politics of depoliticisation takes the form not only of the obscuration of the types of structural factors mentioned above, but as a result of this, the suppression of potential struggles and conflicts over the meaning and causes of unemployment. While in fact remaining fundamentally political insofar as they continue to structure the power relations surrounding unemployment and the fates of the unemployed, questions of political economy, class, the nature of the

13 See D. Campbell, 'Relational Contract and the Nature of Private Ordering: A Comment on Vincent-Jones' (2007) 14(2) Indiana Journal of Global Legal Studies 279–300. In Campbell's view, this 'erosion of the individual dimension of contract', together with the fact that social policy contracts disguise 'the hierarchical coercion that is the identifying feature of state intervention', mean that these 'contracts' are not contracts at all.

14 See, for example, M. Carpenter, B. Freda and S. Speeden (eds) Beyond the Workfare State: Labour Markets, Equality and Human Rights (Bristol: The Policy Press, 2007).

labour market, education, and the bureaucratic compulsion to meet targets are removed from the state's politics of unemployment via a social policy that succeeds in reducing this phenomenon to an issue of morality. Moreover, the state's power to shape the mental structures and classifications surrounding unemployment tends to naturalise our thinking about, and response to, it and removes the need to challenge the manner in which it is constructed. It is the resurrection of this agonistic dimension of politics in the sphere of welfare and social policy that must be reasserted as a means of challenging the politics of depoliticisation that characterise the neoliberal state.

Health care

It was noted earlier that markets are creatures of law and that neoliberal theorists stress the importance of a legal framework of formal abstract general rules for the establishment and successful operation of the market order. While those theorists mainly had in mind markets in which private actors or agencies competed for market share, this section will consider the role of markets and the private sector in a sphere in which, traditionally, they have been absent. This is the publicly funded health care system in the UK – the National Health Service (NHS). Since the 1990s, social services have become subject to the market imperative, as guiding neoliberal norms – such as competition and individual choice – have spread from the private to the public sector. But what role has law played in this development? This section addresses this question by identifying some of the ways in which law is constitutive of markets and facilitates the increasing involvement of the private sector within the NHS. Like the discussion of workfare earlier, the focus will not merely be on identifying the types of law that are involved here; it will extend to incorporate reflection on the forms and logics that structure those laws. Let us begin, though, with two examples that illustrate the expanding role of markets and the private sector within the NHS.

The Health and Social Care Act 2012 puts the norm of competition at the heart of the Coalition Government's vision for the NHS. One of the Act's key provisions is the replacement of Primary Care Trusts with clinical commissioning groups (CCGs) as the bodies responsible for commissioning (purchasing) most health care services within the NHS (a task that will involve responsibility for spending £80bn of NHS resources). By 2016, it will become possible for CCGs to outsource their commissioning work to non-public bodies – including private firms. A market will therefore effectively be created for such services and be funded from the NHS budget. The legislation also promotes the 'any qualified provider' approach to the provision of NHS health care services – meaning there will be increased scope for, *inter alia*, private health care providers to become involved in the provision of NHS health care. The opportunity for private sector involvement is also heightened by the promotion of 'fair and effective' competition and the application of competition law to the commissioning of NHS treatment for the first time. The sector-specific regulator for health care – which is called Monitor – is under a duty to promote a provision of health care services which is 'economic, efficient and effective', and to exercise its functions in a manner that will prevent anti-competitive behaviour in health care provision that is against patients' interests.[15] It will also be able to tackle specific abuses and unjustifiable restrictions that demonstrably act against patients' interests by deploying its licensing powers and, where relevant, the Competition Act 1998. The effect will be to alter the current situation, in which the bulk of NHS services are commissioned from public bodies, by creating a level playing field in which private providers of health care can compete to deliver NHS health care services. CCGs will need, in effect, to ensure that a tendering process for the provision of NHS services is in place, if they are not to fall foul of competition law.

The second example is the prominent role public–private partnerships (PPPs; formerly the Private Finance Initiative) have played as ways of funding new NHS hospital buildings. Here, private contractors raise the money to finance the construction of hospitals for the NHS and, via the PPP contract, own and manage the hospital. The NHS Primary Care Trust leases the hospital and staff, such as cleaners, from the contractors, paying what is known as a 'unitary charge' for these from their annual health care budget. Contracts last for periods ranging from 25 to 30 years, although once they are paid off, the NHS does not necessarily end up owning the premises. The PPP scheme has been the object of cogent critique.[16] As well as being a social cost in monetary terms – that is, a mechanism by which to facilitate the accumulation of capital and profit via the redistribution of money from public funds[17] – it also has potential social costs in human terms, as the often onerous contractual obligations to pay for PPP-financed

15 Health and Social Care Act 2012, s.62.

16 See, for instance, A.M. Pollock, NHS plc: The Privatisation of Our Health Care (London: Verso, 2004).

17 An analysis by The Guardian newspaper in 2012 found that the current 717 PFI contracts, while having a total capital value of £54.7bn, would have an ultimate cost of £301bn once paid off. See The Guardian (6 July 2012) pp. 1 and 18. As Hellowell and Pollock note, one of the reasons for this inflated cost is that 'the cost of finance on PFI schemes is higher than is the case for publicly financed schemes…'. M. Hellowell and A.M. Pollock 'The Private Financing of NHS Hospitals: Politics, Policy and Practice' (2009) 29 Economic Affairs 13. There is also evidence of a so-called Secondary Market in PFI shareholdings in hospitals, schools, roads, and prisons. See BBC Radio 4's File on 4 programme 'PFI Profits', broadcast on 19 June 2011.

buildings can jeopardise the existence of NHS hospitals, thereby endangering the treatment of patients.[18]

Competition law and contract law obviously perform important constitutive functions in facilitating the role of competition, markets, and the private sector within the NHS. But beyond identifying those types of law, what can be said about their form and underlying logic? To answer this question it is necessary to widen the frame of analysis.

It is worth beginning by noting the impact the emergence of the welfare state had upon the nature of the form of law. In Max Weber's analysis the formal rational law he identified as characteristic of Western modernity and that corresponded with the emergence of the capitalist economy came under attack with the development of what he called 'the modern class problem'. Unlike formal rational law, the essence of which lay in a system of formal and abstract general rules that framed private actors' conduct and ensured the formal equality of legal subjects before the law, what became known as social law was a legal instrumentalist form of law which was deployed as a means to redress the substantive inequalities between classes.[19] More recently, François Ewald has argued that the concept of social law is underpinned by a distinct political rationality or logic – namely, solidarity – that differs from the classical idea of social contract, which is based on the relationship between autonomous individuals who agree to create a State the purpose of which is simply to guarantee contracts made between those individuals.[20] Social law is a contractual law too, but importantly what Ewald calls solidarity contracts are structured around a logic that differs from contracts of the private law variety. Solidarity contracts, he says, are 'founded on ideas of fair distribution or equitable allocation of social burdens and profits' and are contractual in the sense that they are based upon a contractual relationship of all with each before and beyond any element of intention; in other words, unlike the classical private law of contract it is not the exercise of the will of rational individuals that founds solidarity contracts, but the relationships of interdependence amongst all and each.

This has consequences for our understanding of welfare measures and laws. So, for example, social insurance for industrial accidents is not based on a notion of individual guilt or fault or responsibility (assigning blame to the employer or the co-workers), but on the idea of the 'socialisation of responsibility'. This takes as its focus the collective relationship between,

18 The recent placing of South London Healthcare Trust into administration owing to an unsustainable deficit created by the contractual obligation to pay PFI costs is a case in point. Also, see Hellowell and Pollock, id.

19 M. Weber, Economy and Society: An Outline of Interpretive Sociology (Berkeley, CA: University of California Press, 1978), Vol. II.

20 F. Ewald, 'A Concept of Social Law' in G. Teubner (ed.) Dilemmas of Law in the Welfare State (Berlin: de Gruyter, 1986), pp. 40–75.

say, employers and employees (production is a collective effort), and works on the idea of settlement of conflicting rights between the parties based on notions of fair distribution or equitable allocation of social burdens and profits. Consequently, Ewald describes social law as a law of groups; a law of inequalities, in that there is an assumption that there exist inequalities between human beings and classes and that these must be compensated or corrected – social law restores upset equilibria/balance; a law of positive discriminations; a law of 'mutual concessions' and tolerance between rich and poor, individual and social interests.

In summary, while formal rational law is consistent with the liberal legal form advocated by neoliberal theorists, social law represents a departure from this form. As Ewald's work illustrates, the arrival of the welfare state signalled a transformation in the form of law – from one focused, for example, on the freedom of individuals to set the terms of their own agreements, to one in which courts were prepared to imply terms into contracts in order to reflect policy goals such as the protection of weaker parties against the powerful – tenants vis-à-vis landlords, say; or the curtailment of private property rights in the name of the public interest. This is not to say that liberal law and the liberal legal form disappeared with the emergence of social law and the welfare state; it is, however, to say that the form and underlying logic of social law differed from formal rational law and the liberal legal form with which it is associated.

In light of this exposition of the differing logics of formal rational law and social law, what can be said of the legal form underlying the types of law that have come to prominence in the context of the reforms to the NHS outlined above? On the one hand these laws are indicative of formal rational law. Thus, the possibility of applying competition law to ensure the absence of anti-competitive behaviour introduces a degree of formal equality into the NHS commissioning process; and the use of contract law as the legal mechanism upon which PPPs rest stresses the importance of the formal notion that agreements freely entered into between parties must be upheld. Possible substantive inequalities between the competing parties gain no recognition under a form of law concerned only with formal equality; nor do the concrete detrimental consequences – such as the closure of hospital wards or indeed entire hospitals – that may flow, for instance, from the need of NHS Trusts to settle the high interest payments associated with PPPs. Competition and the honouring of contractual obligations (*pacta sunt servanda*), rather than the ideas of fair distribution or equitable allocation of social burdens and profits that Ewald identifies as structuring social law and solidarity contracts, are the norms underlying the laws that constitute the markets, and entry of the private sector, being facilitated within today's NHS.

This identification of formal rational law in the context of the NHS is somewhat complicated, however, in that, despite appearances, it is not entirely devoid of any element of collectivisation or socialisation. This is apparent, for instance, in the allocation of risk within contracts framing PPPs, which is often assumed by the government rather than the private sector. As an example, Allyson Pollock explains that NHS Trusts that wish to terminate contracts for the provision of services by private consortia on the basis of poor performance must still pay the consortia's financing costs despite their being at fault. Here, it is suggested that contract creates a legal bond between citizens and capital through which responsibility and liability for the economic risks – in the form of the financial debts and interest accrued by the private sector – and associated potential social harms, such as lack of availability of health care, of PPPs, are socialised or collectivised, not between the contracting parties, but amongst citizens themselves. Through the medium of the PPP contract, a strict liability is imposed upon a non-contracting collective body – taxpayers. It is important to note, though, that this form of socialisation could not differ more from the logic of socialisation underpinning the solidarity contracts that Ewald identifies as defining social law – one which is directed towards ameliorating the inequalities, social and economic harms, and skewed distribution of social burdens and profits produced by the operation of capitalism. Rather than pursuing such objectives, the manner in which PPP contracts are framed, and the form of socialisation that structures them, are geared towards the needs of capital rather than towards the protection of those requiring access to publicly funded health care.

As with workfare, one can witness a politics of depoliticisation at work here. For this novel form of socialisation through contract – an essential component of the practical implementation of neoliberalism and the shaping of the neoliberal state in the context of health care – is occluded by a politics of publicly funded health care that is actively constructed around a discourse, *inter alia*, of value for money, the unsustainable costs of the NHS (both in terms of treatments and personnel), bureaucratic inflexibility and mismanagement, and patient empowerment through, amongst other things, the expansion of choice.[21] These forms of discourse not only demonstrate a core function of the neoliberal state – which, in Wacquant's terms, is the fabrication of collective representations of, in this case, the NHS; in doing so, they succeed in both obscuring the structures put in place to facilitate the neoliberal vision for the NHS and suppressing potential conflicts and struggles over the very meaning and shape of the politics of publicly funded health care.

The conclusion that flows from the foregoing analysis is that, while the types of law constitutive of the neoliberal reforms taking place within the

21 Choice amongst NHS health care providers is now a legal right enshrined in the NHS Constitution. See Department of Health, The NHS Constitution: The NHS Belongs to Us All (2013).

NHS are of the formal rational variety – a legal framework of abstract general rules facilitating competition and the operation of freedom of contract – they are also, at least partially, structured by a logic of socialisation or collectivisation. In its objective, however, the latter is diametrically opposed to the logic of socialisation underlying social law.

Conclusion

What preliminary conclusions might be drawn from the foregoing analysis of the relationship between law and neoliberalism in the areas of unemployment and health care?

First, if, as it has been argued here, neoliberalism is best understood as a political project involving the state's creation and deployment of institutional mechanisms geared towards a society founded upon the market, then social policy and the law and legal categories used to implement this must be taken seriously as important, constitutive, elements in this process.

Second, the form of law encountered in the examples discussed is of the formal rational variety that posits a legal framework of abstract general rules that emphasises formal equality and facilitates the liberty of individuals to choose their owns ends rather than these being chosen for them by an omniscient state. While this form of law is materially important in providing the rules necessary to allow for the development of markets and the competition between actors within them, it is also crucial symbolically as it helps the state shape what Wacquant refers to as the 'subjectivities, social relations and collective representations suited to realising markets'.[22] This feature of law and legal categories is especially potent in the workfare context where the deployment of contract along the lines of its classical private law form – underpinned by a liberal political rationality – allows the state to shape the politics of unemployment around a certain form of social relations and subjectivity.

Finally, the symbolic effects that law and legal categories help to produce, obscure important aspects of the neoliberal political project and curtail the possibility, or even the need for, a politics that contests the coordinates of the contemporary politics of unemployment and publicly funded health care. In exploring the types of law and underlying legal forms and logics that structure neoliberal reforms in two areas of today's social policy, the hope is to resurrect a form of agonistic politics that can challenge this politics of depoliticisation characteristic of the neoliberal state by bringing into view alternative principles upon which future social policy and related law might be founded.

22 Wacquant, op. cit., note 2.

References

BBC Radio 4's *File on 4* programme 'PFI Profits', broadcast on 19 June 2011.

Campbell, D. 'Relational Contract and the Nature of Private Ordering: A Comment on Vincent-Jones' (2007) 14(2) *Indiana Journal of Global Legal Studies* 279–300.

Carpenter, M., B. Freda, and S. Speeden (eds) *Beyond the Workfare State: Labour Markets, Equality and Human Rights* (Bristol: The Policy Press, 2007).

Department of Health *The NHS Constitution: The NHS Belongs to Us All* (2013).

Ewald, F. 'A Concept of Social Law' in G. Teubner (ed.) *Dilemmas of Law in the Welfare State* (Berlin: de Gruyter, 1986), 40–75.

Freedland, M. and D. King 'Contractual Governance and Illiberal Contracts: Some Problems of Contractualism as an Instrument of Behaviour Management by Agencies of Government' (2003) 27(3) *Cambridge Journal of Economics* 465–77.

Gentleman, A. '"No one should die penniless and alone": the victims of Britain's harsh welfare sanctions', *The Guardian*, 3 August 2014 (www.theguardian.com/society/2014/aug/03/victims-britains-harsh-welfare-sanctions).

The Guardian (6 July 2012).

Hayek, F.A. *The Road to Serfdom* (London: Routledge, 1944).

Hayek, F.A. *Law, Legislation and Liberty: A New Statement of the Liberal Principles of Justice and Political Economy* (London and New York: Routledge, 2013).

Hellowell, M. and A.M. Pollock 'The Private Financing of NHS Hospitals: Politics, Policy and Practice' (2009) 29 *Economic Affairs* 13.

Jessop, B. *The Future of the Capitalist State* (Cambridge: Polity, 2002).

Jones, J. Walter *Historical Introduction to the Theory of Law* (Oxford: Oxford University Press, 1940).

Lippmann, W. *An Enquiry into the Principles of the Good Society*, quoted in P. Dardot and C. Laval *The New Way of the World: On Neoliberal Society* (London: Verso, 2013).

Pollock, A.M. *NHS plc: The Privatisation of Our Health Care* (London: Verso, 2004).

Vincent-Jones, P. 'Contractual Governance: Institutional and Organizational Analysis' (2000) 20(3) *Oxford Journal of Legal Studies* 317–51.

Vincent-Jones, P. *The New Public Contracting: Regulation, Responsiveness, Relationality* (Oxford: Oxford University Press, 2006).

Wacquant, L. *Punishing the Poor: The Neoliberal Government of Social Insecurity* (Durham, NC and London: Duke University Press, 2009).

Wacquant, L. 'Three Steps to a Historical Anthropology of Actually Existing Neoliberalism' (2012) 20(1) *Social Anthropology* 66–79.

Weber, M. *Economy and Society: An Outline of Interpretive Sociology* (Berkeley, CA: University of California Press, 1978), Vol. II.

Chapter 5

Law, neoliberalism and the constitution of political subjectivity

The case of organised labour

Robert Knox[1]

Introduction

The birth pangs of neoliberalism in the advanced capitalist world were sparked by a series of spectacular confrontations with the bastions of the trade union movement. In 1981, Ronald Reagan successfully took on the powerful Professional Air Traffic Controllers Union (PATCO), firing those of its members who refused to return to work from a strike aimed at improving terms and conditions. This resulted in more than 11,000 workers losing their jobs and the eventual decertification of the union. Similarly, in 1984–1985, the Conservative government in Britain crushed the miners' strike, in the process crippling the powerful National Union of Mineworkers (NUM). These cases were symbolic of the wider attack on organised labour that characterised the beginnings of neoliberalism.

In *A Brief History of Neoliberalism*, David Harvey – following Duménil and Lévy (2004) – sees this attack as part of the '*political* project to re-establish the conditions for capital accumulation and to restore the power of economic elites' which for him defines neoliberalism (Harvey 2005, 19). In Harvey's telling, neoliberalism emerged in the wake of the failure of the class-compromise of 'embedded liberalism' to deliver high rates of growth and profit. In response to this, a fraction of the ruling class sought to remove impediments to profit-making at home, and enable capitalists in the advanced capitalist countries to draw on surpluses extracted from the rest of the world (Harvey 2005, 33). This required the destruction of embedded liberalism and the opening up of new areas to the logic of

1 Lecturer, School of Law and Social Justice, University of Liverpool. My thanks to Tor Krever for his incisive comments on the first version of this piece; his suggestions and sheer pedantry have helped sharpen its arguments considerably. My thanks also to Claire Mummé, whose actual knowledge of the field addressed within this chapter has helped camouflage my utter dilettantism; many of the more insightful comments in this chapter are down to her. Alas, since the material conditions of academia have interpellated me as an individualistic neoliberal subject, I must act as if all errors of style and substance are my own responsibility.

capital accumulation. By extension, it also required the dismantling of organised labour, which had – in various guises – been at the heart of the project of embedded liberalism. Trade unions were frequently the defenders of nationalised industries, were able to secure higher wages and had imposed limits on the ability of capitalists to flexibly exploit their labour forces.

In focusing on prosaic, class-based concerns, Harvey is keen to stress that neoliberalism should not be seen as a '*utopian* project to realize a theoretical design for the reorganization of international capitalism'. For him, whenever 'neoliberal principles clash with the need to restore or sustain elite power, then the principles are either abandoned or become so twisted as to be unrecognizable' (Harvey 2005, 19). There is a lot of sense to this position. It seems difficult to speak of some ideal type 'neoliberalism', especially given its uneven geographical and political implementation throughout the world. Equally, the anti-statist and 'free market' rhetoric of the original theorists of neoliberalism is vastly at odds with the expansion and reconfiguration of state-power that was needed to birth and secure it.

However, there is a sense in which Harvey's position misses something important. Even if one cannot ascribe some overall 'pure' economic content to neoliberalism, the neoliberal period has nonetheless seen fundamental transformations at every level of social organisation. As Dardot and Laval point out, neoliberalism 'is not merely destructive of rules, institutions and rights' but is also '*productive* of certain kinds of social relations, certain ways of living, certain subjectivities' (Dardot and Laval 2014, 3). Drawing on Foucault, they argue that neoliberalism is a *rationality* which 'tends to structure and organize not only the action of rulers, but also the conduct of the ruled' (Dardot and Laval 2014, 4). The main feature of this neoliberal rationality 'is the generalization of competition as a behavioural norm and of the enterprise as a model of subjectivation', with neoliberalism ultimately creating 'a new mode of government of human beings in accordance with the universal principle of competition' (Dardot and Laval 2014, 4). In other words, neoliberalism produces neoliberal *subjects*.

One need not agree with the whole of this analysis to acknowledge that it raises some important points. Vitally, Dardot and Laval draw attention to the fact that neoliberalism simply *could not function* 'economically' without also creating individual subjects conditioned to implement and perpetuate it. Even with Harvey's more prosaic understanding of neoliberalism as a 'restoration of class power', it is necessary to explain the phenomenal *success* and stability of this restoration. Harvey himself foregrounds 'the cultivation of a middle class that relished the joys of home ownership, private property, individualism, and the liberation of entrepreneurial opportunities' and the spread of these values to the working class as an important component of neoliberalism (Harvey 2005, 61–62).

In essence, Dardot and Laval insist that neoliberalism is *productive* (and not just destructive) and that an important aspect of this productivity involves the creation of individual neoliberal subjects. Yet when it comes to the collective organisations of the working class, they do not carry this argument through. Although they mention trade unions, it is primarily to remark on their *marginalisation* under neoliberalism. For them, neoliberalism was accompanied by 'a political desire to weaken trade-union power' (Dardot and Laval 2014, 173) in order to secure trade unions' compliance with managerial demands. In their view, therefore, neoliberalism's relationship to the trade union movement appears almost wholly 'destructive'. However, this misses something vital. Trade unions are not simply 'economic' bodies. They are also collective political organisations, which shape the lives of their members, hold political positions, intervene in the workplace and create a sense of class identity. They are, in other words, *collective political subjects.* If neoliberalism is marked by the emergence of a particular form of individual subjectivity, then one would expect it to also involve changes to subjectivity at a collective level.

This chapter builds on this insight, arguing that the attacks on organised labour described above were not simply aimed at crushing the strength of the trade union movement. Rather, they were part of a wider process of reconstituting the political subjectivity of organised labour into a form that was compatible with neoliberalism. Here, it is argued, law played an absolutely central role. Law created a series of material compulsions and incentives which pushed the organisations of the British working class to organise themselves in ways that undercut their wider mission of building class solidarity and articulating an alternative political project to untrammelled capitalism.

The chapter begins by reconstructing the 'pre-neoliberal' settlement. It first examines the legal regime that existed prior to the social democratic advances generated by the British labour movement. It then turns to the post-War social democratic consensus of 'collective laissez-faire'. Turning to Gramsci's account of different forms of collective political organisation it traces how the various institutional arrangements produced distinctive conceptions of the role of trade unions in 'representing' the political identity of the working class. In particular, it argues that the legal regime of collective-laissez faire (and its accompanying collective bargaining) created the conditions for a trade union movement that represented the working class *as a whole.*

The chapter moves on to the legislative changes introduced by the Thatcher government and retained by subsequent (Conservative and Labour) governments. It argues that, aside from directly restricting the abilities of unions to engage in industrial action, these laws also fundamentally reshaped the representative function of organised labour, transforming trade unions into narrow organisations representing only the immediate interests of their members. It further demonstrates how these legal changes fundamentally reoriented the political relationship between trade unions and the Labour Party. Finally, the chapter turns to more general reflections on the relationship between law, capitalism and the formation of political subjectivity. Examining the work of Duncan Kennedy, it argues that the changing forms of collective political subjectivity ultimately all remained within the coordinates of capitalist social relations. Accordingly, it argues, one of law's key roles is to integrate the working class into capitalism. The chapter ends by unpacking the strategic consequences of law's role in constituting political subjectivity.

British labour law before neoliberalism

The development of British labour law

Given the early and intensive growth of capitalism in Britain, and Britain's importance to the internationalisation of capitalism, it is unsurprising that British labour law has a long and complex history. What we can observe in this history is the fundamental role that law has played in regulating the relationship between workers and employers and in shaping the character of organised labour. Initially, this took place simply through rendering union organising *illegal*. This changed over the course of the 1800s as working class militancy – and the fear of what this militancy might achieve – forced successive governments to recognise trade union activity and allow for collective bargaining. Thus, we can observe a pattern of explosions in class struggle being contained and managed through legal interventions. These legal interventions produced distinct forms of collective political subjectivity, which – it will later be argued – corresponded to different political projects and possibilities.

To simplify grossly, from 1351, trade unions (or 'combinations') had been outlawed under the Statute of Labourers and a series of Acts that followed it (Lewis 1976, 2). The prohibition on union organisation was achieved through piecemeal, inconsistent legislation which – under the shadow of Jacobin radicalism in the French revolution – was codified and systematised in the Combination Acts (1799–1800) (Thompson 1966, 506). Despite these Acts, combinations still existed, since employers were not always willing to rely on their legal entitlements and since workers formed extra-legal combinations, deploying 'moral' and other sanctions to enforce their demands. This situation continued until 1824, when the Combination Acts were repealed by the Combination of Workmen Act. However, in an attempt to curtail the surge in industrial action that ensued in the wake of their repeal, The Combination of Workmen Act was itself limited by the 1825 Combination Laws Repeal Amendment Act (Lewis 1976, 2).

At this point, on the formal legislative level, trade unions were, with various restrictions, relatively free to organise and negotiate. However, they were hemmed in by a number of 'common law crimes' developed and deployed by an active and conservative judiciary. Important in this respect were the crimes of 'conspiracy' and 'restraint of trade', which essentially rendered industrial organising and action criminal (Lowry *et al.* 1979, 6).

Despite these common law crimes, trade unions were able to survive. They organised legal defences against the common law crimes, and were gaining greater public traction. However, in order to translate this into a more stable legal change, the trade unions needed to gain influence within Parliament (Lewis 1976, 2). The chance to achieve this influence arrived in 1867 when the government established a Royal Commission on Trade Unions to look into the question of how trade unions could be regulated (Brodie 2003, 1). In their final report, produced in 1869, the majority of Commissioners took a conservative line, arguing that union rules should not be allowed to restrain trade, enforce closed shops or allow action in support of other workers. The minority, influenced by a 'group of leading officials from the amalgamated skills union of the day' argued that unions be given immunity from criminal laws and restraint of trade laws, and for little ability to regulate union rules (Lewis 1976, 3).

It was the minority report that proved most influential on the Liberal government. The report was instrumental in securing the passage of a number of Acts throughout the 1870s which provided combinations with immunity from the common law crimes in instances where a combination was 'in contemplation or furtherance of a trade dispute' (Brodie 2003, 1–15). This formulation, known as the 'Golden Formula', was to become central in the development of British labour law (Barrow 2013, 326).

Again the British judiciary reacted against these developments. Rather than criminal liability, the judiciary now argued that trade union activities would amount to *torts*. Conspiracy was recast as a tort, and – most importantly – the tort of 'inducing breach of contract' came to the fore. Here, if a union was said to have induced workers to breach their employment contracts to the detriment of their employer, their employer could sue for damages. This was reinforced by the *Taff Vale*[2] case, which held unions to be liable for such damages *qua* unions (independently of their individual members) (Kay and Mott 1982, 116). This created a severe financial disincentive for trade unions to engage in industrial action.

The landmark 1906 Trades Disputes Act was an attempt to undermine this situation in favour of collective bargaining. This Act was a result of a great deal of trade union lobbying, which had led to a landslide Liberal victory and the election of 29 Labour Members of Parliament. Like the Acts of the 1870s that resulted from the Royal Commission, this Act gave

2 Taff Vale Railway Co v. Amalgamated Society of Railway Servants [1901] UKHL 1.

unions immunity from tortious liability insofar as they were acting 'in contemplation or furtherance of a trade dispute'.

The 1906 Trades Disputes Act set the frame for the basic shape of British labour law throughout the rest of the twentieth and twenty-first centuries. During the first three decades of the twentieth century, the legal status of trade unions and industrial action was strongly contested, as one would expect given the turbulent – and indeed revolutionary – global relationship between capital and labour throughout that period. Following the 1926 General Strike, the 1927 Trades Disputes and Trades Union Act was passed, which excluded 'political strikes' from the Golden Formula and restricted lawful picketing. Yet, in practice the effect of this Act was negligible. It was definitively repealed in 1946 by the newly elected post-war Labour government.

Thus far, one can observe a basic periodisation in the legal forms that trade union activism took. Up to the 1800s, the law largely assumed a directly repressive function, banning the formation of trade unions and their activities. Of course, this did not stop workers from banding together, and it was largely pressure from below, as well as the fear that illegality was breeding radicalism, which eventually pushed the state towards recognising trade unions (Lewis 1976, 3). The period following this, from the 1870s to the 1940s, was one of heightened flux; however one can perceive a distinct direction, which was first embodied in the 1906 Trades Disputes Act and was consolidated in the post-World War II settlement, following the repeal of the Trades Disputes and Trades Union Act. Here, we see a move towards a system in which the government legislated to protect trade unions from the adverse legal consequences of industrial action, whilst avoiding direct legislation on substantive workplace issues.

The post-war settlement

In Otto Kahn-Freud's famous formulation, the post-war settlement was one of 'collective laissez-faire' (Dukes 2009, 221). In this arrangement, the relationship between workers and capitalists was not directly regulated through government legislation, in part because the trade unions 'were too suspicious of the law and lawyers to accept any tight system of legal regulation' (Lewis 1976, 4; see also Collins 1997, 299–300). It was this 'legal abstentionism' that was described as 'laissez-faire'. Instead – and it is here that the 'collective' aspect comes to the fore – the relationship between workers and capitalists was regulated by collective agreements between trade unions and employers. These collective agreements were incorporated into individual contracts of employment by an 'implied bridging term', which meant that members in the workplace or industry that was covered by the agreement would have these terms as part of their own contracts (Deery and Mitchell 1999, 136).

Industrial action represented a crucial aspect of this post-war settlement. It was industrial action, and the threat thereof, which gave trade unions sufficient bargaining power to extract concessions from employers when negotiating these collective agreements. This was where the law took on a direct and immediate importance. On the one hand, the law in Britain has very little to say about the 'right' to strike. There is no right to strike. Neither is any strike per se illegal. On the other hand, industrial action will – at common law – be a breach of contract and attract tortious liability in the form of the tort of inducing a breach of contract. Such breaches will have legal consequences. The breach of contract involved in a strike can be characterised as a repudiatory breach, which entitles the employer to terminate the striking workers, and such tortious liability can entail heavy damages. Similarly, picketing is able to incur civil liability through trespass and nuisance.

The settlement first embodied in the 1906 Trades Disputes Act, and fully concretised in the post-war period, was designed to circumvent these legal restrictions and penalties. The Act, and the subsequent post-War settlement, granted unions immunity from tortious liability and prevented the termination of the workforce when industrial action was taken 'in contemplation or furtherance of a trade dispute'. Similarly, picketing would be protected under these circumstances. Thus, collective laissez-faire was undergirded and framed by a web of primary legislation that guaranteed the ability of trade unions to take industrial action and so enabled them to conduct collective bargaining (Ewing 1998; Deakin and Wilkinson 2005, 201).

Vitally then, coterminously with the 'embedded liberalism' of the welfare state was a particular model of industrial relations in which trade unions performed a very specific role. Because of the legal abstentionism at the heart of collective laissez-faire, the state did not directly intervene in or structure workplace relations. Rather, it was trade unions, through their collective negotiating power, that directly organised the workplace and secured the benefits and protections that workers would receive in the employment relationship. Thus, in 1979, Britain had a union density of 55.4 per cent, with around 85 per cent of the working population covered by collective bargaining (Howell 2005, 131). Of course, there were gaps since not all workplaces were unionised, and accordingly there was a tendency for a basic 'floor' of rights, such as health and safety and the minimum wage, to be legislated. But the fact remains that, in general, under collective laissez-faire, trade unions exercised a quasi-governmental function within the workplace, regulating both directly and indirectly the conditions for the majority of working people.[3] In this way, therefore,

3 In the Canadian context (which was very similar to that of Britain) Harry W. Arthurs characterised this legal regime as one of 'industrial citizenship', in which the mechanisms of collective bargaining functioned to create a kind of 'state within a state (Arthurs 1967, 787).

collective bargaining formed an integral part of the welfare state, serving as a vehicle for a number of important social protections.

The corollary to this system was a trade union movement that was extremely confident, engaging in activities that extended far beyond the immediate workplace. Crucially, the 1946 Trades Disputes and Trades Union Act repealed the ban on secondary action, meaning that unions could engage in industrial action unrelated to their own immediate trade disputes. Consequently, trade unions were able to engage in solidarity actions with workers outside of their immediate sphere of representation. This meant that trade unions served a wider *representative* role. They could engage in industrial action not just to defend their own members, but also in solidarity with other workers and in order to further the cause of the trade union movement as a whole. In this way, different workplaces and occupations could be seen as constituent elements of a wider working class with common interests that were represented by trade unions.

The combination of these quasi-governmental and representative roles meant that, for the trade unions in the post-war settlement, 'politics' and 'economics' frequently came together. This was obviously true insofar as trade unions were able to exercise a 'governance' function within workplaces. Equally, the industrial power of the trade unions could be turned to political ends, given the possibility of secondary action. This was exemplified in the trade unions' opposition to the 1971 Industrial Relations Act passed by the Conservative government.

The Industrial Relations Act 1971, which was a precursor to the later Thatcherite reforms, aimed at replacing collective laissez-faire with a framework modelled closely on the North American model, centred around the 'belief that collective bargaining exists for the sake of the individual' and active legal intervention into the workplace (Hall 1972, 14). This was to be achieved through a system of voluntary registration, whereby registered trade unions would have legally enforceable collective agreements (Weekes *et al.* 1975, 3–5). However, these registered unions would also have their internal regimes regulated by a Chief Registrar (Weekes *et al.* 1975, 64). The Act also established a series of new liabilities linked to industrial action: in particular secondary action and action in support of closed-shop agreements were rendered illegal (Weekes *et al.* 1975, 188–189). These were to be enforced by a new court – the National Industrial Relations Court – which had the power to issue injunctions when the law was breached.

Many trade unions saw this as a threat to their ability to organise and negotiate, and strongly opposed the Act. The Trades Union Congress initially opted for a campaign of non-registration (Moran 1977, 128–138). However, this opposition was radicalised in 1972 when, during the course of a dockers' strike, the Transport and General Workers Union (TGWU) refused to be represented before the NIRC and was subsequently fined

(Moran 1977, 139–140). The TGWU argued that this was the fault of its individual shop stewards, and that it would otherwise be prepared to appear, but the NIRC held that the union was still liable. This was reversed by the Court of Appeal, resulting in the jailing of five dock workers for not obeying the law. The outrage at this imprisonment quickly escalated into a national dispute, bringing the docks to a standstill and causing the TUC General Council to call for a general strike (Moran 1977, 142).

This willingness to flout the law, as well as use industrial muscle to support political objectives, put Britain on the brink of a constitutional crisis. The Conservative government was forced to place the Act 'on ice' for 'virtually … the rest of its term of office' (Panitch 1976, 225).

Interlude: the politics of collective laissez-faire

Thus, in examining this history, we can see a change. In the initial period, trade unions led a scattered and precarious existence. Yet with the rise of collective laissez-faire unions began to serve a different role, in effect *governing* their workplaces, and representing the working class *as a whole*, that is to say, as a class that had interests and needs distinct from the capitalist class. What we see here, then, is that collective laissez-faire also gave rise to a specific configuration of political subjectivity, in which trade unions played a distinct political, economic and representative role (Miéville 2005, 109). In order to understand the particularities of this form of collective subjectivity, it is useful to turn to Antonio Gramsci's understandings of the various collective roles that could be assumed by social classes.

In 'The Modern Prince', Gramsci famously distinguished between different degrees of 'homogeneity, self-awareness, and organisation attained' by social classes which 'correspond[ed] to the various moments of collective political consciousness'. He understood these different degrees as – schematically – comprising three distinct 'moments':

> The first and most elementary of these is the economic–corporate level: a tradesman feels obliged to stand by another tradesman, a manufacturer by another manufacturer, etc., but the tradesman does not yet feel solidarity with the manufacturer; in other words, the members of the professional group are conscious of its unity and homogeneity, and of the need to organise it, but in the case of the wider social group this is not yet so. A second moment is that in which consciousness is reached of the solidarity of interests among all the members of a social class – but still in the purely economic field. Already at this juncture the problem of the State is posed – but only in terms of winning politico-juridical equality with the ruling groups … A third moment is that in which one becomes aware that one's own corporate interests, in their present and future development, transcend

> the corporate limits of the purely economic class, and can and must become the interests of other subordinate groups too.
>
> (Gramsci 1971, 181)

To return to the discussion in the introduction of this chapter, we can understand Gramsci here as describing different modes of collective subjectivity. The previous account suggests that, under the post-war settlement, the conditions were set for the formation of the second mode of consciousness described by Gramsci. Trade unions had the possibility of acting with the 'solidarity of interests' amongst wider layers of the working class, organising their workplaces and engaging in industrial actions that went beyond economic–corporate struggle. The legal regime of collective laissez-faire made it possible for trade unions to perform this function by allowing secondary industrial action and putting the state and government at one remove from the governance of workplace relations.

This form of collective subjectivity had a wider resonance in another collective political organisation of the working class – the Labour Party. Historically, the relationship between the Labour Party and the trade union movement was 'an exceptionally close one', with the Labour Party conceived of as 'the political arm of the labor movement' and unions having 'an institutional role in the constitutional structure of the party' (Howell and Vale 1992, 19). The legal form of collective laissez-faire underscored this relationship. Given that the majority of workplace regulation was achieved through collective bargaining, the job of the Labour Party involved maintaining the *background legal conditions* for the continuation of collective laissez-faire, and legislating a 'minimum floor' of workplace regulation. This meant that, in terms of organising the lives of the working class, the Labour Party was in a symbiotic relationship with the trade union movement. The Labour Party enabled collective bargaining to take place, and in exchange received funding, party activists and was – to some degree – able to rely on industrial support for its policies. Accordingly, the political balance between the two was a delicate one, with neither definitively having the upper hand.

Although the post-war settlement can hardly be described as a radical one, it nonetheless formed the foundation for a more radical critique of capitalism. As Marxists have noted, one of capitalism's defining tendencies is the *formal* separation between politics and economics. Under capitalism (unlike other social systems) social needs are not fulfilled through the direct control of production and consumption; rather, they are indirectly fulfilled through market competition (Wood 2003, 10–12). Because of this, conscious social organisation – the 'political' sphere – can be understood as separate from the sphere of material production and reproduction – the 'economic' sphere.

Radicals have always sought to undermine this separation and bring the fulfilment of social needs under conscious social control. In these radical visions the working class was always seen to play a central role. This is because the working class serves a central economic role in the reproduction of capitalism such that if it – as a whole – did not engage in production, then the capitalist system would grind to a halt. At the same time, since the exploitation of the working class is a structural dimension of the capitalist system, the working class as a whole must articulate a political project that goes beyond capitalism. Thus, although the post-war regime was not a radical one, it enabled the possibility of a working class movement in which the economic and the political were unified. That is, the political subjectivity of the trade union movement under the post-war settlement meant that it served as the potential bearer of an *alternative political project* to capitalism. This political project was intimately linked to social democracy and even contained the seeds of a project that might push beyond it.

If, as Dardot and Laval argue, neoliberalism is structured by a rationality aimed at generalising 'competition as a behavioural norm', one can see how this would clash with the post-war collective subjectivity of the trade union movement (Dardot and Laval, 2014, 4). The latter emphasised the solidarity of individuals in a wider working class movement, with a political mission aimed at managing or reducing capitalist competition. The reason for this clash was not simply that trade unions were too powerful; rather, they also represented a kind of 'counter-rationality' to that which neoliberalism was to create. As such, the birth and consolidation of neoliberalism would have to fundamentally restructure the collective subjectivity of the trade union movement.

Indeed, for the 'theorists' of neoliberalism, the idea that trade unions could represent the wider working class was anathema. For them, there was no working class 'as such' with any common set of interests to represent. Rather, workers were just another set of economic actors seeking to maximise their own interests. Accordingly, trade unions represented *narrow* interest groups who had clothed 'their demands with the aura of legitimacy ... by representing them as a requirement of "social justice"' (Hayek 2012, 141). The legal settlement under Thatcher went a long way towards making this neoliberal account a *reality*.

Thatcher and after

The Conservatives' legislative assault

The Conservative Party that came to power in 1979 did so against the background of a wave of industrial militancy. The previous Labour government, elected in 1974, had promised that it could use its links with the trade union movement to repress wages. This was in order to reduce surging levels of inflation and shore up the fragile state of the British economy. Accordingly, once in government, it attempted a negotiated incomes policy under the rubric of the Social Contract, whereby trade unions would agree to restrain wage demands in exchange for greater state intervention in the economy. This agreement quickly fell apart, as the government refused to commit to interventionism and the trade unions were unable to restrain their rank and file. All of this culminated in the so-called Winter of Discontent of 1978–1979, in which concerted and sustained trade union action brought much of Britain to a halt (Howell and Vale 1992, 23).

In the 1979 election, the Conservative Party's electoral platform was based on curbing the right to strike and ensuring industrial 'peace and stability' (Ewing 1982, 11). This promise was very quickly implemented through the Employment Act 1980, which restricted picketing and explicitly removed secondary action from the purview of trade disputes. This was followed by the Employment Act 1982, which further narrowed the definition of a trade dispute to one 'between workers and their employers' which 'relates wholly or mainly to' terms and conditions of employment; termination of workers; matters of discipline and trade union matter (s.18(2)). The Act also explicitly stated that worker refers to 'a worker employed by that employer' or 'a person who has ceased to be employed by that employer' (s.18(6)).

The cumulative effect of these provisions was to render secondary and political industrial action outside the protection of the 'Golden Formula'. Under the terms of the 1982 Act (s.15), the union *itself* would be liable in tort for any loss from an industrial action that fell outside the trade dispute formula (reinstating the *Taff Vale* case). This would be the case if *any* union official endorsed the action (s.15(4)) and this endorsement was not repudiated by the union 'as soon as reasonably practicable' (s.15(5)).

Alongside their curtailment of the ability of trade unions to take industrial action, the Employment Acts also weakened the ability of trade unions to 'govern' workplaces. The 1980 Act (s.7(3)) allowed employees who had been dismissed for not being members of a trade union to claim compensation for unfair dismissal, unless 80 per cent 'of those entitled to vote in the ballot' had agreed to a closed shop. Equally, any industrial action designed to ensure that employers only dealt with unionised suppliers was no longer protected, again undermining the ability of unions to project their influence beyond their own workplaces and fight to increase unionisation rates (Lewis and Simpson 1982, 227–230).

Of course, as previously observed, changes in the law do not necessarily 'take' on the ground. In the early history of British trade unionism, as well during the opposition to the 1971 Industrial Relations Act, trade unions had deliberately flouted the law. Similar calls were raised in relation to the Employment Act 1982 and some of the more militant trade unionists – such as Arthur Scargill – called for defiance of the law. However, this flew somewhat in the face of the weakened economic position of the trade unions, as well as the fall in public support they had experienced owing to the 'Winter of Discontent' (Wrigley 2002, 73). Consequently, opposition to the Employment Acts was much more cautious.

When the Conservative government won another electoral victory in 1983, partly as a result of enflamed national sentiment around the Falklands War, it continued with its legislative assault on trade unions. Most famously, the 1984 Trade Union Act required that, in order for a strike to be protected, a union would first need to ballot its membership on strike action. In this way, legal interventions began to be made directly into the internal lives of trade unions.

This was accompanied by a direct assault on one of the bastions of the organised labour movement – the NUM. The facts of the miners' strike are well known. However, it is worth noting that, although there was a dispute as to whether the NUM needed to call a national ballot, this concerned the union's internal constitution and *not* the Trade Union Act (Ewing 1985, 160). However, as Benedictus noted, the success of these legal actions may well have contributed to the very quick uptake by employers of their new rights under the 1984 Act, with 'more than a dozen instances' of employers obtaining 'interlocutory injunctions to restrain unions from initiating industrial action' within the first nine months of the Act coming into effect (Benedictus 1985, 188).

With the defeat of the miners' strike, organised opposition to the Conservative industrial relations policy was severely weakened. A series of Acts were passed which deepened the trends of the first five years of Conservative government. The Employment Acts of 1988 and 1990 forbade unions from disciplining or expelling members who refused to participate in industrial action and finally made the closed shop illegal. All of this was codified in the 1992 Trade Union and Labour Relations Consolidation Act (TULRCA), which remains in force to this day. The basic set of industrial relations put into place by successive Conservative governments was also accepted by the 1997 Labour government and those which followed it.

Neoliberal subjectivity?

The net result of these legislative transformations was 'the decollectivization of industrial relations and the spread of individualized institutions' such as individual contracts of employment, individual rights derived from statute and employment tribunals 'for the regulation of social relations in the workplace' (Howell 2005, 14). Essentially, the regime of collective laissez-faire had been dismantled, and the power of the trade unions utterly diminished. This was achieved on a number of levels. First, and most obviously, trade union membership declined heavily under the Conservative governments, with union density falling to 38.6 per cent in 1989 and reaching a low of 23.5 per cent in 2013. Whilst it was a combination of many circumstances that led to this fall – including 'globalisation', the decline of previously unionised industries and changes in the composition of the workforce – legislation nonetheless played a central role (Freeman and Pelletier 1990). Key in this respect were the outlawing of the closed shop, and the removal of pro-unionisation action from the protection of the 'Golden Formula' (Deakin and Wilkinson 2005, 266–267). This undermined the ability of trade unions to project their power beyond their own workplaces and secure increased unionisation.

Second, the new restrictions on industrial action also severely weakened the bargaining power of trade unions. By forcing unions to undergo expensive and complex balloting procedures, industrial action was made much less attractive. Moreover, given the time it takes to arrange these ballots, this system gives employers the advantage of knowing well in advance when strikes will take place, enabling them to pre-emptively lessen the impact of industrial action. This is reinforced by the willingness of the courts to pass interlocutory injunctions when – on the balance of probabilities – it appears a strike would not be protected under the 'Golden Formula' (Barrow 2013, 356). As such, the strike, the main weapon that enabled trade unions to secure concessions from employers, was severely undermined.

Thus, following these legislative transformations, trade unions were unable to push for unionisation throughout the labour force and had their bargaining power severely attenuated. Accordingly, although collective bargaining remained (and remains) a not insubstantial part of the system of British industrial relations, it could not continue as the predominant form of labour regulation.

However, as this chapter has insisted, collective laissez-faire was not just a system of industrial relations; it also provided the conditions of a particular form of collective political subjectivity. This form of subjectivity was one fiercely opposed by neoliberals: in theoretical terms they understood unions as simply the representatives of particular interest groups, and in practical terms the unions represented a form of organisation intrinsically opposed to neoliberalism. Whilst a crucial goal of the Conservative legislative assault on unions was to make taking industrial action more difficult, industrial action was not banned outright. Rather, the legislation rearticulated the conditions under which industrial action could occur and, in so doing, fundamentally reshaped the *form* that trade union action was to take.

Simply put, under the new legislative regime, trade unions would not be protected from civil liability when engaging in solidarity action, or when attempting to engage in actions designed to protect and promote trade unionism more generally. To return to Gramsci's typology, this legislation made it almost impossible for trade unions to act upon the consciousness 'of the solidarity of interests among all the members of a social class' (his second form of 'collective political consciousness'), let alone advance a hegemonic conception, which characterises his third form. The new laws created a set of material (and ultimately penal) compulsions, which encouraged unions to act as 'economic–corporate' organisations, whose sole function was to represent their members' *immediate* interests as against their immediate employers.

There are two nuances to this picture. First, as mentioned above, it is always possible for organisations to defy the law, particularly when pressure is applied from the rank and file. Here, however, the particular structure of the laws comes into play quite effectively. By opening unions up directly to liability for any loss occasioned by industrial action, the law creates a profoundly serious material incentive for compliance with the 'economic–corporate' form of mobilisation. The level of damages that can potentially be levied against a union might bankrupt it, thus forming an existential threat. Such actions have therefore become an all-or-nothing proposition. The only way in which a union could 'win' such a struggle is if it triggered some kind of a political crisis resulting in the law not being applied as in the case of the 1971 Industrial Relations Act.

Reinforcing this, under TULRCA 1992 (s.20(2)), a trade union will become liable for damages insofar as *any* 'official' of the union has endorsed or authorised an unprotected union action. An official is taken to have endorsed or authorised an action – as *per* s.20(3)(b) – if it was 'authorised or endorsed by, or by any member of, any group of persons of which he was at the material time a member, the purposes of which included organising or co-ordinating industrial action'.

The net effect of these provisions is extremely important. In general, trade unions will face an almost existential threat if they go beyond economic–corporate organising. As such, it will only be in situations of political crisis where they might consider doing so. Obviously, these situations will not obtain during their day-to-day practice. At the same time, any solidarity actions by union members with the merest hint of 'official' union involvement will – unless swiftly repudiated by the union's leadership – also render the union liable. In this way, the law forces unions to actively disavow any attempt to go beyond economic–corporate struggles, creating a wedge between more and less radical members of the unions.

Here there is a fundamental difference between the neoliberal legal settlement and that which preceded collective laissez-faire. Although both effectively banned secondary or political industrial action, in the latter case this was part of a general ban on trade union activities. This perversely *encouraged* more radical trade union activity, insofar as members of a combination were already committing a crime and so had less to lose in moving in a more radical direction. Carving out a sphere of 'legitimate' economic–corporate union activity has been much more effective at blunting the collective subjectivity represented by trade unions in the neoliberal period.

The second important nuance is the question of how the above changes played out at the broader political level of trade unions. Whilst trade unions have been confined to economic–corporate forms of industrial action, it is also true that trade unions have not entirely 'internalised' this perspective. The Trades Union Congress still exists, embodying the idea that the various trade unions have a collective identity above and beyond their individual workplaces and trades. Trade unions continue to make 'political' interventions – both through the TUC and its congresses and in an individual capacity – and attempt to pressure governments. However, these interventions are now separate from the unions' concrete day-to-day functions. Whereas under collective laissez-faire, trade unions had – to some degree – unified their economic and political power, neoliberal legislation forced the two apart. That is, unions can use their economic power to defend the immediate interests of their own members. Alongside this, but separate from it, they also have political or rhetorical weight with which to push for political alternatives, or fight for wider changes in regulating work.

If this isolation of political mobilisation sounds familiar, it is because – in a less cynical vein – it accords precisely with the definition that Hayek gave to trade unions: 'special interest groups' who concretely advance the interests of their members but mobilise the language of 'social justice'. The dismantling of the post-war settlement created a series of material compulsions that forced unions to become such 'Hayekian subjects'.

The death of social democracy

None of this is to say that the demands advanced by trade unions – health and safety protections, wages increases, etc. – have been wholly banished from the British political scene. However, the neoliberal settlement gave rise to a distinct configuration of the relationship between the Labour Party and the trade unions. It is said that, when Margaret Thatcher was once asked her greatest achievement, she replied 'New Labour'.[4] Generally, this is taken to mean that successive Conservative governments shifted the political climate sufficiently that, on a *substantive* level, the Labour governments which followed them were forced to adopt their policies. There is some truth to this. However, there is another dimension to this claim. By fundamentally restructuring the role that trade unions played in industrial and political life, Conservative legislation also rearticulated the relationship between the Labour Party and the trade union movement.

4 See www.independent.co.uk/news/uk/politics/margaret-thatchers-legacy-spilt-milk-new-labour-and-the-big-bang-she-changed-everything-8564541.html.

As previously noted, under collective laissez-faire, the primary role of the Labour Party was to maintain the underlying legislative conditions that enabled collective bargaining. The majority of law *directly* governing workplace relations was generated through collective agreements. This was conducive to a relationship of relative equality between trade unions and the Labour Party. However, with the end of collective laissez-faire, unions lost their ability to 'govern' workplaces and their ability to act directly in the interests of the wider working class. In this new situation, it became the responsibility of the Labour Party to pass primary legislation regulating the workplace and stand in as the 'representative' for the wider working class.

The vital point here is that progressive demands in the workplace were not simply 'abandoned' by New Labour. Instead, just as with industrial action, the new configuration transformed the form in which these demands were articulated. Rather than be achieved *directly* through the collective power of trade unions, progressive demands were now introduced through legislation. As such, issues relating to working time, minimum wages, anti-discrimination, redundancy, etc. were all addressed at the level of *statutes* (many of which implemented directives from the European Union). These statutes granted individual workers' rights that they could invoke against their employers.

In this way, the split between politics and economics earlier identified was further entrenched. In terms of specific, narrow economic–corporate disputes, the economic power of the trade unions could still be leveraged. In terms of wider issues – including the basic framework within which industrial action would take place – action would need to be channelled through the Labour Party. This disturbed the delicate symbiosis between the trade unions and the Labour Party. Although unions remain large 'voluntary organisations', they are now wholly reliant on the Labour Party to enact *political* change. Conversely, the Labour Party now relies on unions solely for *financial* support, since industrial action can no longer be leveraged to support Labour Party policy. A trade union is now much more akin to a lobby or special interest group which uses its financial clout to persuade the parliamentary party to back certain initiatives. As such, the old settlement, in which both the unions and the Party conceptualised themselves as different wings of a wider 'labour movement', has given way to a much more fragmented picture. This is reflected in the various constitutional changes to the Labour Party that have decreased the influence of trade unions within the Party.[5]

This shift is profoundly important in terms of re-articulating the collective subjectivity of the labour movement. Under collective laissez-faire,

5 See, for example, www.theguardian.com/politics/2014/mar/01/labour-ed-miliband-reforms-links-trade-unions.

there was a concrete link between collective 'economic' action and governance of the workplace, as well as wider political issues. By contrast, in the new regime, the majority of workplace regulation is mediated through individual rights conferred by the government. Thus, there is a doubly alienated move here. First, in a real sense, 'progressive' gains (in terms of wages, anti-discrimination, etc.) are channelled into the form of individual rights-claims, which robs them of their collective dimension.[6] Insofar as these individual rights are violated, the recourse is no longer industrial action. Instead, it is recourse to the *courts*. Second, in order to establish new rights, there it is no longer collective industrial struggle that results in an improved workplace contract, but rather lobbying and perhaps – at best – protests and demonstrations designed to force political parties into action. In this way, the arena of political contestation becomes more removed from people's concrete collective existence and experience.

In this way political action is recast in a direction fundamentally amenable to neoliberalism: politics are pursued by 'interest groups' that lobby those in power to implement new individualistic rights proposals. Again, what is crucial here is that, rather than simply *ban* union action or the social democratic demands that might flow therefrom, the neoliberal regime partially integrates and redirects these energies. In this way, it avoids the trap of the pre-collective laissez-faire period, in which radical and moderate union members were pushed together by their shared 'illegality'.

The beauty of the neoliberal system is its self-perpetuating nature. Collective laissez-faire was guaranteed through an ultimately fragile system of 'background rules' which protected unions from civil liability in the case of industrial action. The only way to transform this situation (and, with it, to constitute a new form of collective subjectivity), would be to fundamentally restructure the law relating to industrial action. But such a challenge could not be mounted *directly* by the trade union movement itself, given the limitations placed upon it by the present legal order and what the movement would stand to lose if unsuccessful.

Law, subjectivity and politics

From politics to law?

One important consequence of the above analysis is that it challenges those accounts of neoliberalism which stress its 'anti-statism' or 'deregulation'. If

6 As the critical legal studies movement has taught us, rights discourse tends towards channelling demands into an alienated, individualised and depoliticised form which ultimately serves to buttress the existing order. For the classic examples see Gabel 1983; Tushnet 1983; Kennedy 2002. The coincidence of rights discourses with the rise of neoliberalism is suggestive of a wider shift to neoliberal forms of subjectivity.

anything, the neoliberal regime has been marked by the contrary. If the 'pre-neoliberal' industrial relations regime was one of 'collective laissez-faire', then what followed was its antithesis; what we might call 'individualist *interventionism*'. The neoliberal regime has necessitated more direct state intervention in those areas of the workplace which would have previously been the subject of collective agreements. In place of these agreements has been legislation on health and safety, the minimum wage, anti-discrimination, etc. Thus, in this area neoliberalism has seen a flurry of *juridification*, with law coming to *directly* regulate more aspects of the social totality. This juridification has had a profoundly individualising and depoliticising effect, replacing the collective action of trade unions with legal action in the court room.

However, if this argument illustrates that the equation of neoliberalism and 'less regulation' is incorrect, it would also be a mistake to argue that neoliberalism simply involves the replacement of politics by law. If one thing is clear from the historical sketch above, it is that law was involved *at every single step of the process* of forming labour as a collective subject. In the initial period, law served a directly repressive function, attempting to quash the collective identification of the working class. The subsequent arrangement of collective laissez-faire was no less saturated in law. Collective bargaining – and its attendant form of collective subjectivity – was only possible in this period because of a series of legislative interventions that established a framework for its existence. The centrality of the role of law is evidenced by how fragile this system ultimately proved in the wake of the Conservatives' legislative assault on trade unions and the later entrenchment of this assault by the Labour Party.

Rather than seeing neoliberalism as a withdrawal of politics and extension of law, we need to understand that the relationship between 'politics' and 'law' is itself a *juridical question*. That is to say, it is particular legal frameworks that constitute how direct a role that law will play in governing social life. These legal frameworks are – as above – the outcome of wider political and economic struggles and relations, but also play a part in constituting and governing those relations. Accordingly, it is necessary to understand 'the legal process' as 'one of the primary forms ... through which the actual relationships embodying class power ... [are] created and articulated' (Klare 1979, 130).

Perhaps the most rigorous attempt to think through this phenomenon is Duncan Kennedy's article 'The Stakes of Law, or Hale and Foucault!'. Examining – and criticising – his argument in some detail helps elucidate the general role that law plays in constituting political subjectivity. Kennedy attempts to understand the role that law plays in the distribution of income. He starts from the observation that '[n]othing tells us a priori how the value of the joint product [of capital and labour] will be divided', instead it is the relative strength and bargaining power of capital and labour that determine how income is distributed (Kennedy 1991, 328–329).

For Kennedy – drawing on Robert Hale – law is crucial to determining the relative strength of capital and labour. Law does this 'directly', through the rules that regulate strikes and picketing, and 'indirectly' through the rules that influence the availability of alternative employment and alternatives *to* employment. In the latter case, welfare law, law about property in land or food, etc. will influence whether workers can plausibly threaten to leave their jobs and how long they might maintain industrial action (Kennedy 1991, 339–341). If the law is more 'restrictive' in these areas, then employers will be in a much stronger bargaining position. As such, a number of legal 'background rules' subtly constitute the bargaining position of labour and capital (Kennedy 1991, 331). Crucially, this is never a matter of 'more' or 'less' law since, '[o]nce there is a legal system, the choice of any particular set of background rules is a choice of a set of distributive outcomes, whether achieved through many rules or only a few' (Kennedy 1991, 334).

The above history has attempted to illustrate that Kennedy's insights into the distribution of income can be said to apply more widely, with law playing a key role in shaping the *political forms* that the 'bargaining units' in economic processes will take. The particular 'background rules' create a series of material compulsions and incentives which shape the way in which collective political subjectivity is formed.

However, such a perspective is absent from Kennedy's analysis. This makes sense. One of the main targets of Kennedy's argument is the Marxist tradition. He argues that Marxists cannot adequately grasp the dynamics of income distribution, since, for them

> distribution is determined by 'the relations of production'.... There are a capitalist class and a proletariat, defined by their ownership or non-ownership of the means of production [and] the capitalists expropriate the whole joint product except for what is necessary to reproduce the working class.
>
> (Kennedy 1991, 332)

One might cast doubt on this position,[7] but it underlines the fact that Kennedy is not that interested in *relations of production*. Capitalism is essentially the horizon of his analysis, making him inattentive to the wider political concerns of movements beyond their distributive aims.

7 As Althusser notes, for Marx, the amount needed to 'reproduce' the working class, including a historical element, including 'the historical needs imposed by the proletarian class struggle' (Althusser 1971, 131).

Against nostalgia

In Kennedy's analysis, capitalism figures as 'a particular legal regime' which could be changed – bringing about a wholly different distribution of income. As a result, for him, it is necessary to abandon 'the one/off all-or-nothing understanding of capitalism and private property' and acknowledge the existence of a '"mixed" capitalist system' (Kennedy 1991, 338–339). Again, one could dispute this, but Kennedy draws our attention to something that ought not to be neglected. Although this chapter has insisted that different legal regimes have given rise to different forms of collective subjectivity, this should not be overstated. Ultimately, all of these forms of subjectivity have remained *within the coordinates of capitalist social relations.*

On this basis, it would be unwise to gloss over the manifold problems of collective laissez-faire. Trade unions did not cover *all* workplaces, particularly those in low-waged and less 'respectable' fields. They also were reflective of a workplace with an undeniable racial and gender composition, a problem which continues to dog the trade union movement to this day. Thus, insofar as there was a collective political subject, it was one primarily understood as white, male and in relatively steady employment. Most importantly, collective laissez-faire, whilst creating a distinct class identity, did so with the aim of integrating this class into the structures of capitalism.

Here, Karl Klare's account of the New Deal in the United States is instructive. He argues that the National Labor Relations Act was both a radical intervention into US capitalism and an attempt to contain that radical potential. In particular, the courts

> articulated and advanced certain crucial rights of workers and yet, at the same time, defused or 'deradicalized' the latent anti-capitalist potential of the Act, thereby laying the cultural, and later the institutional foundations of the architecture of the post-War administered and regulated class struggle.
>
> (Klare 1979, 141)

The pattern that Klare describes here seems to hold for Britain too. The brief history above shows that, prior to the neoliberal period, British labour law was marked by explosions in class struggle followed by legal attempts to integrate and manage this struggle. The early attempts to completely outlaw 'combinations' met with resistance from the nascent working classes, who pushed hard to secure their legal recognition. It was the fear that these struggles might spill over into open insurrection which eventually allowed their legalisation. This legalisation, whilst a clear victory, meant that these struggles did not spill over into wider demands for social transformation.

Similar considerations operated over the long period of the consolidation of collective laissez-faire that followed. This period was marked by Europe-wide labour struggles, of which the Bolshevik Revolution formed the most potent example. The political instability created by these struggles came to a head following the Second World War when – throughout Europe – an interventionist set of elites, in tandem with a relatively cowed capitalist class, sought to forestall any further political and economic upheavals (Lang 2011, 194). Collective laissez-faire was part of a compromise regime that attempted to create and integrate the British working class into the system of industrial capitalism by offering it a material stake in this system (Knox and Kotiaho 2014, 428).

Thus, although collective laissez-faire was marked by a form of collective subjectivity in which trade unions represented a wider working class with a distinct set of interests, these interests were not – on the whole – understood as intrinsically antagonistic to the capitalist class or capitalist system. Indeed, insofar as this identity was one rooted in collective *bargaining*, it presupposed the legitimacy of the capitalist class's right to own the means of production and appropriate surplus value.[8] The issue was – as with Kennedy – one of distribution. Accordingly, although unions were enabled to intervene in 'political' issues (with their economic power), economic processes were not brought under conscious political control. The basic separation at the heart of capitalism between the political and economic remained in place.[9]

In this way, political subjectivity under collective laissez-faire shared something fundamental with that of neoliberalism – it functioned to channel political energies into a space that ultimately maintained capitalist social relations. When – as in the Winter of Discontent – the class struggle boiled over into open militancy, it was met with a new neoliberal legal regime, which both aggressively restricted the ability of trade unions to engage in industrial action and also more subtly reconfigured their political functionality.

It is in this context that the specific role of law becomes particularly interesting. The foregoing account tells us two things: first that law has played a crucial role in shaping the forms of political subjectivity of the labour movement, and second that it has done so in such a way as to incorporate the working class into capitalist social relations. Here, it is useful to return to Kennedy. He treats it as intuitive that law and capitalism are coextensive. But why is this? *Why*, one might ask, does law assume such

8 As Chris Arthur caustically notes: 'No amount of reformist factory legislation can overcome the basic presupposition of the law: that a property freely alienated belongs to the purchaser, and hence that the living labour of the worker becomes, through exchange, available for exploitation through capital' (Arthur 1978, 31).

9 Of course, one should note that some radical trade unionists viewed their activities as the first step along the road to a more radical solution to this problem. Thanks to Claire Mummé for this point, for more on which see the conclusion to this chapter.

an important 'distributive' role under capitalism? Does law play this role in all social systems?

It is here that the Marxist tradition can be of some use. Marxists have always argued that – under capitalism particularly – law takes on a vital role in shaping 'subjectivity'. Althusser, for instance, famously stated that the function of ideology was to constitute '*concrete individuals as subjects*', with the 'rise of legal ideology' being the central element of this dynamic (Althusser 1971, 170–171). Similarly, Pashukanis argued that:

> Law is simultaneously a form of external authoritative regulation and a form of subjective private autonomy. The basic and essential characteristic of the former is unconditional obligation and external coercion, while freedom is ensured and recognized within definite boundaries. Law appears both as the basis of social organization and as the means for individuals 'to be disassociated, yet integrated in society'.
>
> (Pashukanis 1980, 70)

In this passage Pashukanis draws our attention to the dual dynamic of law. On the one hand, law serves as a kind of 'external' force, doling out punishment and censure. Yet at the same time, law is *constitutive* of 'subjective private autonomy', and – we can add – of different forms of subjectivity more generally. However, for Pashukanis, law as a *form* is a direct product of commodity exchange, and thus capitalism. Accordingly, we can add that the particular types of subjectivity that law produces are *rooted* in this form and share its characteristics (Knox 2009, 429–433). In particular, as Klare noted, this 'distinctive *form* of legal practice in liberal capitalist culture ... is itself an alienation' owing to its constant attempt to separate morals and politics from judicial action, its impersonal and abstract character, and its constant focus on formal equality (Klare 1979, 132).

In this way, those collective subjects constituted through the legal form ultimately are 'dissociated yet integrated in [capitalist] society'. This is why the political subject produced by both collective laissez-faire and neoliberalism ultimately channelled working class energies towards the maintenance of capitalist social relations.

Conclusion: unite and fight?

What, then, is to be done?

This chapter has argued that law has played a key role in shaping and articulating the collective subjectivity of labour under capitalism, culminating in its current neoliberal incarnation. It has argued that key to this process has been the shift from the model of collective laissez-faire – in which trade unions had the capacity to act as wider organisations of the working class as a whole, governed workplace life and levied their 'economic' power for political goals – to the neoliberal model – in which trade unions are economic–corporate bodies, which represent their members' immediate interests and then separately serve as interest groups to 'lobby' governments to achieve political objectives. In this new vision, the workplace is primarily regulated through individual, rights-based legislation, with political action centralised in the Labour Party.

Although this change is marked, this chapter has also stressed that one ought not to overstate these differences. Ultimately both regimes of collective subjectivity remain within the bounds of capitalism and represent an alienated form of 'doing politics'. A large part of this, the chapter concluded, arises from law's intimate interconnection with capitalism. Owing to this *legal form*, those identities generated by law tend to be equally abstract and alienated, and so incapable of challenging capitalism.

Does this mean there is *no* difference between the two regimes? In order to think about this question, it is worth recalling Marx's reflections on struggles for wages and the regulation of the working day.[10] In *Value Price and Profit*, Marx warned that the working class should not exaggerate the importance of everyday struggles for wages. To do so, he argued, would mean confusing causes with effects, and ignoring the *inevitable* limits of capitalism. Against the *conservative* motto: '*A fair day's wage for a fair day's work!*', he argued that it was necessary to argue for the *revolutionary* watchword: '*Abolition of the wages system!*' (Marx 2006, 61). At the same time, though, Marx was not blind to the importance that these struggles could have. Thus, in *Capital*, Marx talked in superlative language about the struggle to limit the working day, arguing that it had caused the labourers to 'put their heads together, and, *as a class*, compel the passing of a law' (emphasis added) (Marx 1999, 181–182).

To recast Marx's language in that of this chapter, the struggle to limit the working day helped to constitute a new form of political subjectivity that went beyond 'economic–corporate' organisation. This was vital because it was only through such recognition that *further* advances could be made. It is here that we begin to see a difference. Both collective laissez-faire and neoliberalism articulated forms of collective subjectivity that were ultimately compatible with capitalism. However, the former case was clearly a *more favourable set of conditions* for building a wider movement. Insofar as – even in a limited sense – collective laissez-faire encouraged a form of political subjectivity which recognised the common interests and collective economic power of the working class, it opened up the possibility of *deepening* this identification.

This was precisely one of the reasons that neoliberals so bitterly opposed it: this form of consciousness was the residue of a political alternative, and a possible site for its regeneration.

10 This point is developed more systematically in Knox 2010. See also Baars 2011.

It is here that we can discern a political possibility. Clearly, simply 'reversing' neoliberalism – and its attendant form of collective political subjectivity – cannot be the goal of those who oppose neoliberalism. Aside from the fact that this may well be impossible (since it took a very extraordinary set of conditions to give rise to the social democratic compromise), it ultimately would not break with the logic of capitalism. Thus, collective laissez-faire cannot be treated as a static goal to reach on its own terms. At the same time, however, such a system – and the struggle for it – can create the conditions for a wider challenge to capitalism.

This will directly play out in the question of law. The above considerations point to a broader tension. On the one hand, law is *constitutive* of the social field; it creates particular forms of subjectivity which can more or less effectively fight for given political goals. On the other hand, it is not *neutral*; all of the forms of subjectivity constituted by law bear its mark. Accordingly, as I have argued elsewhere, the strategic goal of radicals must be to transcend law (as we know it), but, tactically, law cannot simply be 'discarded' (Knox 2010).

Thus, it is vital to understand that legal reforms will have huge *organisational* consequences for those who seek to challenge capitalism. However, in fighting to secure a terrain fertile for the reproduction of radical forms of collective political subjectivity, it must be borne in mind that the law ultimately limits this. Accordingly, it must be mobilised in such a way as to openly subordinate it to the wider movement for radical change (Knox 2011).

References

Althusser, Louis. 1971. *Lenin and Philosophy and Other Essays.* New York and London: New Left Books.

Arthur, Chris. 1978. 'Introduction.' In *Law and Marxism: A General Theory,* by Evgeny Bronislavovich Pashukanis. London: Ink Links.

Arthurs, H.W. 1967. 'Developing Industrial Citizenship: A Challenge for Canada's Second Century.' *The Canadian Bar Review* 45 (4): 786–830.

Baars, Grietje. 2011. 'Reform or Revolution – Polanyian versus Marxism Perspectives on the Regulation of the Economic.' *Northern Ireland Legal Quarterly* 62: 415–431.

Barrow, Charles. 2013. *Industrial Relations Law.* London: Routledge.

Benedictus, Roger. 1985. 'The Use of the Law of Tort in the Miners' Dispute.' *Industrial Law Journal* 14: 176.

Brodie, Douglas. 2003. *A History of British Labour Law, 1867–1945.* Oxford: Hart Publishing.

Collins, Hugh. 1997. 'The Productive Disintegration of Labour Law.' *Industrial Law Journal* 26 (4): 295–309. doi:10.1093/ilj/26.4.295.

Dardot, Pierre and Christian Laval. 2014. *The New Way of the World: On Neoliberal Society.* Translated by Gregory Elliot. London; New York: Verso Books.

Deakin, Simon F. and Frank Wilkinson. 2005. *The Law of the Labour Market: Industrialization, Employment, and Legal Evolution*. Oxford: Oxford University Press.

Deery, Stephen and Richard Mitchell. 1999. *Employment Relations: Individualisation and Union Exclusion: An International Study*. Sydney: Federation Press.

Dukes, Ruth. 2009. 'Otto Kahn-Freund and Collective Laissez-Faire: An Edifice without a Keystone?' *The Modern Law Review* 72 (2): 220–246. doi:10.1111/j.1468-2230.2009.00741.x.

Duménil, Gérard and Dominique Lévy. 2004. *Capital Resurgent: Roots of the Neoliberal Revolution*. Cambridge, MA: Harvard University Press.

Ewing, K.D. 1982. 'Industrial Action: Another Step in the Right Direction.' *Industrial Law Journal* 11: 209.

Ewing, K.D. 1985. 'The Strike, the Courts and the Rule-Books.' *Industrial Law Journal* 14: 160.

Ewing, K.D. 1998. 'The State and Industrial Relations: "Collective Laissez-Faire" Revisited.' *Historical Studies in Industrial Relations* 5: 1.

Freeman, Richard and Jeffrey Pelletier. 1990. 'The Impact of Industrial Relations Legislation on British Union Density.' *British Journal of Industrial Relations* 28 (2): 141–164. doi:10.1111/j.1467-8543.1990.tb00360.x.

Gabel, Peter. 1983. 'Phenomenology of Rights-Consciousness and the Pact of the Withdrawn Selves.' *Texas Law Review* 62: 1563.

Gramsci, Antonio. 1971. *Selections from the Prison Notebooks*. Edited by Quintin Hoare and Geoffrey Nowell Smith. New York: International Publishers Co.

Hall, D.J. 1972. *Industrial Relations Problems and the Industrial Relations Act*. London: Kogan Page.

Harvey, David. 2005. *A Brief History of Neoliberalism*. Oxford: Oxford University Press.

Hayek, F.A. 2012. *Law, Legislation and Liberty, Volume 2: The Mirage of Social Justice*. Chicago: University of Chicago Press.

Howell, Chris. 2005. *Trade Unions and the State: The Construction of Industrial Relations Institutions in Britain, 1890–2000*. Princeton, NJ: Princeton University Press.

Howell, Chris and Michel Vale. 1992. 'Family or Just Good Friends? The Changing Labour Party-Trade Union Relationship in Britain since 1979.' *International Journal of Political Economy* 22 (4): 17–35.

Kay, G. and J. Mott. 1982. *Political Order and the Law of Labour*. London: Palgrave Macmillan.

Kennedy, Duncan. 1991. 'The Stakes of Law, or Hale and Foucault!' *Legal Stud. F.* 15: 327.

Kennedy, Duncan. 2002. 'The Critique of Rights in Critical Legal Studies.' In *Left Legalism/Left Critique*, edited by Wendy Brown and Janet E. Halley, 178–228. Durham, NC: Duke University Press.

Klare, K. 1979. 'Law-Making as Praxis.' *Telos* 1979 (40): 123–135. doi:10.3817/0679040123.

Knox, Robert. 2009. 'Marxism, International Law, and Political Strategy.' *Leiden Journal of International Law* 22 (3): 413–436. doi:10.1017/S0922156509990021.

Knox, Robert. 2010. 'Strategy and Tactics.' *Finnish Yearbook of International Law* 21: 193–229.

Knox, Robert. 2011. 'What Is to Be Done (With Critical Legal Theory)?' *Finnish Yearbook of International Law* 22: 31–47.

Knox, Robert and Paavo Kotiaho. 2014. 'Beyond Competing Liberalisms: The World Trade Organization as Class Project.' *Social & Legal Studies* 23 (3): 426–433.

Lang, Andrew. 2011. *World Trade Law after Neoliberalism: Reimagining the Global Economic Order.* Oxford: Oxford University Press.

Lewis, Roy. 1976. 'The Historical Development of Labour Law.' *British Journal of Industrial Relations* 14 (1): 1–17.

Lewis, Roy and Bob Simpson. 1982. 'Disorganising Industrial Relations: An Analysis of Sections 2–8 and 10–14 of the Employment Act of 1982.' *Industrial Law Journal* 11: 227.

Lowry, David R., Anthony F. Bartlett and Timothy J. Heinsz. 1979. 'Legal Intervention in Industrial Relations in the United States and Britain – A Comparative Analysis.' *Marquette Law Review* 63: 1.

Marx, Karl. 1999. *Capital: An Abridged Edition.* Edited by David McLellan. Abridged edition. Oxford: Oxford Paperbacks.

Marx, Karl. 2006. *Wage Labour and Capital and Value Price and Profit.* New York: International Publishers Co.

Miéville, China. 2005. *Between Equal Rights: A Marxist Theory of International Law.* Leiden: Brill.

Moran, Michael. 1977. *The Politics of Industrial Relations: The Origins, Life, and Death of the 1971 Industrial Relations Act.* London: Macmillan.

Panitch, Leo. 1976. *Social Democracy and Industrial Militancy: The Labour Party, the Trade Unions and Incomes Policy, 1945–1974.* 1st edition. Cambridge: Cambridge University Press.

Pashukanis, Evgeny Bronislavovich. 1980. *Pashukanis, Selected Writings on Marxism and Law.* Edited by Piers Beirne and Robert Sharlet. London: Academic Press.

Thompson, E.P. 1966. *The Making of the English Working Class.* New York: Vintage.

Tushnet, Mark. 1983. 'Essay on Rights.' *Texas Law Review* 62: 1363.

Weekes, Brian, Michael Mellish, Linda Dickens and John Lloyd, eds. 1975. *Industrial Relations and the Limits of the Law: Industrial Effects of the Industrial Relations Act, 1971.* Oxford: Wiley-Blackwell.

Wood, Ellen Meiksins. 2003. *Empire of Capital.* London and New York: Verso.

Wrigley, Chris. 2002. *British Trade Unions Since 1933.* Cambridge: Cambridge University Press.

Chapter 6

Continuity and rupture in restraining the right to strike

Ntina Tzouvala

Introduction

This contribution is based on the following presumption: neoliberalism must be understood and analysed on two distinct and interrelated levels: first, neoliberalism can be understood as an intellectual current stemming from the crisis of classical *laissez-faire* liberalism that was initiated already in the late nineteenth century and second, as a class strategy to revive capitalist profitability and hegemony in the last quarter of the twentieth century. This duality is essential in order to comprehend the peculiarities of neoliberal legality. First, the intellectual novelty of neoliberalism and its attempt to respond to genuine problems of classical liberalism hints at the existence of a specifically neoliberal genre of legality that corresponds to the richness (and the contradictions) of the most influential intellectual tradition of our times. Hence, the idea that neoliberal legality is a 'return' to the archetypical liberal paradigm appears oversimplified. At the same time, we need to keep in mind that the rise of neoliberalism from an ensemble of intellectuals marginal to the mainstream ideology and governance technique of our time can only be explained in reference to the political and economic interests it is anchored to. In a nutshell, neoliberalism should also be understood as a strategy of the ruling capitalist class to re-establish their profitability and consolidate their dominance in turbulent times. Consequently, neoliberal legality should be analysed through its continuity with previous forms of capitalist legality. This dual approach enables us to conceptualise neoliberal legality both as novel and as immanent, as intellectually ground-breaking and socially integrated in a nexus of capitalist relations of power and exploitation. Because the right to strike is situated at the heart of class confrontation and has gone through multiple stages of regulation, limitation and restriction in the course of the last decades, it provides us with a good case study to examine the above sketched assumption. More specifically, the focus of this chapter will be the diachronically diverse utilisation of the exact same legal framework in Greece to achieve different social outcomes in relation to the right to strike. In turn this points to legal indeterminacy of law as the quality that enables bridging the gap between liberal and neoliberal forms of legality.

This chapter consists of three parts. First, I am going to provide an account of neoliberal thought on trade unions, strikes and their legitimate regulation through law. Here, it is explained how the confrontation between ordo-liberals and the American 'branch' of neoliberalism concluded with the decisive victory of the latter, who were openly averse toward trade unions and their legal protections. Second, I will try to show how Greek legislation on the right to strike as implemented during the last five years of intense austerity constitutes an impressively faithful application and, importantly, a further deepening of the neoliberal understanding of the right to strike. Third, I will attempt to theorise the functions of law vis-à-vis industrial disputes in the era of neoliberalism. To do so, Poulantzas' conceptualisation of *authoritarian statism* will be invoked. My argument here is that the concept of authoritarian statism enables us to comprehend the expansive role of the state in restraining trade unions' actions in a context of capitalist crisis and to theorise neoliberal legality as a continuum of norms and practices that draws from past arrangements and, anchoring itself to the inherent indeterminacy of law, establishes a new, draconian framework for strike action. The point of departure here is that since law incorporates varying and conflicting morals, values and – significantly – interests, it is unable to provide a rational and coherent body of norms.[1] This openness in turn means that the same legal framework can acquire widely divergent meanings. In this specific case, it is argued that a provision originally designed to establish the outer limits of class confrontation in a Keynesian context was re-invented in the era of neoliberalism as a means of aggressive confrontation with trade unions.

Trade unions as monopolies and private coercion agents: from theory to programme

Since the gradual rise of the workers' movement from the end of the nineteenth century onwards and especially after the passing of legislation in many Western states that protected and facilitated collective bargaining, the problem of trade unions became of significance to neoliberal thought. Two main strands of understanding can be traced. On the one hand, ordo-liberals were ready to accept the power of trade unions to the extent

1 'The many conflicts of interest and vision that lawmaking involves, fought out by countless minds and wills working at cross-purposes, would have to be the vehicle of an immanent moral rationality whose message could be articulated by a single cohesive theory.' Roberto Mangabeira Unger, 'The Critical Legal Studies Movement', 96 Harvard Law Review, p. 571.

that they understood them as agents of social peace and stability. On the other hand, an intellectual current dating back to Hutt and Simons, which was elaborated by Hayek and reached its apogee with Machlup, advocated fiercely against the then prominent social role of trade unions.

Ordo-liberal economists like William E. Rappard invoked the example of Switzerland, where in 1937 employees and employers signed a pact (widely known as *La Paix du Travail*) that prohibited strikes and public protests on behalf of unions. Thus, ordo-liberal sympathy towards the workers' movement stemmed from their conviction that organised labour could operate as a venue of collaboration between employees and employers, and therefore, as agents of class reconciliation rather than of class confrontation. In Rappard's understanding the role of neoliberal think tanks should be to 'educate the trade unions leaders, and members, to a conception of solidarity of employers' and employees' interests',[2] rather than to confront them. This point of view was hegemonic in the context of the Mont Pèlerin Society[3] (MPS hereafter) for almost a decade until the end of the 1950s. As Yves Steiner puts it 'one can roughly describe the dominant position on unions within the MPS as entertaining a *not unfriendly* stance toward them'.[4] Nevertheless, a significant faction of neoliberal thinkers, Hayek included, objected to this approach, and by the 1958 meeting of the MPS in Princeton ordo-liberals were already swimming against the tide.

Ben Jackson has argued convincingly that the intellectual matrix of this openly hostile neoliberal view toward unions was the work of W. H. Hutt and Henry Simons.[5] Already before the end of the Second World War, Hutt and Simons put forward their concurring arguments[6] which 'conceptualised unions as monopolies which sought to control the labour supply in order to charge a price for labour in excess of its competitive level'.[7] Both in their opinion and Hayek's, unions tend to benefit their members

2 F. Graham (ed.) Wages and Wage-Policy. Conference Proceedings of the 1st Meeting of the Mont Pèlerin Society at Mont Pèlerin (Hoover Institution Archives, 1947), p. 204.

3 The Mont Pèlerin Society was founded by Friedrich Hayek in 1947 as an exclusive, cosmopolitan neo-liberal think tank against the then hegemonic Keynesian economic policies. The MPS is still active and its official website is available here: https://www.montpelerin.org/montpelerin/home.html See also: Richard Cockett, Thinking the Unthinkable: Think Tanks and the Economic Counter-Revolution 1931–1983 (Fontana Press, 1995).

4 Yves Steiner, 'The Neoliberals Confront the Trade Unions', in: Philip Mirowski and Dieter Plehwe (eds), The Road From Mont Pelerin: The Making of the Neoliberal Thought Collective (Harvard University Press, 2009), p. 183.

5 Ben Jackson, 'An Ideology of Class: Neo-Liberalism and the Trade Unions, c. 1930–79', in: C. Griffiths, J. Nott and W. Whyte (eds), Classes, Cultures and Politics: Essays for Ross McKibbin (Oxford University Press, 2011), pp. 263–81.

6 W. H. Hutt, The Theory of Collective Bargaining (Institute of Economic Affairs, 1930); H. Simons, 'Some Reflections on Syndicalism', 52 Journal of Political Economy 1.

7 Jackson (note 5), p. 268.

in the short term by setting money wages at a level higher than that which would have occurred 'naturally' according to the market process. In order to do so, though, unions allegedly have to exclude those willing to work for lower wages. Hence, they contribute to increasing unemployment and harm those in genuine need, who are obliged to opt for non-unionised professions. In Simons's words a union 'enables an aristocracy of labour to build fences around their occupations, restricting entry, raising arbitrarily the costs and prices of their products, and lowering the wages and incomes of those outside, and of the poor especially'.[8]

Crucially, unlike Hutt and Simons, and even Friedman, Hayek argued further that, under Keynesianism, this situation is also directly related to inflation. If the starting point is that trade unions give rise to unemployment, Keynesian governments are seen to counteract this trend by enacting full employment policies. In Hayek's view, the only remedy to too high wages imposed by unions is the relaxation of money supply, which in turn leads to inflation.[9] Hence, trade unions do not even contribute to higher real wages, since their gains are temporary and countered by inflationary policies. As a consequence, the orthodox neoliberal argument goes, unions tend to harm the most vulnerable workers, along with consumers and employers, only to the precarious benefit of a fraction of workers, and, therefore, they cannot be said to bear substantial economic benefits.

Stretching his point even further, Hayek argued against trade unions, accusing them of something he otherwise was quite hesitant to accept the very existence of: private coercion. Citing Dicey himself, Hayek advances that the legal position of unions after the final decades of the nineteenth century constituted a flagrant violation of the rule of law.[10] In his view, unions acquired an (unacceptable) level of power since they were equipped by law with significant coercion powers, such as the privilege to bind workers who did not consent individually or through extensive exceptions from tort liability. Importantly, even non-violent picketing is understood by Hayek as coercive to the extent that it exerts unacceptable moral pressure upon workers. This is in stark contrast with the bulk of neoliberal thought which generally equates coercion with physical violence and insists that non-coerced decisions taken, for example, under the threat of

8 Simons (note 6), p. 12. See also: F. A. Hayek, The Constitution of Liberty (The University of Chicago Press, 1960), p. 389.

9 '[T]here can be little doubt that current union policies must lead to continuous and progressive inflation. The chief reason for this is that the dominant "full employment" doctrines explicitly relieve the unions of the responsibility for any unemployment and place the duty of preserving full employment on the monetary and fiscal authorities.' Ibid., p. 399.

10 Ibid., p. 385 note 3.

starvation are still valid and compatible with freedom.[11] Further, Hayek departed from the conceptualisations of Hutt and Simons to the extent that he targeted 'labour monopoly' consistently, whereas he was clear that 'enterprise monopoly' was different and less problematic.

Hence, by the 1960s trade unions were elevated into a distinct problem in the framework of neoliberal thought, and, on a policy level, confronting trade unions was singled out as the most pressing project. Hayek's words are elucidating:

> I believe I have myself in the past used the tactical argument that we cannot hope to curb the coercive powers of labour unions unless we at the same time attack enterprise monopoly. I have, however, become convinced that it would be disingenuous to represent the existing monopolies in the field of labour and those in the field of enterprise as being of the same kind.[12]

What is of direct interest here is that, unlike Hutt and Simons, neoliberals from the 1950s onwards proposed concrete legal reforms in order to tackle the 'union problem'. In their attempt to transform political theory into political programme, proponents of neoliberalism began to put forward numerous ideas, including the removal of what they understood to be trade union privileges and the deliberate restraint of the extent of these privileges.[13] What is of relevance here is their understanding of the right to strike and its limitations in a 'free society'. As mentioned already, picketing was seen as problematic, even when it did not involve physical coercion of any kind.

Furthermore, Hayek manifested an evident suspicion regarding the right to strike. Even though he acknowledged its existence, he went on to submit it to extensive qualifications, as he stated emphatically that it is not an inalienable right.[14] Even though Hayek did not provide any justification for this assertion, he drew generous conclusions from it. More specifically, he went on to argue that long-term obligations on the part of workers could justify outlawing recourse to strike. Arguably, this is a particularly

11 Mirowski summarises this neoliberal position as follows: 'They seek to paint all "coercion" as evil, but without admitting into consideration any backstory of the determinants of our intentions. Everyone is treated as expressing context-free hankering, as if they were born yesterday into solitary confinement; [...] This commandment cashes out: no market can ever be coercive.' Philip Mirowski, Never Let a Serious Crisis Go Wasted: How Neoliberalism Survived the Financial Meltdown (Verso, 2013), p. 61.

12 Hayek (note 8), p. 381.

13 Already in the 1958 MPS meeting Lewis had advocated for a 'limitist approach' to prohibit sector or nationwide union action and restrain organised labour at the plant level. See: H. G. Lewis 'Labor Unions and Labor Monopoly in the United States' (Mont Pèlerin Society, 9th General Reunion, 1958).

14 Hayek (note 8), p. 388.

open-ended exception which could substantially curtail the exercise of this right. If we assume that Hayek discusses the right to strike as a non-coercive practice – that is, as voluntary abstention from work as a bargaining strategy on the part of a group of individuals – then it follows that even in theory neoliberals did not simply aim to strip unions from their coercive powers and restore the rule of law. Rather, there is an evident bias against collective action, even when it conforms to the general standards of conduct set by the same theorists (voluntariness, compatibility with the rule of law, etc.). This understanding might be expressed cryptically in Hayek's *Constitution of Liberty*, which focuses on the immediate issue of removing union privileges, but this can be attributed to the hostile political environment of the time. Published in 1960, *Constitution of Liberty* was a challenge to the Keynesian orthodoxy of its time and it only set Hayek's outline of the emerging competing paradigm. Hence, some moderation and even some uncertainty about specific policies to be followed were to be expected.

Unsurprisingly, the election of the first solidly neoliberal governments in the UK and the US in 1979 and 1981 respectively initiated a phase of creativity and explosion of the neoliberal political imagination. Charles Hanson displayed such creativity when he published a short, yet sharp, intervention in *Economic Affairs* in 1983.[15] Directly addressed to the UK Secretary of State for Employment, Norman Tebbit, his piece aimed to push for more radical reform in the area of collective bargaining. His principal argument was that Thatcher's government had not been brave enough in confronting union power and it kept surrendering to unions' demands. In order to tackle this perceived problem, Hanson argued that the right to strike in the so-called 'essential industries' should be drastically limited. Importantly, Hanson provided a non-exhaustive list of sectors including health services, gas, water, electricity and telephones or any other sector in which a disruption poses a direct threat to public health and safety.[16]

Once again, it became clear that the neoliberal agenda for trade unions manifested a clear hostility toward collective bargaining practices and went far beyond the removal of privileges. By invoking the 'essential industries' argument Hanson attempted to introduce an ever-widening hole at the heart of the right to strike. His definition of 'essential industries' is so vague that it allows for expansive interpretation, which in turn effectively erodes the right to strike. Crucially, since his argument was articulated in an era of rapid privatisations, these 'essential industries' did not have to be public in nature to be covered by the strike ban.

To sum up, the choice by prominent neoliberals to depart from Hutt's and Simons's critique of both capital and labour monopolies should be

15 C. Hanson, 'Trade Unions Reform: Tebbit's Next Step', 4 Economic Affairs 18.
16 Ibid, p. 19.

understood as indicative of the dual character of neoliberalism as sketched above. To comprehend how trade unions were initially elevated to a field of inquiry for neoliberals, we need to acknowledge how monopolies became a conceptual problem for liberal thought. Classical liberalism advocated by Adam Smith was based on exchange relations between autonomous actors and, therefore, failed to describe the complicated reality of capital concentration and organised labour that had arisen already in the nineteenth century.[17]

Nonetheless, this very real theoretical problem does not explain the choice of Hayek and of subsequent neoliberals to focus their attack almost exclusively on trade unions and lapse into significant contradictions, for example by pointing out that, in the case of strikes, non-violent private actions can be repressive and therefore, non-permissible. This contradiction can only be explained if we accept that neoliberalism, apart from an intellectual trend for the renewal of liberalism, was also elevated to the dominant bourgeois political strategy, in order to restore profitability and delimit the power of organised labour and the political Left. Moreover, the gradual concretisation of neoliberal engagement with trade unions is significant in its own right. The passage of neoliberalism from political theory to policy-making and to the emergence of specific legal arrangements, including the emergence of a particular neoliberal legality, coincides with the unravelling triumph of neoliberalism.

The Greek example: from self-restraint to class militancy

Let us now move to a concrete example of the neoliberal understanding of the right to strike by examining the case of post-crisis Greece. More specifically, the analysis will focus on the evolution of the governmental prerogative to intervene and stop legally decided and executed strikes by invoking 'public good'-related reasons. This example points at elements of continuity between liberal and neoliberal legal form to the extent that the neoliberal affront to trade unions was materialised by using legal frameworks already in place. Hence, the rapid process of neoliberalisation of Greek society that took place through the bailout agreements[18] at least

17 'The inadequacy of liberal formulas to the imperatives of changing the condition of wage-labour, their incompatibility with occasional attempts at social reform, represented another factor in the crisis of dogmatic liberalism. ... The idea that the wage-relation was a contract involving two independent, equal wills increasingly seemed to be a fiction completely divorced from social reality at a time of major industrial and urban concentration.' Pierre Dardot and Christian Laval, The New Way of the World: On Neo-liberal Society (Verso, 2013), p. 24.

18 Amongst many: Jérémy Morales, Yves Gendronb and Henri Guénin-Paracini, 'State Privatization and the Unrelenting Expansion of Neoliberalism: The Case of the Greek Financial

partly utilised laws promulgated when the Keynesian arrangement was at its apogee.

In order to fully grasp the interplay between law and neoliberalism in this specific case, it needs to be stressed that the periodisation of Greek capitalism differs crucially from the homologous story in Western Europe and the US. Due to historical peculiarities mainly associated with the Greek Civil War (1946–1949) and the subsequent oppression and exclusion of left-of-centre political forces from mainstream politics, Greece did not go through the 'golden decades' of Keynesian capitalism when Western Europe did. Rather, such policies were introduced only after the fall of the military dictatorship in 1974 and more consistently during the period 1981–1985 when the Socialist Party (PASOK-Πανελλήνιο Σοσιαλιστικό Κίνημα) first came to power. Hence, even though the 1975 Constitution was drafted during the international decline of Keynesianism and under the hegemony of a right-wing party (New Democracy-Νέα Δημοκρατία) it was largely considered to be progressive, and in no sense can it be seen as a blueprint neoliberal legal document. Property rights are of course protected by this constitution, but they are limited by social clauses; comprehensive protections of social and social action-related rights are introduced, and the nationalisation of crucial industries is allowed. For example, the 1975 Constitution (as amended in 1987, 2001 and 2008) protects the right to strike through a combination of two articles. Art. 22 par. 3 reads as follows:

> Any form of compulsory work is prohibited.
>
> Special laws shall determine the requisition of personal services in case of war or mobilization or to face defence needs of the country or urgent social emergencies resulting from disasters or liable to endanger public health, as well as the contribution of personal work to local government agencies to satisfy local needs.[19]
>
> Accordingly, Art. 23 par. 2 directly regulates the right in question:
>
> Strike constitutes a right to be exercised by lawfully established trade unions in order to protect and promote the financial and the general labour interests of working people.
>
> Strikes of any nature whatsoever are prohibited in the case of judicial functionaries and those serving in the security corps. The right to strike shall be subject to the specific limitations of the law regulating

Crisis', 25 Critical Perspectives on Accounting 423; Özgün Sarimehmet Duman, The Political Economy of Labour Market Reforms Greece, Turkey and the Global Economic Crisis (Palgrave Macmillan, 2014).

19 The Constitution of Greece as revised by the parliamentary resolution of 27 May 2008 of the VIIIth Revisionary Parliament, Article 22 para. 3. Available in English at: www.hellenicparliament.gr/en/Vouli-ton-Ellinon/To-Politevma/Syntagma/ (last accessed: 09/09/2016).

> this right in the case of public servants and employees of local government agencies and of public law legal persons as well as in the case of the employees of all types of enterprises of a public nature or of public benefit, the operation of which is of vital importance in serving the basic needs of the society as a whole. These limitations may not be carried to the point of abolishing the right to strike or hindering the lawful exercise thereof.[20]

However, while the constitution itself was considered to be progressive, these constitutional provisions are accompanied by and operationalised through ordinary legislation. In this case, the legal framework setting the conditions for the requisition of personal services under abnormal circumstances that is mentioned in the above articles of the 1975 Constitution dates back to the era between the fall of the military dictatorship (July 1974) and the election of the first post-dictatorship parliament (November 1974). Legislating under the previous – hardly liberal – constitution of 1952 and being practically unrestrained in the absence of a parliament, the government of the time opted for a decree that disproportionately expanded the prerogative of the government to terminate a legally called and organised strike action. This governmental prerogative is known as 'civil mobilisation' (πολιτική επιστράτευση) and is applicable to otherwise lawful strike action.

More specifically, although the 1975 Constitution only grants the government with this prerogative in exceptional and extreme circumstances, a 1974 ministerial decree expanded these cases in a practically unlimited way. The decree in question (17/1974) provides a notoriously loose definition of emergency that covers events ranging from natural disasters and war to anything that can bring about damage to life or property or 'cause disruption to the economic and social life of the State'.[21] Since the very object and purpose of every efficient strike is to provoke some degree of nuisance and disruption, this latest clause was specifically designed to target industrial action. Further, the decree does not specify any time limits for its application. Consequently, a sector can be under civil mobilisation regime for months or even years, which in turn means that there is a blanket and unlimited ban on striking during this time. This is not just a theoretical scenario. Subway employees were mobilised in June 2013 and the ban was only lifted one year later (July 2014).

20 Ibid., Article 23 para. 2.

21 Legislative Decree 17/1974 'On the Civil Planning of Emergencies' Article 2 para. 5. Available at: www.et.gr/idocsnph/search/pdfViewerForm.html?args=5C7QrtC22wHxY9m0TgvYxHdtvSoClrL8SRL2byguO4d5MXD0LzQTLWPU9yLzB8V68knBzLCmTXKaO6fpVZ6Lx3UnKl3nP8NxdnJ5r9cmWyJWelDvWS_18kAEhATUkJb0x1LIdQ163nV9K-td6SIuSEr9pIgSK-limE1rd4RqzbG-PvNWPL5qeJbJK7dcdbgl (in Greek) (last accessed: 09/09/2016).

This piece of legislation largely operated as a 'sleeping giant' between 1974 and 2010. No parliamentary majority repealed the law, but governments manifested relevant self-restraint and 'only' used it six times to terminate strikes during this period.[22] That being said, it is also important to understand that neoliberal reforms in Greece were initiated during this period. Arguably, the turning point was '1996 under the leadership of PASOK's new leader Kostas Simitis'.[23] This signalled a prolonged crisis for Greek trade unions as their power and ideological appeal gradually declined and the dominance of PASOK among major unions, especially in the public sector, was linked to a less confrontational stance. While precarious labour steadily increased, unions excluded with various techniques this vulnerable part of the workforce. In a nutshell, between 1996 and 2010 civil mobilisation remained a marginal strategy to confront union power. This can be attributed both to the internal transformation of the labour movement, but also to the proactive stance of the judiciary that ruled against the legality of strikes on a regular basis rendering civil mobilisation redundant.

Nonetheless, it is important to note that, when the seafarers were mobilised in 2006, they challenged the constitutionality of the decree before the Council of the State. The Court never ruled on the case, since the government withdrew the decision, and, given that constitutional control in Greece is not of an abstract character, the court no longer had jurisdiction to rule on the question. This withdrawal was largely understood as an indirect acceptance by the government of the unconstitutionality of the decree, but this did not lead to its repeal. Importantly, when such a decision was challenged again in 2013, the government insisted on its stance, and successfully so: Greek courts, which are notoriously hostile towards organised labour and have generally assisted in the implementation of neoliberal reforms since 2010, ruled that civil mobilisation was constitutional.[24]

The turning point for decree 17/1974 occurred after Greece was subjected to one of the most intensive and destructive austerity programmes ever imposed upon a developed state.[25] The so-called 'rescue packages' were first introduced in 2010 as a response to the soaring public debt of

22 Between 1974 and 2010 the decree was applied against the following strikes: banking sector employees (1979), lorry drivers (1983), state-owned aviation company (OLYMPIAKI – Ολυμπιακή) aircrew (1986), bus drivers (1994), seafarers (2002 and 2006).

23 Christos Laskos and Euclid Tsakalotos, Crucible of Resistance: Greece, the Eurozone and the World Economic Crisis (Pluto Press, 2013), p. 22.

24 'The Council of the State rules that teacher's mobilisation is lawful and constitutional.' Available at: www.lawnet.gr/news/ste-nomimi-kai-suntagmatiki-i-epistrateusi-ton-ekpaideutikon-32599.html (in Greek) (last accessed: 09/09/2016).

25 For a very brief report on the impacts of austerity see 'What impact are austerity cuts having in Greece?' Available at: www.bbc.co.uk/news/world-europe-17225278 (last accessed: 09/09/2016).

Greece[26] and were unsurprisingly accompanied by a series of conditionalities, many of which took aim at labour law and collective bargaining.[27] Nevertheless, this aggressive neoliberalisation of the Greek society[28] did not occur only through legislative reform. Novel interpretation of already-existing rules was also a secondary, but perhaps even more effective, means to that end. Between 2010 and July 2014, the government invoked urgent circumstances using the decree to bring a strike to an end six times.[29] During the first six months of 2013 alone, the decree was applied three times. More importantly, it was applied as a precautionary measure before a strike called by high-school teachers had even begun. This decision was considered to be borderline legal, as even the 'generous' 1974 decree only applies to an ongoing strike that has already given rise to tangible problems, rather than a mere decision to take industrial action. In addition to invoking urgent circumstances, the government also argued that the high-school teachers' strike constituted a 'public health hazard'. The argument deployed was that, since the strike was to delay university entrance exams, it would cause serious mental anxiety and distress to the students and would pose a serious threat to public order.[30]

A year later, in July 2014, the decree was applied once again to end a strike by the electrical workers in Greece's partly publicly owned electricity company (DEI-Δημόσια Επιχείρηση Ηλεκτρισμού).[31] Here, the arguments along with the contradictions of Hanson's approach become evident. The mobilisation was clearly decided on the 'essential industries' rationale proposed by Hanson. Ironically, though, the workers were striking against the privatisation of the company. In a nutshell, the government was making two directly contradictory arguments at the same time. On the one hand,

26 For a comprehensive critique of the 'rescue packages' see: Laskos and Tsakalotos (note 23).

27 See: Ioannis Katsaroumpas, 'EU Bailout Conditionality as a De Facto Mode of Government: A Neo-Liberal "Black Hole" for the Greek Collective Labour Law System?' 4 Critical, Quarterly of Legislation and Law 345.

28 For the push of neoliberal reforms in the domain of labour law through the conditionalities attached to the 'rescue package' see: ibid.; Apostolos Dedoussopoulos, Valia Aranitou, Franciscos Koutentakis and Marina Maropoulou, 'Assessing the impact of the memoranda on Greek labour market and labour relations', Working Paper No. 53 Governance and Tripartism Department International Labour Office (November 2013).

29 Between 2010 and 2014 the following sectors were mobilised: owners of lorries (2010), cleaning staff of municipalities (2011), subway employees (2013), seafarers (2013), high-school teachers (2013), electricity company employees (2014).

30 For a short report of the story see: Renee Maltezou and Harry Papachristou, 'Greek workers walk out to protest ban on teachers' strike' (14 May 2013, Reuters) Available at: http://uk.reuters.com/article/2013/05/14/uk-greece-strike-idUKBRE94D053201 30514 (last accessed: 09/09/2016).

31 Kerin Hope, 'Greece orders power workers to end strike' (5 July 2014, Financial Times). Available at: www.ft.com/intl/cms/s/0/dd0538c8-0469-11e4-ab6a-00144feab7de.html# axzz3BCjHgKHl (last accessed: 09/09/2016).

when it came to its privatisation, the electricity company was no different from any other company, and its privatisation was unproblematic. However, when it came to the strike against its privatisation, the company was an 'essential industry' and its employees did not enjoy the constitutionally guaranteed right to strike that employees of other companies did. The immediate problem here is that arguably some conceptualisation of 'public good' is required for these 'essential industries' to be detected. However, neoliberalism is engaged in an attempt to redraw the line between public and private sectors not only by privatising public assets but also by inducing competition as the *modus operandi* of the public sector as well.[32] Hence, in a reversal of logical order, an industry can be identified as 'essential' the moment its employees are banned from striking. Arguably, this is an intellectual move that expands in an unlimited way the power of the executive to regulate industrial relations to the detriment of organised labour.

The situation is further complicated for organised labour to the extent that the above described legal strategy of civil mobilisation is the last resort against strike action and as such is exceptional. This is because Greek courts tend to rule that strikes called in Greece are unlawful and/or constitute an abuse of the right to strike. This was a standard practice of the Greek courts that was aggravated after 2010. As a result, any group willing to strike needs to overcome two main legal obstacles: first, the question of legality, and, second, the question of emergency. As has already been indicated, this double legal move has created considerable burdens for the emergence of a confrontational labour movement in a time of acute significance. In conclusion, it is worth taking note of the fact that the legal framework promulgated during the period of Keynesianism was mobilised to materialise the neoliberal agenda which was determined to diminish radically the power of organised labour. The invocation of the 'public good' is an exemplary case of the inherent indeterminacy of legal language, especially to the extent that the concept incorporates conflicting values and interests without being able to resolve their tension. Hence, the concept has been historically invoked to perform widely divergent functions ranging from the Keynesian check on union militancy to neoliberal aggressiveness toward organised labour.

Neoliberal legality: between continuity and rupture

What does the example of the right to strike in Greece say about neoliberal legality? Many theorists and political commentators attempt to the-

32 'State action must therefore be submitted to economic analysis, in order to discriminate not only between agenda and non-agenda, but also between ways of accomplishing the agenda', Dardot and Laval (note 17), p. 216.

orise the management of the 2008 crisis by reference to the Schmittian scheme of the state of exception.[33] Within this paradigm, the idea that 2008 initiated a 'state of exception' when the sovereign decided to suspend 'normal' liberal legality is prevalent. Much more to the point, the argument that neoliberalism does not just entail a 'return' to classical liberalism nor can it only be explained in all its complexity in reference to specific class interests needs to be taken seriously. For example, Dardot's and Laval's critique of (certain) Marxist approaches to neoliberalism summarises the complexity of the phenomenon and the intellectual poverty of simplistic approaches:

> Trapped in a conception that makes the 'logic of capital' an autonomous motor of history, they reduce the latter to a sheer repetition of the same scenarios, with the same characters in new costumes and the same plots in new settings.[34]

This argument needs to be taken seriously as it safeguards (to the extent anything does) against the perils of reductionism. Nevertheless, the significance of continuity deserves to be stressed as well. My argument here is that neoliberal legality manifests at least some significant aspects of continuity with pre-existing legal forms. The neoliberal agenda can be realised to a significant degree by *twisting, stretching and creatively interpreting* the ordinary legal framework of a functional liberal Keynesian state. Admittedly, ruptures can and must be traced within this continuity for neoliberal legality to be conceptualised properly. Neoliberalism is not simply the return of classical liberalism, a truth admitted expressly by neoliberals themselves in the early days of the neoliberal current. For instance, neoliberals were quick to replace free exchange with competition as the central concept and cohesive force of free economies and societies. Milton Friedman has summarised this crucial departure as follows: 'But instead of the 19th century understanding that laissez-faire is the means to achieve this goal, neoliberalism proposes that competition will lead the way.'[35]

This intellectual move was of immense political and social impact. As Wendy Brown has noted, unlike free exchange, competition does not bear the promise of a final equilibrium. Competition has its winners and its losers, and accepting competition as the central feature of our societies

33 Karl Schmitt, Political Theology: Four Chapters on the Concept of Sovereignty (The University of Chicago Press, 2005). For an analysis of the management of the crisis that applies the Schmittian scheme see: Leonidas Kyriakopoulos, 'The State of Exception as Precondition for Crisis', in Beyond the 'Greek Crisis': Histories, Rhetorics, Politics. Available at: http://production.culanth.org/fieldsights/255-the-state-of-exception-as-precondition-for-crisis (last accessed: 09/09/2016).

34 Dardot and Laval (note 17).

35 Milton Friedman, 'Neoliberalism and its Prospects', 17 Farmand 89.

means accepting the permanent exclusion and relative (or absolute) deprivation of those not capable of adjusting to competition.[36] Further, in terms of legality, neoliberalism is not reducible to a simple return to the abstract, general and formal forms of law that dictated much of the nineteenth century, even though this is definitely part of the picture.[37] Since neoliberalism advocates the limitless expansion of competition as a way of living and mode of governing, the state itself must be modelled after the market. It is a unique feature of the neoliberal society that public law is increasingly modelled after, and interpreted in accordance with, market and private law principles to the extent that the public and the private even merge in the concept of 'governance'.[38] These, and many more, innovations are undeniable and need to be taken seriously.

Nevertheless, a crucial question remains: what is the unifying principle that could help us to make sense of the neoliberal chaos? Or to rephrase: what is the common feature of inter-war German ordo-liberals who first articulated the argument for a competition-driven society and the Chilean Chicago Boys who established the first neoliberal government, which nonetheless provoked some (limited) embarrassment for its dictatorial character? Why do we claim that Scandinavian *flexicurity* and post-1978 China have something in common, despite their immense differences? Why did the *Constitution of Liberty*, written more than 40 years ago, gain such prominence in the late 1970s and then again after the 2008 crisis, when neoliberalism supposedly had been discredited?[39] My argument is that, apart from some shared theoretical premises, neoliberalism gains coherence through its political orientation: the restoration and deepening of class power in favour of capital on the national and international level. It is no coincidence that, while neoliberalism was first articulated in the 1930s and was a fully developed political and economic current by the 1960s, it only gained political momentum in the late 1970s. Neoliberal arguments, once mocked even by the mainstream Right, were elevated to a new orthodoxy at this time not because of their inherent rationality or because they delivered on their promises. Rather, it was the combination of an extremely unfavourable balance of social

36 See: Wendy Brown, 'American Nightmare: Neoliberalism, Neoconservatism, and De-Democratisation', 34 Political Theory, p. 695.

37 The return to general, abstract rules is evident in areas like international trade or investment law. Amongst others: Andrew Lang, World Trade Law After Neoliberalism: Re-imagining the Global Economic Order (Oxford University Press, 2011), pp. 240–53.

38 'It is precisely this new generalised hybridization of so-called "public" action that explains the promotion of the category of "governance" to think state functions and practices, instead of the categories of pubic law, starting with sovereignty.' Dadrot and Laval (note 17), p. 220.

39 Mirowski has convincingly demonstrated how 2008 brought about a deepening rather than a serious crisis of neoliberalism: Mirowski (note 11), pp. 157–238.

powers both domestically and internationally that brought about its triumph.

If we accept that neoliberalism is a new mode of governance not reducible yet closely tied to the enhancement of capitalist power,[40] the question of neoliberal legality becomes interlinked with the question of capitalist law and the capitalist state. The inquiry about the character and functions of the capitalist state take us to the work of the Marxist philosopher and political theorist Nicos Poulantzas, who has provided us with one of the most elaborate arguments within the Marxian paradigm. In his final and seminal work *State, Power, Socialism*, he makes two potentially relevant observations. The first concerns the transformations of capitalist law and the capitalist state in accordance with the requirements of capitalist accumulation, a process known as *authoritarian statism*. The second observation is interlinked with the first and concerns the limits of legality in the context of the modern state.

In Poulantzas's work, authoritarian statism was 'a new historical form of the capitalist state'.[41] Initially the concept was developed to provide an explanation for the military dictatorships of Southern Europe, but it was expanded gradually far beyond these regimes to grasp the transformation of the state and law in Western Keynesian democracies. More specifically, during the post-war era the transformations of the state could be said to be generally attributable to the rise of popular struggles, to the crisis of the power bloc, to the alleged dominance of the monopolistic faction of capital over other factions and, importantly, to the necessities, modalities and antinomies of the welfare state. Accordingly, the authoritarian state of western capitalism manifested one or more of the following attributes:

> the subordination of the legislative branch to the executive (usually plebiscitarian in character), the abolition of separation of powers, the rise of the administrative-bureaucratic state, the crisis of the rule of law, where general, abstract, and universal laws are replaced by discretionary and arbitrary decrees...[42]

40 'Thirty years later, in the midst of the 1970s, the neoliberals suddenly and surprisingly found in the economic crisis of the welfarist project an opening for their views. The rest of neoliberalism's history since that breakthrough moment is well-known: the evisceration of the regulatory state in the North Atlantic industrial zone together with an international program towards the global south (as well as, perhaps most spectacularly, formerly communist Eastern Europe) to facilitate capital movement to the detriment of opposing forces.' Samuel Moyn, 'A Powerless Companion: Human Rights in the Age of Neoliberalism', 77 Law and Contemporary Problems 147.

41 Andreas Kalyvas, 'The Stateless Theory. Poulantzas' Challenge to Postmodernism', in: Stanley Aronowitz and Peter Bratsis (eds), State-theory Reconsidered: Paradigm Lost (University of Minnesota Press, 2002), p. 124.

42 Ibid.

What is of direct relevance here is that Poulantzas specifically stressed the importance of this transformation of the state for the form and function of legality. The crucial attribute of authoritarian statism for Poulantzas was the increasing domination of the executive over the legislative branch of the state, which marked the end of 'the predominance of the parliament as the sanctuary of law'.[43] This domination unfolded gradually with the emergence of the welfare state and the multiplicity and complexity of the socio-economic problems tackled by the state in this context. This turn was marked by a (temporary) departure from the general and universal form of law, which was and still is largely considered to be the distinctive characteristic of modern law. This did not amount to the formal disappearance of formal and general legal rules. Nevertheless, these rules co-existed with the extensive use of ministerial decrees and, more importantly, with a series of administrative decisions by the extensive bureaucratic state mechanisms that were concretising and essentially distorting the rules, in order to apply them. In practice, state bureaucracy became the main locus for the interpretation and application of laws. Given that most of the time it is extremely difficult to distinguish between the interpretation of an existing rule and the creation of a new rule, this reality decisively enhanced the role of the executive, which in turn radically modified the character of the law itself. Arguably, since the days of Poulantzas, authoritarian statism has been transformed following the transformation from Keynesian to neoliberal capitalism.[44] In any case, though, the executive has retained, and in many cases expanded, its prerogatives in the interpretation and application of laws.

Poulantzas' second relevant observation concerns the ability of the capitalist state to exit legality whenever necessary. Let us turn to Poulantzas' exact words at some length:

> Every juridical system includes illegality in the additional sense that gaps, blanks or 'loopholes' form an integral part of its discourse ... Many laws would never have existed in their present form if a certain rate of ruling-class violation had not been anticipated by, and written into, the workings of the state machinery.[45]

This was not to imply that legality for capitalist states is unimportant, a mere façade. Rather, along with Poulantzas I am arguing that given the historically unprecedented concentration of legality and legitimate coercion at the

43 Nicos Poulantzas, State, Power, Socialism (Verso, 2000), p. 218.

44 For example, Kalyvas has suggested that after the 1990s we partly moved away from the paradigm Poulantzas described towards the 'liberal authoritarian legalism', marked by the rise of the judiciary. See Kalyvas (note 41).

45 Poulantzas (note 43), pp. 84–5.

hands of the state, there is no external force other than the balance of social powers to ensure compliance with those laws that were imposed through social struggles. In a nutshell, the modern capitalist state knows no competitor in the field of prescribing legal rules. Therefore, and if we take the separation of powers less seriously than liberal theory invites us to do for a second, we can conceive the wide room for manoeuvre the capitalist state has for creating, selectively applying and liberally interpreting legality, to the extent that there is no point external to the state to assume a competitive function. This potential is accentuated by the very indeterminacy of the liberal legal form already discussed. If indeed there is not one right answer for every legal question, then the room for manoeuvre available to the state broadens significantly. This means that indeterminacy allows the state to remain within the realm of legality while confronting both social crises and struggles and also its own crises of legitimacy and governmentality.

The case of changes to the right to strike in Greece is illustrative of the trends sketched above. The institutionalisation of the right to strike has generally been an unwelcome element in the fabric of bourgeois legislation to the extent that, going to the core of exploitative relations, it has the potential to destabilise the 'normal' process of capitalist accumulation.[46] That said, in the years of Keynesian conciliation, the role of the state was to *contain* and *channel* class confrontation and generally avoid reaching the point of legal coercion against strikers. In these cases, law operated as the outer limit of class confrontation, given that the state had retained the prerogative to deploy legal coercion against intensified class struggles. Thus, legal restrictions on unions' rights, even when used with prudence, were a means to formulate, enforce and guarantee the Keynesian social contract – a social arrangement much less spontaneous, let alone rosy, than it was later imagined to be.

In the course of the deployment of the neoliberal agenda, the role of legality expanded radically. Unsurprisingly, the aggressive introduction of neoliberal reforms in Greece after 2010 triggered social resistance, and recourse to strike was one of the common means of resistance deployed. What is significant here, though, is that restrictive legislation did not just operate as the outer limit of social confrontation as it had in the Keynesian period. Rather, legal coercion moved to the centre of political and social life. Law no longer operates as a threat leading to persuasion, but it targets directly the actions of working classes. Further, the invocation of laws and legality enables the government to invoke a concept that otherwise sits rather uncomfortably with the neoliberal ideology: the public good. Claiming to be acting in response to a public emergency and promoting general welfare, the government utilises the law to construct a narrative that depicts the strikers as promoting their individualistic interests,

46 See also the points raised by Robert Knox in the present volume.

whereas neoliberal reforms represent the common good. This is a significant aspect of neoliberalism's confrontation with the unions. As has already been noted above, one of the central arguments of Hayek against the unions was that they only promoted the particularistic interests of their members at the expense of the entire society. Hence, through restraining strike actions neoliberals are able to rhetorically juxtapose the universal good of the society to the particularistic, egoistical actions of the unions. This is in turn indispensable for the function of the neoliberal state to the extent that, no matter how committed to individualism a state might be, it is also entrusted with the task to construct the unity of the social body.[47]

Conclusion

At the turn of the twentieth century, legal realists invoked the argument of the inherent indeterminacy of the law to challenge the *laissez-faire* bias – commonly known as *Lochnerism* – of the US Supreme Court.[48] According to their arguments,

> the Supreme Court, as final arbiter of the law, does not simply state the appropriate interpretation of the law, but actively generates it, in a move best understood as performative. The content of law is only knowable at the moment when the court enunciates it.[49]

Arguably, this performativity extends to the executive to the extent that the executive interprets and applies the law on a constant basis, thus defining and redefining its content. Ironically, though not necessarily unexpectedly, a century later this indeterminacy performs social functions directly contradictory to the attempt to introduce the New Deal, paving instead the way for the destruction of collective bargaining and re-liberalisation of labour. What is of importance here is that what is nominally the same piece of legislation can be utilised to serve diverse social goals and operationalise different bourgeois strategies, and this is made possible by the indeterminacy inherent in the liberal legal form. This suggests not only that legality has been shaped by neoliberalism but that the liberal

47 'I then saw clearly that dual movement whereby the modern State creates individualizations and privatizations by constituting itself as their unity and homogenization – a movement, that is to say, both of creating modes of isolation (of which the people-nation is composed) and of representing their unity (in the modern national-popular State).' Poulantzas (note 43), p. 70.

48 See: O. Holmes, 'Privilege, Malice, and Intent', 8 Harvard Law Review 1 and O. Holmes, 'The Path of the Law', 10 Harvard Law Review 457.

49 Stephen Humphreys, The Theatre of the Rule of Law: Transnational Legal Intervention in Theory and Practice (Cambridge University Press, 2010), pp. 74–5.

legal form has been essential to the functioning and spread of neoliberal policy around strikes and labour action.

Admittedly, neoliberal legality is not reducible to the liberal paradigm of the nineteenth century nor can it be solely explained in reference to some bare, eternal capitalist logic. Nonetheless, we need to understand how both in the case of Greece and more generally, neoliberal legality has not always arisen out of sweeping reforms but also from creative interpretation and application of already existing legislation. This complicated relationship between continuity and rupture can only be understood properly if we take into consideration the centrality of neoliberalism in the restoration of capitalist power in the last quarter of the twentieth century. Or, as di Lampedussa wrote in *The Leopard*: 'If we want things to stay as they are, things will have to change.'

Acknowledgement

I warmly thank the editor, Honor Brabazon, and Robert Knox for their insightful comments. All errors of substance and style remain my own.

References

Brown, Wendy. 'American Nightmare: Neoliberalism, Neoconservatism, and De-Democratisation', 34 *Political Theory*, p. 695.

Cockett, Richard. *Thinking the Unthinkable: Think Tanks and the Economic Counter-Revolution 1931–1983* (Fontana Press, 1995).

The Constitution of Greece as revised by the parliamentary resolution of 27 May 2008 of the VIIIth Revisionary Parliament, Article 22, para. 3. www.hellenicparliament.gr/en/Vouli-ton-Ellinon/To-Politevma/Syntagma/ (last accessed: 06/07/2014).

Dardot, Pierre and Christian Laval. *The New Way of the World: On Neo-liberal Society* (Verso, 2013), p. 24.

Dedoussopoulos, Apostolos, Valia Aranitou, Franciscos Koutentakis and Marina Maropoulou. 'Assessing the impact of the memoranda on Greek labour market and labour relations', Working Paper No. 53 Governance and Tripartism Department International Labour Office (November 2013).

Duman, Özgün Sarimehmet. *The Political Economy of Labour Market Reforms: Greece, Turkey and the Global Economic Crisis* (Palgrave Macmillan, 2014).

Friedman, Milton. 'Neoliberalism and its Prospects', 17 *Farmand* 89.

Graham, F. (ed.) *Wages and Wage-Policy. Conference Proceedings of the 1st Meeting of the Mont Pèlerin Society at Mont Pèlerin* (Hoover Institution Archives, 1947), p. 204.

Hanson, C. 'Trade Unions Reform: Tebbit's Next Step', 4 *Economic Affairs* 18.

Hayek, F. A. *The Constitution of Liberty* (The University of Chicago Press, 1960), p. 389.

Holmes, O. 'Privilege, Malice, and Intent', 8 *Harvard Law Review* 1.

Holmes, O. 'The Path of the Law', 10 *Harvard Law Review* 457.

Hope, Kerin. 'Greece orders power workers to end strike' (5 July 2014, *Financial*

Times). Available at: www.ft.com/intl/cms/s/0/dd0538c8-0469-11e4-ab6a-00144feab7de.html#axzz3BCjHgKHl (last accessed: 23/08/2014).

Humphreys, Stephen. *The Theatre of the Rule of Law: Transnational Legal Intervention in Theory and Practice* (Cambridge University Press, 2010), pp. 74–5.

Hutt, W. H. *The Theory of Collective Bargaining* (Institute of Economic Affairs, 1930).

Jackson, Ben. 'An Ideology of Class: Neo-Liberalism and the Trade Unions, c. 1930–791', in: C. Griffiths, J. Nott and W. Whyte (eds), *Classes, Cultures and Politics: Essays for Ross McKibbin* (Oxford University Press, 2011), pp. 263–81.

Kalyvas, Andreas. 'The Stateless Theory. Poulantzas' Challenge to Postmodernism', in: Stanley Aronowitz and Peter Bratsis (eds), *State-theory Reconsidered: Paradigm Lost* (University of Minnesota Press, 2002), p. 124.

Katsaroumpas, Ioannis. 'EU Bailout Conditionality as a De Facto Mode of Government: A Neo-Liberal "Black Hole" for the Greek Collective Labour Law System?' 4 *Critical Quarterly of Legislation and Law* 345.

Kyriakopoulos, Leonidas. 'The State of Exception as Precondition for Crisis', in *Beyond the 'Greek Crisis': Histories, Rhetorics, Politics.* Available at: http://production.culanth.org/fieldsights/255-the-state-of-exception-as-precondition-for-crisis (last accessed: 23/08/2014).

Lang, Andrew. *World Trade Law After Neoliberalism: Re-imagining the Global Economic Order* (Oxford University Press, 2011), pp. 240–53.

Laskos, Christos and Euclid Tsakalotos. *Crucible of Resistance: Greece, the Eurozone and the World Economic Crisis* (Pluto Press, 2013), p. 22.

Legislative Decree 17/1974 'On the Civil Planning of Emergencies' Article 2, para. 5. Available at: www.et.gr/idocsnph/search/pdfViewerForm.html?args=5-C7QrtC22wHxY9m0TgvYxHdtvSoClrL8SRL2byguO4d5MXD0LzQTLWPU9yLzB8V68knBzLCmTXKaO6fpVZ6Lx3UnKl3nP8NxdnJ5r9cmWyJWelDvWS_18kAEhATUkJb0x1LIdQ163nV9K--td6SIuSEr9pIgSKlimE1rd4RqzbG-PvN-WPL5qeJbJK7dcdbgl (in Greek) (last accessed: 23/08/2014).

Lewis, H. G. 'Labor Unions and Labor Monopoly in the United States' (Mont Pèlerin Society, 9th General Reunion, 1958).

Maltezou, Renee and Harry Papachristou. 'Greek workers walk out to protest ban on teachers' strike' (14 May 2013, Reuters). Available at: http://uk.reuters.com/article/2013/05/14/uk-greece-strike-idUKBRE94D05320130514 (last accessed: 23/08/2014).

Mirowski, Philip. *Never Let a Serious Crisis Go Wasted: How Neoliberalism Survived the Financial Meltdown* (Verso, 2013), p. 61.

Morales, Jérémy, Yves Gendronb and Henri Guénin-Paracini. 'State Privatization and the Unrelenting Expansion of Neoliberalism: The Case of the Greek Financial Crisis', 25 *Critical Perspectives on Accounting* 423.

Moyn, Samuel. 'A Powerless Companion: Human Rights in the Age of Neoliberalism', 77 *Law and Contemporary Problems* 147.

Poulantzas, Nicos. *State, Power, Socialism* (Verso, 2000), p. 218.

Schmitt, Karl. *Political Theology: Four Chapters on the Concept of Sovereignty* (The University of Chicago Press, 2005).

Simons, H. 'Some Reflections on Syndicalism', 52 *Journal of Political Economy* 1.

Steiner, Yves. 'The Neoliberals Confront the Trade Unions', in: Philip Mirowski and Dieter Plehwe (eds), *The Road From Mont Pelerin: The Making of the Neoliberal Thought Collective* (Harvard University Press, 2009), p. 183.

'The Council of the State rules that teacher's mobilisation is lawful and constitutional.' Available at: www.lawnet.gr/news/ste-nomimi-kai-suntagmatiki-i-epistrateusi-ton-ekpaideutikon-32599.html (in Greek) (last accessed: 23/08/2014).

Unger, Roberto Mangabeira. 'The Critical Legal Studies Movement', 96 *Harvard Law Review*, p. 571.

'What impact are austerity cuts having in Greece?' Available at: www.bbc.co.uk/news/world-europe-17225278 (last accessed: 23/08/2014).

Chapter 7

The promise of rights

International indigenous rights in the neoliberal era

Kristin Ciupa

Introduction

In the neoliberal era, threats to indigenous ways of life around the world have reached unprecedented levels. Expanding foreign direct investment and the marketization of new areas of life threaten to privatize and commodify indigenous communal lands, resources, livelihoods and culture, as new locations around the world are subject to the laws and logics of neoliberalism. Arising in the same time period, and part of the broader proliferation of international human rights and focus on multiculturalism that began in the 1970s, international indigenous rights law seeks to protect indigenous identities and ways of life by both extending universal human rights mechanisms to indigenous groups, and by creating specialized rights provisions that protect indigenous interests. Since their creation, indigenous rights discourses have been invoked by states, NGOs and grassroots movements made up of indigenous and non-indigenous people alike in the name of indigenous people. Despite the proliferation of indigenous rights instruments, however, many of the inequalities that prompted a greater focus on indigenous interests continue to exist. These ongoing inequalities necessitate a closer look at the origins, and the effects, of using international rights to protect indigenous interests, as well as the relationship between indigenous rights and the neoliberal system.

This chapter explores certain limitations of international indigenous rights instruments and examines their role in constructing and reproducing the neoliberal system. While mechanisms of international law have been used historically to justify intervention into, and the subordination of, indigenous communities, what is new under neoliberalism is the way in which the potentially empowering discourses of rights and recognition are implicit in advancing the neoliberal project. This chapter argues that international indigenous rights instruments advance the neoliberal project in two ways. First, by incorporating indigenous people into dominant legal frameworks, indigenous rights assimilate indigenous people into the structures and discourses of the neoliberal system. Second, by adopting a normative definition of indigeneity that is compatible with the neoliberal paradigm, indigenous rights instruments circumscribe the category of indigeneity, and thereby manage indigenous identity and resistance. This chapter relies on examples from the United Nations Declaration on the Rights of Indigenous Peoples (UNDRIP) to illustrate these arguments. The UNDRIP is the main international instrument that outlines indigenous rights and serves as a guiding framework for national indigenous rights legislation.

First, this chapter develops a theoretical framework for exploring the characteristics of, and connections between, neoliberalism and human rights. Second, this chapter outlines the history of indigenous rights at the UN, focusing on the UNDRIP. Third, it explores how and why indigenous rights have failed to protect, and improve the conditions of, indigenous people under neoliberalism. Lastly, this chapter argues that instead, by assimilating indigenous people into the neoliberal system and managing indigenous difference, indigenous rights are complicit in constructing and reproducing the neoliberal system.

Foundations

The proliferation of international indigenous rights instruments and institutions, and their effects, can be understood by situating them in the neoliberal context in which they became prevalent. This section first outlines the main arguments of this chapter, and second, explores the origins and characteristics of contemporary neoliberalism and human rights.

While there is an abundance of literature that critiques human rights (Rajagopal 2003; Miéville 2006; Bowring 2008; Young and Perelman 2010), these debates rarely look at the relationship between rights and neoliberalism specifically. Those that do have focused on the ways in which the neoliberal restructuring of the state and conceptions of citizenship and political participation have limited the scope of rights in the neoliberal era (Brown 2003, 2006; Giroux 2005). In particular, analyses of indigenous rights in the neoliberal era have focused on the ways in which official definitions of indigeneity and cultural difference are being used to advance indigenous interests, and the ways in which such conceptualizations limit indigenous activism and identity through narrow and exclusionary definitions of indigeneity (Hale 2002, 2005; Coombe 2005; McCormack 2011, 2012). Rarely, however, do these analyses explore the ways in which the indigenous rights paradigm actually helps to construct the neoliberal system.

This chapter contributes to the critical literature on indigenous rights and neoliberalism by exploring how indigenous rights are not only shaped and limited by the neoliberal order, but also the ways in which the neoliberal order is constructed and perpetuated by indigenous rights. It argues that neoliberalism and indigenous rights are mutually constitutive. The neoliberal era provides the context for, and ultimately influences the content of, the contemporary UN human rights and indigenous rights frameworks. On the other hand, human rights and indigenous rights form part of a legal apparatus that maintains the neoliberal system by reproducing neoliberal rationalities and incorporating rights bearers into the language and legal structures of the neoliberal system.

To make this argument, I rely on two theoretical concepts. First, Partha Chatterjee's 'rule of colonial difference', which refers to the observation that colonialism depended upon the very differences between colonizer and colonized that it purported to overcome (Chatterjee 1993: 10). On the one hand, British administrators justified colonialism in India by arguing that it would eventually eradicate difference by modernising colonized people. On the other hand, however, the continuation of colonial authoritarianism depended upon, and thus reproduced, the subordinate position of the colonized (Kolsky 2005: 636). This created a two-pronged discourse: colonized peoples were deemed rational and capable of being modernized, but at the same time, they were perpetually deemed different in order to justify continued colonial domination. This discourse earned them the status of 'equal, but different'. Legal reforms played an important role in maintaining the 'equal, but different' status of colonized peoples by extending 'universal' legal principles to colonized peoples alongside laws specific to the colonized.

While the role of international law in subordinating indigenous people has a long history, this chapter argues that what is new under neoliberalism is the way in which the potentially empowering discourses of rights and recognition are implicit in both assimilating indigenous people into the neoliberal project, while also circumscribing the very category of indigeneity and indigenous identity. Arguing that relations of colonial and imperial domination are inscribed into the very structures and form of international law (Miéville 2006: 270), this chapter will apply Chatterjee's concept of the 'rule of colonial difference' to explore how, under neoliberalism, indigenous rights construct indigenous people as 'equal, but different'. The implication of this argument is that indigenous rights not only help to construct neoliberalism by incorporating indigenous people into the neoliberal framework via universal human rights mechanisms, but also construct, maintain and depend upon difference, via specialized rights provisions, as a legitimating condition of their very existence.

Second, I rely on Charles Hale's conceptualization of the relationship between neoliberalism and cultural rights to explain how cultural differences circumscribed by indigenous rights help to construct neoliberalism. While cultural rights seem counterintuitive to neoliberal economic imperatives, Hale argues that the neoliberal project relies upon a purposive set of legal and institutional reforms that construct and manage neoliberal subjects and participation in the neoliberal system (Hale 2002: 496). Collective cultural rights, granted as compensatory measures to disadvantaged groups under neoliberalism, are part of these legal reforms in that they induce rights bearers to participate in the neoliberal system, while posing little challenge to the system itself (Hale 2005: 12–13). In fact, the relationship between cultural rights and neoliberal economic reforms is so symbiotic that Hale uses the term 'neoliberal multiculturalism' to refer to the complementary role that cultural rights play in integrating culturally divergent groups into the neoliberal system (Hale 2005: 12). According to this perspective, in the neoliberal era, cultural rights thus function as a means of absorbing, and making room for, certain forms of manageable cultural difference within the political economic rationality of neoliberalism, without disrupting the fundamental principles upon which neoliberalism is based (Melamed 2006: 15). Cultural rights become the avenue through which resistance and difference is channelled, which means that the forms resistance and difference take are mediated by legal norms that are fundamentally compatible with, and thus reproduce, the neoliberal system. Indigenous rights are crucial to this process of assimilation: by granting concessions to marginalized communities, indigenous rights serve the function of incorporating indigenous people in the neoliberal system and managing their behaviour by imposing definitions, criteria and duties that must be followed as conditions for claiming rights.

This chapter thus argues that by both extending universal human rights mechanisms to indigenous groups, and by creating specialized rights provisions that protect indigenous interests, indigenous rights discourses reproduce the conceptualization of indigenous people as 'equal, but different'. This has the effect of constructing and reproducing the neoliberal system by assimilating indigenous people into the discourses and frameworks of the neoliberal paradigm, while also managing and subsuming difference within frameworks compatible with neoliberalism. Most importantly, indigenous rights maintain difference by relegating indigenous principles and goals to the field of difference, perpetually separate from, yet fundamentally compatible with, the dominant ideologies of the neoliberal system. The following sections explore in greater detail the history, and definitions, of neoliberalism, human rights and indigenous rights.

Neoliberalism

Neoliberalism is a form of capitalism that emerged in the 1970s in response to the decline of a period of worldwide economic growth post-Second World War associated with high productivity and accumulation, and a strong welfare-state and economic regulation (McNally 2010: 25;

McCormack 2012: 421). Over-accumulated capital and declining profits in the Global North, alongside mounting debts in the Global South, brought to a head by oil crises and rising interest rates in the 1970s marked the end of the postwar economic boom. Proponents of neoliberalism, such as the members of the Mont Pèlerin Society, argued that the liberal principles of personal freedom, private property, market competition and the rule of law, were key to restoring growth and profitability (Friedman 2002: 2, 8; Brown 2003: 1–2; Harvey 2005: 20). Further, they argued that these principles could be achieved by removing all barriers to free market competition, and in particular, by achieving a minimal and non-interventionist state tasked with supporting economic participation.

In the Global North, neoliberal reforms were first implemented in Britain by Margaret Thatcher and in the United States by Ronald Reagan as a believed alternative to the Keynesian era that would restore economic growth (Harvey 2005: 22). In the Global South, neoliberal reforms were implemented by governments via structural adjustment programmes headed by the IMF and World Bank, which granted loans to countries struggling with crippling debt, upon the condition that recipient countries adopt certain neoliberal reforms. Reforms around the world were meant to remove barriers to, and maximize, market competition globally, including: economic deregulation, privatization, trade and financial liberalization, dismantling of the welfare state and a decline in democratic institutions, reorientation of public spending and fiscal discipline (Macdonald and Ruckert 2009: 3; Walsh 2014: 281). It is important to note, however, that neoliberal reforms were not applied evenly across different countries, with governments instead orienting reform agendas towards state-specific problems and solutions, and with countries in the Global South often having less autonomy to direct neoliberal reform than their counterparts in the Global North (Harvey 2005: 115).

Three features of neoliberalism are crucial to understanding its relationship with liberal rights. First, neoliberalism can be understood as a class-based political project (Harvey 2005; McNally 2010). While neoliberal reforms restored levels of capitalist accumulation and profitability in many cases, they did so at the expense of working classes, indigenous populations and economies in the Global South. Policy reforms that increase labour flexibility, including outsourcing employment facilities to cheaper production locales and increasing temporary, part-time and low-waged employment, as well as cutbacks to social programmes, have increased profitability for a select few while increasing poverty levels for the majority of the world's population. Meanwhile, deregulation and liberalization have opened up economies in the Global South to uneven trade and competition from the Global North, disproportionately affecting local industries and enterprises that cannot compete with the prices of imported goods. As a result of the unequal effects of these reforms, one of the defining features of neoliberalism is that it has increased social inequality and poverty around the world.

Second, neoliberalism is constructivist. Charles Hale and Wendy Brown argue that the main difference between liberalism and neoliberalism lies in the explicitly constructivist nature of the latter (Hale 2002: 495–6; Brown 2003: 4). Under classical liberalism, state interventions are intended to 'free' the individual and to produce forms of consciousness that lead to subjects governing themselves. The neoliberal model, on the other hand, is predicated on the need to recreate or recapture the individualist ethic through specific modifications to everyday life (Hale 2002: 495–6). Under neoliberalism, individuals must be constructed as market actors through economic, social and political reforms that recreate relations of individualized market participation. For citizens, privatization, a decline in social services and public spending, and a decline in democratic institutions has meant a reorientation of citizenship away from political participation towards individual market participation as consumers. In this way, the neoliberal project relies upon a purposive set of legal and institutional reforms that construct and manage rational individualized participation in the free market.

Third, neoliberalism is expansionary. As a result of deregulation and liberalization policies that open up economies around the world to capitalist enterprise, as well as the expansion of global finance capital, neoliberalism has led to the globalization of capitalist relations. Further, neoliberalism has led to the expansion of market rationalities to new areas of social and political life that previously operated outside of the realm of profit-based imperatives, including healthcare, basic services such as water and electricity, and education (Grewal and Purdy 2014: 3). Neoliberalism has thus led to an unprecedented expansion and intensification of capitalist rationalities in economic, social and political relations around the globe. These three features of neoliberalism as a class-based, constructivist and expansionary political project are key to understanding the relationship between neoliberalism and rights outlined below.

Human rights

The origin of contemporary human rights is a contested issue. Some scholars argue that the fundamental principles upon which modern human rights are based have their origins in the philosophical concept of natural rights, or apolitical humanitarian enterprise that has existed for thousands of years (Sargeant 2014: 142). Others are critical of this perspective, arguing that the meanings and assumptions upon which purportedly 'universal' rights are based are always culturally and historically determined (Brown 1995: 97). This chapter takes the latter position, arguing that the content and application of contemporary human rights discourse is the product of the particular late twentieth century context within which they have become prevalent. This section explores how the historical political conditions of neoliberalism have impacted upon, and are impacted by, contemporary human rights discourses.

While the UN Declaration of Human Rights (UNDHR) was signed in 1948, its effects in the 1950s and 1960s were slight (Sargent 2014: 128). This was because the international relations that developed after the Second World War were not based on integration, but rather on state sovereignty as states devastated by war sought to rebuild, and decolonizing countries in the Global South sought to maintain newly achieved sovereignty (Sargeant 2014: 128). As such, universal human rights discourses, and their enforcement within state borders, gained little ground during this period when Western states were reluctant to intervene in the affairs of other nations on the basis of 'human rights violations' (Moyn 2010: 7).

In the 1970s, the conditions that led to the ascendance of neoliberalism also enhanced the status, and framed the substance, of human rights (Eckel 2014: 226–7). States, social movements and NGOs began invoking human rights discourses, although with different ideologies, goals and outcomes (Eckel 2014: 235). The shift to a post-colonial world with the collapse of the last colonial empire in Portugal in 1975, impacted usages of human rights discourses in countries in the Global North and the Global South (Sargeant 2014: 138). In the Global South, developing countries began turning to human rights discourses in their quest for a just and equitable economic order as a way to promote rapid economic growth and counter the effects of colonialism (Rajagopal 2003: 2653). In the Global North, the United States began to promote human rights internationally as part of its foreign policy and could do so without the appearance of colonial intervention into the sovereign affairs of nation-states (Sargeant 2014: 138). Officially framed as a moral humanitarian enterprise, the role of international human rights promotion by the United States in advancing American interests is clear in a quote from Washington's ambassador to the United Nations Daniel Patrick Moynihan in 1975: 'Colonialism is over, human rights is our secret weapon' (Sargeant 2014: 139).

As states sought to define the parameters of international human rights law, increasing economic and political integration led to increasing social and cultural interdependency. While the role of social movements in shaping international law does not typically form part of official historiographies of international law, several scholars have pointed to the importance of social movements in normalizing human rights discourses based on emerging global conceptions of humanity in the 1970s (Rajagopal 2003; Eckel and Moyn 2014). Social movements and newly forming international NGOs, drew on discourses of global connectedness and community, with human rights offering 'a renewed sense of moral purpose' for those seeking social progress (Sargeant 2014: 132–3). NGOs began revealing human rights abuses around the world and constructing international networks to make those abuses known. It is important to note, however, that movements in the Global South were often not recognized by international institutions equally to those in the Global North, resulting in a racialized bias in international rights law regarding who has the authority to speak on human rights abuses (Rajagopal 2003: 1517–18).

Given the diverse articulations of human rights in the 1970s, it is clear that a unique feature of human rights is the malleability of their meaning and application, which is also a key factor to understanding how rights help to construct neoliberalism. In the international arena, where states are deemed formally equal and there is no sovereign arbiter to adjudicate the meanings of international law, China Miéville relies on a quote from Marx to explain how meanings are determined: 'between equal rights, force decides'. By this, Miéville means that while all states are deemed formally equal under international law, the relative power of each determines the outcome in the event of a conflict in interpretation and application of the law (2006: 292). This analysis is useful for exploring how relations of power between states have shaped, and continue to shape, official international discourses on human rights. Since the 1970s, the content of official human rights promoted by the United Nations has been largely shaped by the ideologies of liberal individualism that re-emerged in the Global North as part of the neoliberal framework. Power imbalances between the Global North and South, particularly in the context of newly achieved post-colonialism in the 1970s, meant that individualist conceptions of rights promoted by Western states eclipsed collectivist priorities of the Global South at UN General Assemblies. Official human rights discourses took on an anti-statist thrust, focusing instead on individualism, liberty, limited government and the free movement of ideas and people (Sargeant 2014: 137). In foreign policy, human rights discourses have been invoked by Western states to justify intervention into, and violence within, states in the Global South in the name of anti-authoritarianism, democracy promotion, humanitarian aid and development initiatives (Sargeant 2014: 144; Žižek 2005: 115). Thus, the relations of power that shaped the emergence and spread of neoliberalism also shaped the content of official human rights discourses.

Wendy Brown argues that rights can operate in different ways, depending on the vectors of power that exist in a given time and place. She argues that rights have the potential to emancipate from political disenfranchisement, to be a regulatory discourse, to be a means of obstructing more radical political demands, or to serve as empty promises (Brown 1995: 98). In the neoliberal era, where priority is given to civil and political rights that reflect the principles of neoliberal citizenship at the expense of economic and social rights, official international human rights discourses serve to reproduce neoliberal conceptions of state, individual and capital, and the relations of power between them. As rights remain contested territory, however, this does not preclude interpretations and applications of human rights in ways that advance the interests of marginalized groups. Human rights in the neoliberal era thus operate in all of the ways that Brown suggests to regulate, manage and obstruct, but also to potentially emancipate rights bearers. What is crucial, however, is that under the neoliberal system, even when rights discourses have advanced the interests of marginalized groups, they reproduce and thus fail to challenge the power relations, and systemic nature, of neoliberalism. The next section explores how indigenous rights as a sub-section of human rights emerged in the neoliberal era.

Indigenous rights

Beginnings

This chapter treats international indigenous rights as a subset of collectivist cultural rights that developed out of the same historical conditions that facilitated the broad shift towards human rights discourses in the 1970s. International dialogues on indigenous issues between states, social movements and NGOs became prevalent in the 1970s in the context of increasing globalization accelerated by neoliberal reforms, and decolonization. Elizabeth Povinelli argues that the increasing integration of states and cultures around the world during this time into a global economy via international regulations created a common ground upon which indigenous struggles could be uprooted from their specific localities and discussed as a broad issue in the global arena (Povinelli 2002: 24). Increasing global integration thus set the stage to begin discussing the 'global' implications of various social and cultural issues, including the history of the treatment of indigenous people on a global scale.

Decolonization shaped the international dialogue on indigenous issues as a series of ethical discourses, and the emancipation of indigenous people as a moral and ethical project (Povinelli 2002: 32). Decolonization has resulted in the global acknowledgement that indigenous people were exploited, discriminated against and assimilated during the colonial era, and has created an ethical push for states and the international community to make reparations for the exploitation of indigenous people during colonialism. This has resulted in states apologizing for past injustices (Trouillot 2000: 174) and replacing colonial laws with international indigenous rights legislation (Watson 2002: 259) in order to distance themselves temporally from past injustices and demonstrate their desire to construct a more just and equal present and future (Trouillot 2000: 183).

It was within this global context that the United Nations first began discussing indigenous issues in 1972 when the UN Sub-Commission on the

Prevention of Discrimination and Protection of Minorities (now called the Sub-Commission on the Promotion and Protection of Human Rights), began work on the *Study of the Problem of Discrimination against Indigenous Populations.* The Sub-Commission was formed without the knowledge and participation of indigenous people and after a period of initial activity, it appeared by the mid-1970s that the study would be discontinued due to inactivity and the Sub-Commission's failure to submit annual reports on its progress (Dunbar-Ortiz 2006).

At the same time, there was an increase in transnational indigenous organizing and international NGOs representing indigenous interests, which ultimately helped to revive the study and to propel indigenous rights-building at the UN. In 1977, the International Conference on Indigenous Peoples of the Americas was held in Geneva, organized by indigenous leaders and activists. Among other things, the outcome of the conference was to request that the Sub-Commission establish a Working Group on Indigenous Populations, which it did, integrating for the first time the direct participation of indigenous representatives (Dunbar-Ortiz 2006). Prior to this time, indigenous people were not permitted to participate in UN initiatives on indigenous issues. The Working Group helped to revive the Sub-Commission's study, and the *Martinez Cobo Study* subsequently released in five volumes between 1981 and 1984. It identified the need for the international community to act decisively to improve the conditions of indigenous people.

The United Nations Declaration on the Rights of Indigenous Peoples

After the release of the *Martinez Cobo Study,* the Working Group turned its attention to creating a comprehensive international indigenous rights instrument. After more than 20 years of drafting, the UNDRIP was adopted by the UN General Assembly on 13 September 2007. Rights granted to indigenous people under the UNDRIP fall into two categories. First, the UNDRIP extends the universal human rights granted in the Charter of the United Nations, the UNDHR and other international human rights law to indigenous people (Article 1). Broader human rights principles that are extended to indigenous people under the UNDRIP include: the right to self-determination (Articles 3, 4); the right to life, physical and mental integrity, liberty and security of person (Article 7); and the right to develop priorities and strategies for exercising their right to development (Article 23), all of which illuminate the principle of equality found in Article 2, that 'indigenous peoples and individuals are free and equal to all other peoples and individuals'.

Second, the UNDRIP grants cultural rights specific to indigenous people that are not found in broader human rights discourses, based on a specific conceptualization of indigenous culture. A paper prepared by the Working Group on Indigenous Populations lists the following factors that have been considered relevant to the understanding of the concept of 'indigenous' by international organizations and legal experts: priority in time, with respect to the occupation and use of a specific territory; the voluntary perpetuation of cultural distinctiveness; self-identification, as well as recognition by other groups, or by state authorities, as a distinct collectivity; and an experience of subjugation, marginalization, dispossession, exclusion or discrimination, whether or not these conditions persist (Secretariat of the Permanent Forum on Indigenous Issues (SPFII) 2008: 8). In a 2009 report, the UN recognized the unique cultural attributes of indigenous people to be the following: an understanding of society that is not confined to human beings, and thus a unique and symbiotic relationship between indigenous people and nature; a collective rather than individualistic society, meaning that responsibilities to the collective are equally important as rights for indigenous people; and the values of honour, respect, deference to elders, family and kinship roles, sharing, cooperation, humour, language, customs and traditions, compassion, humility, avoidance of conflict, spirituality and peace and harmony, all of which are 'norms' that guide indigenous societies towards harmonious relations (SPFII 2009b: 190). The UNDRIP includes principles that protect indigenous rights to culture, language, tradition, religion, custom, governance structures, land, development, education, healthcare, environmental protection, intellectual property and labour within the context of the above definition of indigenous culture (Articles 9–35). These rights emerged from the history and struggles of indigenous people and there is a performative element wherein indigenous people must demonstrate their indigeneity according to the criteria outlined by the Working Group in order to claim indigenous rights (Kulchyski 2013: 48). Indigenous rights, according to the UN, are thus captured both within the broad framework of universally applicable human rights, as well as within the narrow framework of rights applicable only to indigenous people, earning indigenous people the legal status of 'equal, but different'.

The promise of rights

Having explored the characteristics of, and relationships between neoliberalism, human rights and indigenous rights, this section explores how and why indigenous rights have failed to live up to the expectations of rights proponents in the neoliberal system. This section first outlines claims made by rights proponents about the role of human rights and indigenous rights in protecting the interests of the oppressed. Second, relying on evidence from UN policy papers, this section explores the ways in which the UNDRIP has fallen short of fulfilling this role. Third, this section offers an explanation for these failures by situating human rights and indigenous rights within the power relations of the neoliberal system.

Rights in theory

Human rights proponents claim that rights represent a form of moral universalism that can be used to advance the interests of the powerless and to protect and enhance individual autonomy from the state (Ignatieff 2001: 4, 7, 19). Arising in the aftermath of the Second World War wherein it was believed that citizens needed to be protected from the oppressive practices of states, human rights gave individuals international legal recognition for the first time and the means to protect themselves against unjust state law or oppressive customary practices (Ignatieff 2001: 5). By becoming signatories to rights instruments, states participate in the fortification of the claim that human rights protect interests and promote equality, while also legitimizing their own role as neutral arbiter and rights-protector both nationally and internationally (Marx 1844: 7).

Indigenous rights in particular, are said to achieve social justice by making reparations for past forms of exploitation against indigenous people and by protecting indigenous interests in the present and future. Types of reparations include national apologies on behalf of offending governments to exploited groups (Trouillot 2000: 171), rejecting national legal principles that were the impetus for colonialism (Watson 2002: 259), and creating new legislation that represents a break from the colonial past and promises a just future. When the international community creates, and states become signatories to, international indigenous rights instruments, states distance themselves temporally from past colonial governments (Trouillot 2000: 174). The symbolic act of invoking indigenous rights legislation is often considered to be enough to demonstrate the international community's and state's commitment to justice for indigenous people.

Rights in practice

An analysis of the UN's narrative on colonialism and the UNDRIP reveals the temporal break that the contemporary international community, made up of international organizations and states, seeks to create between itself and the actions of past colonial governments. The UNDRIP recognizes that the need to protect the unique rights of indigenous people arises in a context where indigenous people have suffered from historic injustices as a result of colonization that has prevented their development (Annex). In a UN informational publication on the United Nations Permanent Forum on Indigenous Issues (UNPFII), a point-by-point historical account of indigenous participation at the UN between 1923 and 2006 is interrupted after the 1994 creation of the UNPFII with the following comment,

> All told, it took 80 years, almost the entire history of the League of Nations and the United Nations together, for indigenous voices to arrive on the podium of an official United Nations meeting. Finally they are speaking in their own voices.
>
> (SPFII 2007: 9)

This break creates a 'before' where all events leading up to it form part of a struggle for indigenous voices to be heard, and an 'after' where indigenous perspectives are now represented and where all subsequent events are simply 'further steps on the road', that is, minor improvements subsequent to the major victory of representation at the UN. In this way, the non-representation of indigenous people at the UN becomes the particular practice that is objectionable and, having overcome that problem, the UN is now able to assert a temporal separation from the UN that only 30 years ago would not hear indigenous perspectives at forums on non-discrimination against indigenous people. Similarly, the act of creating the UNDRIP and the contents of this legal instrument demonstrate the UN's desire to distance itself from its colonial past. By recognizing past dispossession of land as well as impediments to the right to development during colonialism (Annex), and by specifically providing for these rights today (Articles 10, 23), the UNDRIP creates a temporal break between a colonial past where indigenous people had no rights and a present where an international declaration, an international forum and various other resources are dedicated to overcoming historical wrongs.

Yet despite this declared temporal break and the assertions by rights proponents about the emancipatory potential of rights, indigenous people continue to be marginalized under the neoliberal system. An analysis of contemporary indigenous rights legislation and UN reports reveals the disconnect between rights discourses and positive changes to the material conditions under which indigenous people live. The UN *State of the World's Indigenous Peoples* report acknowledges

> Indigenous peoples continue to face serious human rights abuses on a day-to-day basis. Issues of violence and brutality, continuing assimilation policies, marginalization, dispossession of land, forced removal or relocation, denial of land rights, impacts of large-scale development, abuses by military forces and armed conflict, and a host of other abuses, are a reality for indigenous communities around the world.
>
> (SPFII 2009: 203)

Further, the report cites the ascendency of global neoliberalism and entrenchment of corporate power in national and international affairs as a source of deepening inequalities within and between nations, stating that global neoliberalism undermines efforts toward sustainable development through environmental degradation and loss of traditional lands and territories (2009: 16). The UN report, *Indigenous Peoples: A Desk Review 2010*, found that in nine signatory countries, 'the disparate level of attention to indigenous peoples and indigenous issues continues to be a gap' in implementing the Millennium Development Goals and UN Development Assistance Frameworks for indigenous populations (SPFII 2010a: 2).

These violations have occurred despite numerous provisions in the UNDRIP that place a duty on signatory states to protect and enforce indigenous rights. For example, the UNDRIP provides that states should take appropriate measures, in consultation with indigenous people, to achieve the ends of the Declaration (Article 38); that states should ensure that indigenous people have the right to develop contacts and relations (Article 36); that indigenous people have the right to have states honour and respect treaties (Article 37) and that indigenous people have the right to financial and technical assistance from states (Article 39). This discrepancy between the obligations of the state outlined in the UNDRIP and state actions can be explained by the fact that signatory states have no positive obligation under the law to implement mechanisms that prevent or redress actions that violate the UNDRIP and destroy indigenous culture (McCormack 2011: 288). A UN policy paper on the duty of the state to protect indigenous peoples affected by transnational corporations found that the current system caters to codes of conduct that focus on the interests of corporations rather than the well-being of indigenous people (Hasteh 2012: 3 para 5). It is a common practice of corporations to exploit natural resources in indigenous territories for profit, and current laws regarding the state's extraterritorial jurisdiction to deal with corporations and states' duties regarding business remain unclear (Hasteh 2012: 11 para 34, 12 para 37–9). The paper concludes that, at the domestic level, states may not have the capacity to take action against corporate interests, while at the international level states compete for access to markets and investment, which may impede states' position as the international community's public authority to enforce rights (Hasteh 2012: 16 para 53). The result has been that corporations have taken advantage of their position of power (Hasteh 2012: 4 para 12), resulting in non-recognition of property rights, displacement, forced migration, exploitation of natural resources, destruction of ecosystems and loss of traditional territories (Hasteh 2012: 5 para 13).

Rights in the neoliberal era

The disconnect between rights discourses and positive changes to the conditions under which indigenous people live can be understood by exploring the power relations upon which international law is based. Antony Anghie demonstrates how the principles of international law were developed to justify Spanish colonial intervention and war (Anghie 1996: 332). On the one hand, Indians were deemed to possess human reason, and thus be capable of being held to a universal code based on Spanish rules. However, on the other hand, they were deemed to be different due to their specific social and cultural practices (Anghie 1996: 325, 327). By deeming Indians capable of adhering to universal norms, yet at the same time at variance with them, this scheme created a system of norms that was inevitably violated by the Indians, which justified endless Spanish incursion into their society (Anghie 1996: 326, 329–31). According to Anghie, international law is thus not based on neutral universal principles, but rather was created by particular states to justify incursion into, and domination over, other states and peoples.

The power relations inscribed in the legal form continue to shape international law in the present albeit in unique ways under the neoliberalism system. The disconnect between the rhetoric of rights and their practical effects can be understood by exploring the changes to democratic participation, citizenship and the state under the neoliberal system. Rights are premised upon liberal conceptions of citizenship and participation characterized by the separation of the public and private spheres (Marx 1844: 3, 12–13). The public sphere is that of political participation. In the public sphere, individuals put aside social differences and come together as rational political citizens to engage in legitimate debate, and are mediated by a universal state that represents the public interest. The private sphere is where social and cultural differences are accepted; where individuals are understood to have distinct identities and interests. On the one hand, the ideal of universalism has led to universal rights discourses that protect dignity and the equal worth of all people, while, on the other hand, the ideal of individualism has led to rights discourses that protect unique identities and individual choice (Taylor 1994: 37–8).

Conceptualizations of the individual in both the public and private spheres explain why indigenous rights have failed to improve the material conditions of indigenous people. Wendy Brown argues that in order to achieve a universal citizenry that is entirely equal in the public sphere individuals must abstract themselves from the particular conditions of their lives to become political rational citizens only. Universal rights are premised upon the idea that all people are equal, and thus it is these abstracted political rational subjects that are granted universal liberal rights that centre upon freedom, equality and representation in the public sphere (Brown 1995: 106). Since universal rights do not account for or protect difference in the private sphere, the material conditions under which people live in civil society remain outside the scope of universal human rights and thus remain unequal (Brown 1995: 106). The unequal conditions in civil society become naturalized as 'social or cultural difference' and the concerns of individualized persons, which has the effect of encoding the social powers that repress the disenfranchised (Bannerji 2000: 126). Universal human rights thus fail to address the underlying structural and ideological conditions that perpetuate discrimination against indigenous people. Rather, by applying only to indigenous people as abstracted political subjects, human rights serve to perpetuate and naturalize the inequalities enhanced under neoliberalism in the private spheres of indigenous life as 'cultural difference'.

A closer look at the neoliberal state illuminates some of the practical difficulties of placing a duty on the state to protect rights. Marx argues that since the capitalist state gains legitimacy as a neutral arbiter representing all social classes, the state depends upon the very inequalities that it purports to challenge as a signatory to rights instruments (Marx 1844: 7). According to this argument, the state has a vested interest in maintaining unequal social relations as the legitimating condition of its very existence, despite subscribing to the principles of human equality found in human rights discourses. What is new under neoliberalism is that reforms restricting state autonomy, the need to maintain a competitive advantage in a system of global capital, and the fact that states' duties towards corporate interests remain unclear under international law, have combined to limit the state's ability to uphold indigenous rights for non-economic reasons. Subject to neoliberalism's all-encompassing market rationality, discussed throughout this volume, state departments are reorganized in such a way that expands those dealing with economic internationalization and subordinates those dealing with welfare and labour (Albo 2005: 77). While the state continues to gain legitimacy by relying on discourses of democracy and by mediating social interests, the state behaves increasingly like a market actor as its prerogative is to ensure a good investment climate for capital, rather than to protect the interests of its citizens (Brown 2003: 5; Harvey 2005: 7). States are thus often unwilling or unable to enforce indigenous rights that place restrictions on foreign direct investment, or indigenous rights are protected to the extent that they are compatible with the interests of capital. For example, in some cases states observe indigenous intellectual property rights not for the purpose of protecting indigenous rights to culture and knowledge, but to strategically protect national culture and knowledge economies to maintain a competitive advantage in the global market (Coombe 2005: 41–2). Thus, while states have become signatories to, and adopted the language of, indigenous rights legislation, this act has been largely symbolic. When state autonomy is limited under neoliberalism by reforms that scale back the state, or is limited by the imperatives of capital accumulation, it becomes increasingly difficult for states to enforce indigenous rights.

'Equal, but different'

Having explored how the features of neoliberalism have shaped, and limit, the scope of indigenous rights, this section builds on the previous analysis to explore the ways in which indigenous rights both assimilate indigenous people into the neoliberal system and structure indigenous difference in ways that are compatible with neoliberal power relations. It will rely on Partha Chatterjee's concept of the 'rule of colonial difference' to argue that indigenous rights law constructs indigenous people as 'equal, but different'.

Universal rights, sameness and the homo economicus

This section explores how neoliberal conceptualizations of the market, state and subject inform the character of universal human rights, and analyses the implications of these assumptions for extending universal rights to indigenous people. Several scholars have pointed to the economic rationality that pervades universal human rights discourses in the neoliberal era (Brown 1995; Rajagopal 2003; Miéville 2006). Far from being 'universal' as the law suggests, Rajagopal argues that the 'human' posited in human rights is the *homo economicus*, an abstracted liberal Western conceptualization of human beings as fully rational market actors who realize their interests within the confines of the state and the conditions of the market (Rajagopal 2003: 2419). The *homo economicus* exercises its freedoms by rationally pursuing its interests in the marketplace as a consumer and producer (Giroux 2005: 2; Faulk 2013: 7–8; Grewal and Purdy 2014: 6). Rajagopal argues that the idea of *homo economicus* is based on scarcity of resources, which explains the prioritization of some rights over others and some rights-bearers over others (Rajagopal 2003: 2421). Resource scarcity explains the priority given to civil and political rights over economic and social rights, a priority that is not inscribed within the law itself, but is a context-specific interpretation of rights in the neoliberal system. Civil and political rights are prioritized by states because they maintain the conditions necessary for market participation of the *homo economicus*, including the rule of law and order, and the creation and extension of infrastructure (Rajagopal 2003: 2428).

Rajagopal's argument explains why universal rights are an integral part of the UNDRIP. If the fundamental understanding of 'human' in human rights is based on the concept of *homo economicus*, and if adopting this conceptualization of the individual is essential to being recognized as a rights holder, then universal rights in the UNDRIP play a necessary role in ensuring the recognition of indigenous people under the law. The UNDRIP can be seen to integrate indigenous people into the neoliberal system by declaring them to be 'free and equal to other peoples and individuals' and thereby entitled to universal rights protections (Annex). This declaration of equality between indigenous and non-indigenous people provides the justification for incorporating indigenous people into a set of rights discourses that reproduce and apply neoliberal conceptions of the individual, community, property, culture and resistance to indigenous people. For example, the UNDRIP encourages indigenous people to think of themselves as self-interested individuals through rights that, for example, grant life, liberty and security of the person (Article 7); and as property holders through provisions that grant the right not to have their property arbitrarily interfered with (Annex). These conceptualizations of personhood and property ownership are not only at odds with indigenous conceptions of community and communal property, but also fail to account for the collective and systemic nature of poverty and dispossession from land and natural resources that indigenous communities experience. Indigenous people are constructed as rational market actors under the UNDRIP, wherein indigenous forms of subsistence, medicine, customs and art are commodified, becoming 'cultural heritage', 'traditional knowledge' and 'traditional cultural expressions' to which indigenous people are granted intellectual property rights (Article 31). Drawn into the global market, indigenous people are granted the right to profit financially from these forms of culture and are encouraged to use them in their own self-interest when traditional forms of subsistence become unsustainable due to displacement from their lands or dwindling natural resources.

While the UNDRIP constructs indigenous people as the *homo economicus* and integrates them into the neoliberal system, it also limits resistance. By subscribing to the discourses of international indigenous rights, indigenous people are discouraged from engaging in collective forms of action like protesting, and instead are encouraged to follow standardized legal conflict resolution processes (Rajagopal 2003: 605, Article 40). In particular, Rajagopal argues that because the *homo economicus* is assumed as the subject of rights law, violence caused by the market or state is treated as out of the bounds of human rights law (Rajagopal 2003: 2419). The assumption in rights discourses that rights holders are rational and equal individuals that fulfil their interests through market participation is necessarily blind to the structural inequalities experienced by indigenous people that make their participation unequal, and to the fact that indigenous conceptions of self may not fit within the *homo economicus* model. This helps to explain why states have been unable to take action against corporations exploiting natural resources on indigenous territory and why the indigenous right to prior and informed consent regarding such exploitation is being violated (see Hasteh 2012).

'Sameness' and 'universal' rights granted by the UNDRIP thus encourage indigenous people to define themselves according to the *homo economicus* model through conceptions of individual, property, state and the market that are compatible with neoliberal ideology. The impact on indigenous people is to integrate them as the *homo economicus* into the neoliberal system, while ignoring and thus perpetuating the systemic inequalities that make their economic participation unequal.

Indigenous difference

In counterpoint to recognizing 'sameness' the UNDRIP also accounts for indigenous difference through cultural rights granted specifically to indigenous people. While the official discourse on cultural rights is that they reflect pre-existing cultural difference (Taylor 1994: 72), many scholars have argued that cultural rights actually construct difference and do so in ways that are oppressive to rights holders (Brown 1995; Hale 2002, 2005; Melamed 2006). This section focuses on two features of indigenous cultural difference that are constructed in the UNDRIP. First, it argues that the forms of difference that are recognized under the UNDRIP and the types of cultural rights claims that are successful are those that are compatible with the neoliberal framework. Second, it argues that the performative element of indigenous rights, wherein rights holders must adhere to a particular definition of 'authentic indigeneity' in order to be protected by the UNDRIP, constructs and maintains indigenous difference. By defining the terms upon which difference must be demonstrated and is recognized, this section argues that indigenous cultural rights under the UNDRIP have the potential to oppress indigenous people.

Acceptable difference

First, cultural difference is structured in a way that makes it compatible with the neoliberal normative framework. Charles Hale's concept of neoliberal multiculturalism illuminates the complementary role that cultural rights play in integrating divergent groups into the neoliberal system. By acting as compensatory measures, cultural rights induce rights holders to participate in the neoliberal system, while posing little challenge to the system itself (Hale 2005: 12–13). However, this process of granting some concessions that are compatible with neoliberalism means that customary practices that are incompatible with the neoliberal framework must necessarily be excluded (Povinelli 2002: 3). For example, exploring the relationship between the Nunga Aboriginal people and the state in Australia, Irene Watson argues that Aboriginal conceptions of law, land and sovereignty are fundamentally incompatible with those of the state and have thus been excluded by the Australian state. For the Nunga, law is part of the universal order; it is not created, but rather is from the land, and knowledge of the law comes through living it (Watson 2002: 254). European conceptions of state sovereignty, ownership of land and retaliatory action for violating laws are based upon using power and force of arms to determine boundaries and invoke closures that are foreign to the Nunga understanding of the law that involves the balanced co-existence of people and nature, and which is boundary-less (Watson 2002: 255). A second example can be found in the work of Megan Ybarra who lived with the Q'eqchi' Mayan community in Guatemala as they struggled for recognition from the state and control over sacred caves threatened by an ecotourism operator (Ybarra 2013: 585). Ybarra points to a number of conceptual differences between the Q'eqchi' and liberal laws that impeded the Q'eqchi's claims. These include the difficulty of measuring land to claim property ownership given the Q'eqchi' understanding that spirits are the only legitimate land owners. Further, the Q'eqchi' do not conform to liberal distinctions between politics and religion, resulting in the frequent claim of state analysts that the Q'eqchi' relied upon religion to make political claims (Ybarra 2013: 585, 594).

Limiting official cultural rights discourses to those that are compatible with the neoliberal framework is problematic for indigenous people because it excludes rights claims based on non-recognized cultural difference. Rajagopal argues that groups that attempt to invoke, for example, their right to forms of education or to healthcare that are outside of the modern Western conceptions upon which these rights are based have been largely unsuccessful in their claims (Rajagopal 2003: 2719–20). Rather, in order to make successful rights claims against the state, indigenous people have been forced to reconceptualize their claims to be compatible with liberal rights discourses. For example, Ybarra reflects on how NGOs and Peace Corps volunteers helped the Q'eqchi' to frame their cultural rights claims to be compatible with liberal rights discourses. This was done by making reference to their ancestors' practices on the land to demonstrate a claim to property ownership, and by arguing that their spiritual practices have always been political and territorial (Ybarra 2013: 595). This practice is problematic for two reasons. First, it means that Western volunteers are often more capable of framing successful indigenous rights claims than indigenous people themselves (Ybarra 2013: 590), which creates a racialized hierarchy in terms of who can legitimately speak of rights violations in the international arena (Rajagopal 2003: 1517–18). Second, reframing the meanings of, and relationships between, indigenous groups, cultural objects, and practices, to be recognized by the law and state, can permanently alter indigenous conceptions of self, community and culture over time. The effect of cultural rights under neoliberalism is thus that they frame cultural difference in ways that are compatible with the neoliberal normative framework. This serves both to construct and reproduce the neoliberal system, and to limit resistance to it.

Performing 'authentic indigeneity'

A second way in which indigenous rights discourses construct cultural difference is that they rely on a particular definition of indigenous identity to which indigenous people must subscribe in order to be recognized as indigenous and make indigenous rights claims. Most problematic for indigenous people wishing to demonstrate 'authentic indigeneity' has been demonstrating a connection with pre-colonial societies given the destruction of indigenous culture during colonization and afterwards through assimilative state-led programmes. Writing on the Cucapa indigenous people in Mexico, Muehlmann explains that Mexican state policies in the 1980s and 1990s discouraged indigenous identification and aimed for assimilation, largely wiping out indigenous language, clothing and customs (Muehlmann 2009: 469). To have been granted fishing rights in the mid-2000s, however, the Cucapa had to show the use of traditional fishing methods. Further, the Cucapa could not use more contemporary and efficient fishing methods, had to stop fishing with non-indigenous Mexicans, and were advised by their lawyers to wear traditional skirts and speak their language to be taken seriously as 'Indians' at their hearing (Muehlmann 2009: 468). In this way, indigenous people have had to perform, or conform to, stereotypical conceptualizations of indigeneity in order to be recognized by the state (Muehlmann 2009: 473). When indigenous people fail to articulate this stereotypical indigeneity, indigenous rights serve as a policy framework that denies indigenous identity and rights.

In addition to the difficulties of demonstrating indigeneity under the law, some scholars have argued that the authentic indigeneity posited in indigenous rights discourses is an 'oppressive authenticity' because it maintains current relations of power and the subordination of indigenous people (McCormack 2011: 286). First, the UN definition of indigeneity necessarily incorporates the colonial encounter, thereby inscribing the subjugation of indigenous people as a defining feature of their collective identity. While states can distance themselves from their colonial past through apology and by becoming signatories to the UNDRIP, it is impossible for indigenous people to overcome the collective identity of pain and subjugation inscribed on them by the UN's reconciliatory approach to indigenous issues. Second, negative stereotypes about the primitive ways of life of indigenous people are used to justify poor working and living conditions by labelling them as 'traditional ways of life' (Muehlmann 2009: 476). For instance, the Cucapa were not permitted by the Mexican government to simultaneously use more efficient fishing techniques and claim rights on the basis of indigeneity because these were not the traditional methods used in pre-colonial societies. These stereotypes not only prevent the development of indigenous people by maintaining cultural difference based on subordination; they are also at odds with the UN's human rights-based approach to development, wherein development is achieved through the progressive realization of rights. In this way, indigenous rights presuppose and reproduce the very inequalities that they purport to overcome (Hale 2005: 13). Demonstrating an authentic indigenous identity can mean that indigenous people cannot develop and improve their living conditions or methods for engaging in subsistence activities like fishing or hunting over time because they must show an ongoing connection with pre-colonial societies.

The problematic for indigenous people wishing to rely upon indigenous rights law is thus that they must moderate their behaviour to adhere to the neoliberal normative framework, while at the same time performing indigeneity and inhabiting 'the impossible object of an authentic self' as it is articulated under the law, in order to be protected by indigenous rights legislation (Povinelli 2002: 13, 6). This involves demonstrating both sameness and difference, but ultimately, demonstrating both within the acceptable ideological boundaries of the neoliberal system. The implication of extending both universal human rights and particularized cultural rights that are compatible with neoliberalism under the UNDRIP, and thereby declaring indigenous people as 'same, but different', is that indigenous rights discourses reproduce, and fail to challenge, the power relations upon which neoliberalism is based. While indigenous rights may serve to advance the interests of indigenous people in particular contexts, in their current official form, they fail to challenge the systemic nature of indigenous oppression in the neoliberal system, and thus serve to construct and reproduce the neoliberal system.

Why rights?

Given that the field of rights is fraught with difficulties, why then do indigenous people use rights discourses to represent their interests? The most straightforward answer is that the language of rights reflects, at least to some extent, the goals and interests of indigenous people. Drafted in consultation with indigenous people and NGOs, and offering indigenous people the collective right to self-determination, recognition of their unique cultural identity and the right to maintain their cultures, languages, lands and customs, indigenous rights represent a moral-ethical discourse that is considered a legitimate and recognized form of resistance by the international community, including states, corporations and international organizations. Further, indigenous rights claims, have in some instances, been used effectively to advance the interests of indigenous people (Young and Perelman 2010). For example, in the case of the Q'eqchi' indigenous people of Guatemala, the Guatemalan state now recognizes that the caves in question are a sacred place in Q'eqchi' cosmology and the Q'eqchi' have been recognized as the legal owners of the caves (Ybarra 2013: 598).

This explains why indigenous people may use indigenous rights from time to time, but not why human rights discourse has become the 'go-to' language of resistance to oppression and emancipation, leading to what Louis Henkin has deemed 'the age of rights' (Henkin in Rajagopal 2003: 2063). Rajagopal explains the prevalence of rights as a form of resistance, arguing that modern human rights discourse has become the sole approved discourse of resistance, prompting movements to rely on it in order to be officially recognized by states and the international community (Rajagopal 2003: 1984). The principles of international law, reflecting the liberal distinction between public and private, distinguish between routine institutional politics associated with rights claims and extra-institutional forms of protest seen as 'private', 'simply social' or 'illegitimate' (Rajagopal 2003: 1999). As discussed further in Chapter 8, in this way, international and national laws increasingly treat popular protests outside the realm of rights claims as 'outside' the state and therefore illegitimate and unruly. The monopoly that rights claims now have in the field of resistance suits the neoliberal project very well in that resistance is limited to mainstream institutional frameworks that adjudicate based on approved legal discourses and that recognize certain groups and individuals while having the power to not recognize others. This limits resistance against dominant relations of power to the legal frameworks created by, and complicit with, dominant forms of power. Thus, while indigenous rights claims have resulted in victories in some cases for indigenous people, the fact that such claims are adjudicated within a legal framework that maintains current relations of power, and the malleability of international rights law, mean that official rights discourses will be ineffective as a means of improving the conditions of indigenous people in the long term.

Moving forward

Despite the limitations of rights discourses in the neoliberal system, there has been substantial debate about whether rights are redeemable. In fact, many scholars argue that the potential of rights discourses to become an emancipatory tool lies in exactly the same characteristic that has made rights a useful tool for perpetuating neoliberalism: the malleability of their interpretation and application (Brown 1995: Rajagopal 2003; Miéville 2006; Young and Perelman 2010). While rights discourses tend to reflect and perpetuate the principles constituting the neoliberal paradigm, they are sufficiently open-ended to incorporate and reflect alternative principles advocated by social movements and communities such as indigenous people.

In order to develop alternative rights discourses the spectrum of international legal actors and concepts must be broadened. Rajagopal argues that a social movement perspective on international law-making must be adopted so that social movement resistance can be incorporated into mainstream discussions and actions that shape international law rather than working from outside those debates (Rajagopal 2003: 3548). Once the international legal field is open to the perspective of social movements, Rajagopal argues that this will infuse new perspectives into international law, thereby redefining rights discourses to reflect local understandings and interests.

Additionally, local identities and beliefs must be preserved, and indigenous communities must play an active role in advocating alternative discourses outside of the neoliberal framework if they wish to minimize the contradictions of official rights discourses outlined above. For example, in the Australian case, Watson argues that it is up to the Nunga Aboriginal people to explain why native land title does not fit within their conceptualization of the law and how native land title sanctifies non-Aboriginal land titles through continued forms of colonialism (Watson 2002: 265–6). Further, Brown argues that discourses that define cultural groups based on past exploitation only serve to inscribe that subjugation and thus argues that identity politics discourses should look forward, focusing on future emancipatory goals (Brown 1995: 75). The value and potential of rights discourses today can thus be said to lie in 'the egalitarian imaginary that they could engender outside of the particular power relations in which they are articulated' (Brown 2005: 134), meaning that their value lies in their potential to be rearticulated based on egalitarian principles distinct from the neoliberal framework.

References

Albo, Gregory. 'Contesting the "New Capitalism".' In *Varieties of Capitalism, Varieties of Approaches*, edited by David Coates. Basingstoke: Palgrave Macmillan, 2005.

Anghie, Antony. 'Francisco De Vitoria and the Colonial Origins of International Law.' *Social and Legal Studies* 5, no. 3 (1996): 321–36.

Bannerji, Himani. 'Charles Taylor's Politics of Recognition: A Critique.' In *The Dark Side of the Nation: Essays on Multiculturalism, Nationalism and Gender*, 125–50. Toronto, Ontario: Canadian Scholars Press, 2000.

Bowring, Bill. *The Degradation of the International Legal Order? The Rehabilitation of Law and the Possibility of Politics.* New York: Routledge-Cavendish, 2008, Kindle edition.

Brown, Wendy. *States of Injury: Power and Freedom in Late Modernity.* New Jersey: Princeton University Press, 1995.

Brown, Wendy. 'Neo-Liberalism and the End of Liberal Democracy.' *Theory and Event* 7, no. 1 (2003).

Brown, Wendy. 'American Nightmare: Neoliberalism, Neoconservatism, and De-Democratization.' *Political Theory* 34, no. 6 (2006): 690–714.

Chatterjee, Partha. *The Nation and Its Fragments: Colonial and Postcolonial Histories.* Princeton, NJ: Princeton University Press, 1993.

Coombe, Rosemary. 'Legal Claims to Culture in and against the Market: Neoliberalism and the Global Proliferation of Meaningful Difference.' *Law, Culture and the Humanities* 1 (2005): 35–52.
Duménil, Gerard and Dominique Levy. *Capital Resurgent.* Cambridge, MA: Harvard University Press, 2004.
Dunbar-Ortiz, Roxanne. 'What Brought Evo Morales to Power? The Role of the International Indigenous Movement and What the Left Is Missing.' *Monthly Review* (2006). http://mrzine.monthlyreview.org/2006/dunbarortiz060206.html.
Eckel, Jan. 'The Rebirth of Politics from the Spirit of Morality: Explaining the Human Rights Revolution of the 1970s.' In *The Breakthrough: Human Rights in the 1970s,* edited by Jan Eckel and Samuel Moyn. Philadelphia: University of Pennsylvania Press, 2014, Kindle edition.
Eckel, Jan and Samuel Moyn (eds) *The Breakthrough: Human Rights in the 1970s,* Philadelphia: University of Pennsylvania Press, 2014, Kindle edition.
Faulk, Karen Ann. *In the Wake of Neoliberalism: Citizenship and Human Rights in Argentina.* Stanford, CA: Stanford University Press, 2013.
Friedman, Milton. *Capitalism and Freedom.* Chicago: University of Chicago Press, 2002.
Giroux, Henry A. 'The Terror of Neoliberalism: Rethinking the Significance of Cultural Politics.' *College Literature* 32, no. 1 (2005): 1–19.
Grewal, David Singh and Jedediah Purdy. 'Introduction: Law and Neoliberalism.' In Law and Contemporary Problems: Yale Law School, Public Law Research Paper No. 313, 2014.
Hale, Charles R. 'Does Multiculturalism Menace? Governance, Cultural Rights and the Politics of Identity in Guatemala.' *Journal of Latin America Studies* 34, no. 3 (2002): 485–524.
Hale, Charles R. 'Neoliberal Multiculturalism: The Remaking of Cultural Rights and Racial Dominance in Central America.' *Political and Legal Anthropology Review* 28, no. 1 (2005): 10–28.
Harvey, David. *A Brief History of Neoliberalism.* Oxford: Oxford University Press, 2005.
Hasteh, Paimaneh. 'Analysis of the Duty of the State to Protect Indigenous Peoples Affected by Transnational Corporation and Other Business Enterprises.' In Permanent Forum on Indigenous Issues, Eleventh session, 7–18 May 2012. New York: United Nations Economic and Social Council, 23 February 2012.
Ignatieff, Michael. 'Human Rights as Political Rights.' In *Human Rights: As Politics and Idolatry,* edited by Amy Gutmann, 2–52. Princeton, NJ: Princeton University Press, 2001.
Kolsky, Elizabeth. 'Codification and the Rule of Colonial Difference: Criminal Procedure in British India.' *Law and History Review* 23, no. 3 (2005): 631–83.
Kulchyski, Peter. *Aboriginal Rights Are Not Human Rights: In Defence of Indigenous Struggles.* Semaphore Series. Winnipeg, Manitoba: ARP Books, 2013.
Macdonald, Laura and Arne Ruckert. 'Post-Neoliberalism in the Americas: An Introduction.' In *Post-Neoliberalism in the Americas,* edited by Laura Macdonald and Arne Ruckert, 1–18. Basingstoke, UK: Palgrave Macmillan, 2009.
Marx, Karl. 'On the Jewish Question'. Marxists Online Archive (1844). https://www.marxists.org/archive/marx/works/1844/jewish-question/index.htm.

McCormack, Fiona. 'Levels of Indigeneity: The Maori and Neoliberalism.' *Journal of the Royal Anthropological Society* 17 (2011): 281–300.

McCormack, Fiona. 'Indigeneity as Process: Maori Claims and Neoliberalism.' *Social Identities* 18, no. 4 (2012): 417–34.

McNally, David. *Global Slump: The Economics and Politics of Crisis and Resistance.* Oakland, CA: PM Press, 2010.

Melamed, Jodi. 'The Spirit of Neoliberalism: From Racial Liberalism to Neoliberal Multiculturalism.' *Social Text* 24, no. 4 (2006): 1–24.

Miéville, China. *Between Equal Rights: A Marxist Theory of International Law.* Chicago: Haymarket Books, 2006.

Moyn, Samuel. *The Last Utopia: Human Rights in History.* London, England: The Belknap Press of Harvard University Press, 2010.

Muehlmann, Shaylih. 'How Do Real Indians Fish? Neoliberal Multiculturalism and Contested Indigeneities in the Colorado Delta.' *American Anthropologist* 111, no. 4 (2009): 468–79.

Povinelli, Elizabeth A. *The Cunning of Recognition: Indigenous Alterities and the Making of Australian Multiculturalism.* London, England: Duke University Press, 2002.

Rajagopal, Balakrishnan. *International Law from Below: Development, Social Movements, and Third World Resistance.* Cambridge, UK: Cambridge University Press, 2003, Kindle edition.

Sargeant, Daniel. 'Oasis in the Desert? America's Human Rights Rediscovery.' In *The Breakthrough: Human Rights in the 1970s,* edited by Jan Eckel and Samuel Moyn. Philadelphia: University of Pennsylvania Press, 2014, Kindle edition.

Secretariat of the Permanent Forum on Indigenous Issues (SPFII). 'Engaging Indigenous Peoples in Governance Processes: International Legal and Policy Frameworks for Engagement.' In International Conference on Engaging Communities, UN Workshop on Engaging the Marginalized: Partnerships between Indigenous Peoples, governments and civil society. Brisbane, Australia Division for Social Policy and Development/UN Department of Economic and Social Affairs, 15 August 2005.

SPFII. 'Indigenous Peoples, Indigenous Voices.' Edited by United Nations Permanent Forum on Indigenous Issues: Department of Economic and Social Affairs/ Division for Social Policy and Development, 2007.

SPFII. 'Resource Kit on Indigenous Peoples' Issues.' Edited by United Nations Department of Economic and Social Affairs. New York, 2008.

SPFII. 'Guidelines on Indigenous Peoples' Issues.' Edited by United Nations Development Group. New York and Geneva: United Nations, 2009a.

SPFII. 'State of the World's Indigenous Peoples.' Edited by Permanent Forum on Indigenous Issues: Department of Economic and Social Affairs/Division for Social Policy and Development, 2009b.

SPFII. 'Mdg Reports, CCAs, UNDAFs and Indigenous Peoples: A Desk Review 2010.' Edited by United Nations Permanent Forum on Indigenous Issues, 2010a.

SPFII. 'Training Module on Indigenous Peoples' Issues: Facilitator's Handbook.' Edited by United Nations Department of Economic and Social Affairs. New York, 2010b.

SPFII. 'Review of World Bank Operational Policies.' In Permanent Forum on Indigenous Issues, Twelfth session, 20–31 May 2013. New York: United Nations Economic and Social Council, 20 February 2013.

Taylor, Charles. 'The Politics of Recognition.' In *Multiculturalism: Examining the Politics of Recognition*, edited by Amy Gutmann. Princeton, NJ: Princeton University Press, 1994.

Trouillot, Michel-Rolph. 'Abortive Rituals: Historical Apologies in a Global Era.' *Interventions* 2, no. 2 (2000): 171–86.

United Nations. 'Declaration on the Rights of Indigenous Peoples.' In GA Res 61/295, edited by United Nations Permanent Forum on Indigenous Issues, 13 September 2007.

United Nations. 'Permanent Forum on Indigenous Issues.' United Nations, http://undesadspd.org/IndigenousPeoples/SecondDecade.aspx.

Walsh, James P. 'The Marketization of Multiculturalism: Neoliberal Restructuring and Cultural Difference in Australia.' *Ethic and Racial Studies* 37, no. 2 (2014): 280–301.

Watson, Irene. 'Buried Alive.' *Law and Critique* 13, no. 3 (2002): 253–69.

Ybarra, Megan. '"You Cannot Measure a Tzuultaq'a": Cultural Politics at the Limits of Liberal Legality.' *Antipode* 45, no. 3 (2013): 584–601.

Young, Katharine and Jeremy Perelman. 'Rights as Footprints: A New Metaphor for Contemporary Human Rights Practice.' *Northwestern Journal of International Human Rights* 9, no. 1 (Fall 2010): 27–58.

Žižek, Slavoj. 'Against Human Rights.' *New Left Review* 34 (July–August 2005).

Chapter 8

Dissent in a juridified political sphere

Honor Brabazon

Introduction

Law is generally considered to be a vehicle through which neoliberal change is brought about: what is neoliberal about neoliberal law is the *content* of the laws enacted during the neoliberal period. This chapter shifts attention to the role played by the *form* of law. It argues that not just the individual laws we pass but the way we understand law itself has been essential to the neoliberal project.

Neoliberalism is the vague shorthand that has come to denote the dominant ideology, political economy, and policy approach in much of the world from the 1980s onward. Beneath this broad usage lie two largely complementary and overlapping projects that are at times contradictory: on the one hand, an internally disputed theoretical project pursued by a small group of thinkers in Europe and the United States from the 1930s to the 1950s; on the other hand, a pragmatic and adaptive political project by the upper fractions of ruling classes to restore their income and class power following their decline during the post-war Keynesian compromise (Harvey, 2006; Mirowski, 2009; Duménil and Lévy, 2011). Despite sustained use of the term neoliberalism, much remains unknown about both projects and about their interrelationships, including the role of law therein.

David Harvey (2006) has observed that neoliberalism has 'become hegemonic as a mode of discourse ... to the point where it has become incorporated into the common-sense way we interpret, live in and understand the world' (145). This chapter explores the role of the legal form in shaping this common sense. Specifically, it investigates the role of the legal form in the neoliberal reconstitution of the *political sphere*, understood in rough terms as the publicly accessible state and non-state forums in which people assemble, discuss, and struggle over social needs and the distribution of social goods. The chapter demonstrates that the legal form has not only provided institutional support for a particular paradigm of the political sphere but has also shaped and modelled this paradigm and the subjectivities required by it. The chapter further suggests that the legal form has done so in a manner that at times bridges and helps cohere contradictions between neoliberalism as a theoretical project and neoliberalism as a political project.

The chapter proceeds by discussing the nature of the legal form before outlining four ways in which the political sphere has been reframed in the neoliberal period and how the logic of the legal form has enabled and modelled these shifts, as well as the implications of this juridification for public debate and dissent – including resistance to neoliberalism.

The (neo?)liberal form of law

Marxist and other critical legal scholarship has long critiqued Marx's initial base-superstructure dichotomy, which relegated law to a superstructural add-on that is ultimately determined by the economic base (Hay, 1975; Thompson, 1975; Balbus, 1977). However, it is unfortunate that the alternative far more nuanced and rigorous idea that law has played an active and constitutive role in the development of capitalism has been slow to gain traction in other fields, as this constitutive conception of law reveals much about neoliberalism.

In this view, the transformation in the form of law during the transition from feudalism to capitalism highlights how the specificities of the liberal capitalist legal form are co-constitutive of capitalist relations. Under feudalism, law was chaotic and intermingled with religious and political authority. It was not a set of abstract normative judgments but was embedded in concrete social relationships between specific people. Local law was an extension of political (feudal) power. It was used primarily by lords in their own manorial courts to ensure that feudal services were rendered to them, and it was enforced by those lords through direct coercion. Importantly, law and its enforcement were dependent upon the parties' *unequal* positions in the feudal hierarchy, and there was no pretence to law's neutrality (Tigar, 1977; Fine, 1984).

The same social processes that led to the gradual degeneration of the feudal order and the development of capitalist imperatives of production and exchange (see Wood, 2009) also led to gradual changes in the form of law. In order to conceive of a commodity in the capitalist sense, or of the process of buying and selling commodities, a particular type of property right was necessary – one that no longer referred to specific people but was general and interchangeable. At the same time, law started to become abstracted from specific relationships in a manner that allowed it to mediate relations between all potential buyers and sellers of property, as *equals* before the law. Legal subjects were still substantively unequal, but the reorientation and abstraction of law concealed their substantive inequality. Similarly, law was no more neutral and less political than it had been in feudal times, but its legitimacy now depended upon its ability to mystify its political nature. The enforcement of law eventually became indirect, not applied by property owners themselves but mediated by law. Power and authority were seen less to be inflicted by one person on another and more as the mutual subordination of both parties to the independent reason of a neutral and rational authority: the law (Tigar, 1977; Pashukanis, 1978[1929]; Fine, 1984).

Importantly, in this account, the capitalist form of law did not develop ideationally, separate from capitalist relations of production and exchange. Nor did it develop subsequently to, and as a mere extension of, or institutional framework for, capitalist relations of production and exchange. Instead, this account emphasises that capitalist economic and juridical relations developed in tandem as two equally essential expressions of capitalist relations (Fine, 1984: 207).

Nonetheless, it is clear that each also contains elements of its own logic. For instance, the specificities of the liberal-capitalist legal form enable law to depoliticise the social relations that are mediated through it: the abstraction of laws from the specific social contexts in which they arise obscures their indeterminacy, their historical contingency, and the power relations underpinning them.[1] This enables laws to appear to be universal and fixed, independent of historical conjuncture and political will, and legal decisions to appear to be technical matters of the interpretation of universal and fixed legal texts in a very formalist sense. In Karl Klare's (1982) words,

> legal discourse ... tends to ... induce the belief that our evolving social arrangements are just and rational, or at least inevitable, and therefore legitimate. The *modus operandi* of law as legitimating ideology is to make the historically contingent appear necessary.
>
> (1358)

This chapter argues that the neoliberal period illustrates that law not only constitutes particular social relations through its established ideological, repressive, and facilitative roles (Klare, 1979: 130–132; also Pashukanis, 1978[1929]); it can also perform an important modelling function, as the subjectivities and social relations at the core of neoliberal thought mirror those produced through the legal form. For instance, '[s]ubjects of

1 Importantly, the term depoliticisation in this chapter is not meant to imply that certain subjects become any more or less political, in the sense that they are thereby insulated from critical analysis of power or patterns of distribution, but merely to signal a diminution of the facility with which their political nature is recognisable and these questions contestable on the public stage.

a legal relation relate to each other as autonomous entities, mutually competitive, self-involved, for whom (in Hobbes's image) the law provides the *only* form in which they take into consideration the interests of others' (Fine, 1984: 142). Legal relations frustrate the pursuit of collective social goals, 'express[ing] and reproduc[ing] social relations based on the conflict of private interests, mutual indifference and all-round competitiveness rather than relations based on mutual co-operation, love, comradeship, and collective pursuit of a common goal' (156). Moreover, content is subordinated to form in the liberal legal configuration (Klare, 1982; Fine, 1984). Formal equality is emphasised over substantive equality, and a just legal process is prioritised over just results: law structures the form of social relations whilst appearing indifferent to (and mystifying) the content of these relations. As the remainder of this chapter demonstrates, these characteristics of the legal form, and of its particular impact on the social relations it mediates, are consistent with – and constitutive of – the social relations envisioned in the neoliberal *theoretical* project.

To appreciate how the legal form similarly shapes and supports the neoliberal *political* project, it is crucial to understand the impact of the legal form, and of the rule of law specifically, in an unequal society. The creation of formal equal rights between non-equals does not eliminate their substantive inequality; rather, it ensures that their substantive inequality is perpetuated and extended (Pashukanis, 1978[1929]: 125; Fine, 1984: 118). This arises from a combination of the abstracted formal equality of legal subjects, which hinders efforts to reduce their substantive inequality through legal decision-making, and law's indeterminacy, through which it is posited that legal arguments can always be met with equally valid counter-arguments such that legal decisions often consider extra-legal factors and are influenced by the substantive inequality between legal subjects (Anghie, 2004; Miéville, 2004; Koskenniemi, 2005a, 2005b): in Marx's words, 'between equal rights, force decides' (in Miéville, 2005: 8).

Thus, the legal form, and the rule of law specifically, shape social relations in a manner that tends to perpetuate inequalities between parties, whilst the image that law embodies the universal rights of all and applies equally to all allows relations between unequal parties to appear to be merely the equal subjection of all to reason. Herein lies the political popularity of the call for government by laws and not by people in Hayek's neoliberal theory.

The following examination of neoliberal shifts in the political sphere illustrates how the increased mediation and modelling of political social relations by law in the neoliberal period both reflects and guides neoliberalism and also lends the appearance of coherence to contradictions that arise between neoliberalism's theoretical and political projects. This analysis contends that the legal form, and the expansion of the rule of law in particular, are fundamentally constitutive of neoliberalism. It further contends that neoliberalism is a juridical process of the expansion of the rule of law and other components of the capitalist legal form as much as it is an economic process.

The neoliberal juridification of the political

The broad shifts in the political sphere in the neoliberal period discussed in this chapter can be divided loosely into four overlapping reframings: (1) a reframing of the role of the state; (2) a reframing of dissent; (3) a reframing of the relationship of the state to dissent and (4) a reframing of social concerns. Through each of these reframings, the legal form has both modelled and enabled political subjectivities and political relations that are conducive and constitutive of both the neoliberal theoretical and political projects.

These shifts or 'reframings' are deeply enmeshed, but they are examined sequentially for clarity. They are considered in the context of the transition from the Keynesian welfare state model to the neoliberal model, which are sketched in broad strokes as ideal types; there are of course many variations in the way these models have been developed and applied around the world (see Ban, 2016) to the extent that the term 'model' is itself contestable. The focus on this transition should not be interpreted as an uncritical endorsement of the Keynesian model. Nor do the changes identified represent a complete break with the Keynesian model or what preceded it as many of these processes and logics were present in the political sphere prior to neoliberal restructuring. Continuities and divergences are noted throughout the analysis that follows.

Reframing the role of the state

The first shift involves a reframing of the role of the state. The neoliberal state is usually discussed in terms of the laws it has passed mandating various components of neoliberal restructuring – such as the privatisation of social services – and in terms of the institutional infrastructure it has provided to facilitate the functioning of competitive markets. However, the neoliberal state also fosters social relations and subjectivities necessary for this market society to function (Wacquant, 2009), which are conducive to competitive markets and other neoliberal priorities, and which are in many ways shaped by the legal form.

The Keynesian post-war compromise was built upon a consensual and continual agreement between capital and labour (Oliver, 1989: 37). The state certainly upheld a market economy, but it was also seen as a mediator between the interests of capital and labour (in an effort to control both), and even at times as a boundary protecting society from the uninhibited functioning of the market (Jessop *et al.*, 1988; Rose, 1997; Isin,

1998). The state had a mandate not only to *protect* the collective public interest but also to actively pursue social change in the public interest, which was understood to include various (albeit limited) goals of social justice, equality, and redistribution.

In contrast, neoliberal theorists conceived of the state as an agent for facilitating, rather than tempering, the uninhibited functioning of the market. They tended to envision a strong state capable of constructing competitive market relations and consolidating political power, in contrast to the classical liberal principle of laissez-faire (Jessop *et al.*, 1988; Rose, 1997; Isin, 1998; Mirowski, 2009).

Moreover, neoliberal theorists opposed the idea of a common public interest. Hayek considered the notion to presuppose both a uniform and complete ethical code and the ability of individuals to imagine and evaluate the needs of all other individuals, neither of which exists. In his view, when a state claims to act in the common interest, the needs of individuals are being dictated by others, which is coercive and undemocratic. Instead, individuals should be free to act in their own limited self-interest, which is best realised through the uninhibited functioning of the market – a 'common interest' only to the extent that it represents the coincidence of the individual interests of all (Hayek, 1944: 62–63).

In practice, the regulatory and spending activity of the state has increased where it aims to promote market-based competition and individual choice, whilst state activity has decreased in the pursuit of progressive social goals (Langille, 1987; Jessop *et al.*, 1988; Isin, 1998). In this sense, the privatisation of public sector programmes and services reflects not only the neoliberal preference for market-based competition but also the invalidity of the notion of a common good, which had legitimised public social spending in the welfare state period.

More than the state's social functions, however, social interaction itself is meant to take place mainly in the private sphere in the neoliberal model. In the post-war period, the state mediated between the market and society, 'politicising' both in an expansive public sphere. In the neoliberal model, 'society' outside the market is a fiction, and social interaction is recast as private transactions between isolated individuals. In their interactions with the state, citizens are considered to be clients obtaining services from the government (Isin, 1998: 174), not participants engaging in ongoing and meaningful dialogue. In this context, privatisation also reinforces a minimal political sphere by shifting decision-making power and authority from public actors to private actors in the family or the market, who are removed from electoral politics, public contestation, and public accountability (Clarke *et al.*, 1996: 17, 20).

Law plays an essential role in conceiving these different spheres and in enabling activity to shift from one to the other. The division between private and public law embodies and models this division. In the post-war period, public law was emphasised and took on a legal realist/instrumentalist role as a tool of the state in its intervention into the economy and its pursuit of progressive social change (Trubek and Santos, 2006: 2). In the neoliberal model, however, law is considered to be independent of progressive social goals, and private law is emphasised over public law. Private law traditionally more closely embodies the image of the liberal legal form, and these attributes are played up in the neoliberal period, portraying private law as a neutral framework free from distributional consequences, rather than a framework that reflects (unequal) private interests (Trubek, 2006: 87). This conception of law as objective, fixed, and pre-existing independent of history and power dynamics depoliticises the social interactions that law mediates, allowing them to seem like isolated incidences between individuals. When social relations are mediated by private law, they are recast as apolitical relations between atomised individuals. Moreover, the increased mediation of social relations by law reconceives individuals themselves as atomised and formally equal, isolated from broader patterns and political contexts – in the image of legal subjects.

In the neoliberal period, then, the state is reframed from a centre of public deliberation in an expansive political sphere into a service administrator that no longer possesses a mandate for broad social change in the public interest. As the state's social functions, and social interaction in general, are increasingly carried out in the private sphere, social relations are increasingly mediated by and modelled on the liberal legal form. The public/private distinction embodied in law and the formalist image of private law have both modelled and enabled this privatisation, recasting social interaction as distinct relations between atomised individuals independent of historical or political context and contestation, and without a common social interest. Far beyond just reducing opportunities for public contestation and accountability, this reframing also depoliticises social interaction itself, concealing its political nature. This depoliticisation hinders any kind of progressive distributive claims or other appeals to common goals and reduces opportunities for the development of collective consciousness and collective political contestation. This process fosters subjectivities more conducive to unbridled market competition than subjectivities based on social solidarities and notions of a common good. But, crucially, this reframing does not only serve the market economy in a manner consistent with the visions of society profferred in neoliberal thought; it also constrains the spaces and tools for debate and dissent to neoliberal policy, thereby furthering both the neoliberal theoretical *and* political projects.

Reframing dissent

The second shift is a reframing of the legitimate means of dissent. The more expansive sphere of public participation in the post-war period valued and, to varying degrees, institutionally supported citizens' regular involvement in shaping their society through ongoing debate. Participation in the political sphere was certainly limited and was not equally accessible to all, but it was the premise of this democratic model and was supported institutionally. Moreover, interests and rights were advocated collectively, and the advocacy of community groups was seen to contribute more voices, pressure on government, expertise, and points of view to the political sphere (Thorburn, 2001: 389). Community groups were considered to hold the collective public interest at heart, and their participation in public discourse and decision-making was encouraged, at least officially.

In contrast, under neoliberalism, not only is the sphere of public debate more limited, as distribution and social interaction increasingly are relegated to the private realm, but what remains of the political sphere is said to be reconfigured as a market (Mirowski, 2009: 436; Brown, 2015) – an analogy that will be further qualified later in the chapter. For now, the notion of a political market is useful to the extent that, like the capitalist economic market, the political market is constituted by the legal form, and particularly by the image of legal subjects as formally equal; by law's consideration of cases individually, not as social phenomena; and by law's orientation toward evaluating individual actions rather than historical and distributive relationships and processes.

Political subjects are likewise constructed as abstracted, formal equals, and their claims are considered individually, abstracted from their historical and political context. Group identities and collective advocacy are delegitimised as undemocratic attempts to obstruct the political market. Subaltern views are marginalised as 'special interests' speaking only for themselves and not in the public interest, and they are seen not in historical context as traditionally oppressed groups but as stakeholders with views as valuable as any other stakeholders' (Hayek, 1944: 63; Dardot and Laval, 2009: 226). Indeed, as Mirowski (2013) puts it, '[e]veryone is treated as expressing untethered context-free hankering, as if they were born yesterday into solitary confinement...' (61).

Moreover, in contrast to the liberal idea of a free exchange of ideas in the political sphere, the neoliberal political market is rooted in the idea of free *competition* between ideas. This parallels the replacement of free exchange by competition as the central principle of the market in the neoliberal period (Hayek, 1944; Dardot and Laval, 2009: 28), which in fact arguably more closely mirrors the legal process, which itself centres around adversarial competition with definitive winners and losers.

For instance, this competitive individualism characterises the limited neoliberal vision of democracy, which centres primarily on the individual advocacy of ostensibly politically equal citizens through their vote. If neo-liberal citizens are typically considered to be clients who obtain services from the government, rather than participants engaged in ongoing and meaningful dialogue, during elections they are seen as consumers choosing between competing (political) products based on self-interest rather than collective considerations of justice and equality.

Furthermore, street protest is discouraged in the neoliberal model as both a disruption of the economic market (when protests threaten to interrupt consumerism, labour, or supply chain transit) and a disruption of the political market, in the context of which protest is seen as the attempt of a well-organised minority to impose its will on the majority and obstruct one-person-one-vote competition.

In practice, protest is seen increasingly 'as an aberration and in need of repression' (Rajagopal, 2003: 10). In addition to overt repression, protest is increasingly juridified and hyper-regulated. Previously, law identified only the outermost boundaries of protest; now law regulates and mediates seemingly every aspect of protest: where the protest can transpire (e.g. protest zones, perimeter fences); the essential quality of the protest as legal or illegal; the time of the protest (e.g. curfews, permits); the clothing worn at protests (e.g. police targeting those wearing black, prohibiting masks); the degree of politicisation of the protest (e.g. more freedoms for hockey riots than political protests); and the language and frames used to express protest (e.g. recent anti-terrorism legislation restricting the content of speech) (D'Arcy, 2013; Forcese and Roach, 2015; Ligue, 2015).

By mediating protest through law in this way, the liberal image of law as rational and neutral is mobilised to give protest an added moral component. In keeping with the tendency of neoliberal theory to value process over purpose,[2] the legitimacy of protest is now judged less on the moral infraction it seeks to rectify and more on the morality of the means it assumes to do so. This procedural morality is measured by lawfulness, and a protest is handily branded legitimate or illegitimate by the media, police, and government officials based on its ability to navigate this complex web of legal regulation. Protest traditions rooted in disobeying the law (e.g. civil disobedience and direct action) are not considered legitimate. This has hindered protest that does not remain within the confines of the law and which challenges or questions the law and the broader systems of which it is a part.

2 For example, seeing democracy as a means rather than an end (Mirowski, 2009: 446) and conflating socialism and fascism on the grounds that they both subordinate individuals to collective goals (Hayek, 1944).

Dissent that cannot be expressed through voting can acceptably assume the form of court challenges and human rights claims, which again mobilise the legal form. Literature on the 'judicialisation of politics' details how political and social claims increasingly are articulated through the law and resolved through the courts rather than in the sphere of political contestation and debate (Tate and Vallinder, 1995; Faundez, 2005; Sieder *et al.*, 2005; Smulovitz, 2005; Huneeus *et al.*, 2010).

However, the specificities of the liberal legal form create certain restrictions on social change that is pursued through law, as the example of human rights illustrates. Human rights is now considered in many instances to provide 'the sole approved discourse of resistance' (Rajagopal, 2003: 9; also Riles, 2000; Goodale, 2005; Merry, 2005). Yet critical legal scholars have pointed out that the dominant human rights discourse is limited to a liberal conception of human rights which centres on individual – not collective – advocacy and on winning protections for the individual through adversarial rather than solidaristic social relations (Glendon, 1991; Piore, 1995; Rajagopal, 2003; Smulovitz, 2005).

This approach portrays human rights as detached from economic relations and interests and as if they are bestowed benevolently by the state, which eclipses the role of political struggle in their actualisation (Panitch and Swartz, 1993; Goodale, 2005; Clarke interview, 2012). This reflects and reinforces the neoliberal view that law should mediate social relations outside of broader goals of equality or community building. It also reflects a conception of politics in which political activity and political goals are limited to what is possible within the parameters of the existing institutional sphere, which constitutes what Balakrishnan Rajagopal (2003) has identified as a 'sharply delimited arena of the "political"' (241).

Moreover, the focus on the courtroom directs the strategic outlook of movements away from political mobilisation and into the juridical arena, where they forfeit their strategic advantage (Panitch and Swartz, 1993; Palmer, 2005; Kuhling and Levant, 2006). This shift mediates activism not only through a juridical setting but also through a juridical rationality which restricts activists to tactics and discussions sanctioned and controlled by the state. It also diverts the energy and resources of marginalised groups from social action to lengthy litigation strategies, often demobilising their movements (Arthurs, 2003: 20–21).

The reconception of the political sphere as a market thus involves recasting democratic subjects and democratic engagement to mirror legal subjects and the legal process. Collective advocacy is replaced by the advocacy of competing self-interested individuals, much like in the courtroom, which generates a false equality between citizens, dissenting views, and political opportunities. Dissent is expressed through voting or litigation, both of which atomise, abstract, and equalise dissenters in the manner of legal subjects and abstract contentious claims from their historical context (such as a group seeking special collective consideration as redress for historical injustices); from the power differentials between parties; and from the root causes of the rights violation being claimed. Dissenters are seen as formally equal to other (often more powerful) stakeholders, and their dissent is considered an aberration instead of the encouraged collective participation of a conscientious minority, as in the welfare state model. Political debate and dissent are structured and understood using the logic of the legal form, which fosters subjectivities conducive to the neoliberal vision of competitive markets and also reduces the means and the horizon of dissent to neoliberal restructuring. This is particularly useful in reducing the power of the left and of the labour movement by discrediting the collective identity and solidarity of workers and by channelling their activism into less effective forums, and it thereby furthers both the neoliberal theoretical and political projects.

Reframing the relationship of the state to dissent

The third shift involves a reframing of the relationship of the state to dissent. In the post-war welfare state model, dissent was, if not welcomed, considered in theory to be part of the fabric of a rich democracy. Progressive social change was enacted even by conservative governments that were ideologically opposed to the changes themselves because the legitimacy of the government depended to some extent upon its ability not only to maintain political stability but also to engage, if not address, the views of a dissenting minority – particularly minorities who were historically disadvantaged. Indeed, it was considered in the public interest to do so.

This relationship between the state and dissent – limited as it might have been in practice – has been reframed in the neoliberal period. As discussed above, the state no longer has a mandate to pursue a broad conception of the public interest, and political advocacy is meant to be individual, not collective. In practice, collective advocacy is often portrayed by government officials as akin to bullying and as a circumvention of the democratic process rather than a quintessential feature of it (D'Arcy, 2013). This language of 'bullying' and 'intimidation' can be seen in state responses to strikes, protests, and social movement demands, and it is often accentuated in responses to the collective action of unions (e.g. Dominiczak and Riley-Smith, 2015), as seen in the epigraph of this book.

Likewise, historically disadvantaged groups are considered to be stakeholders with interests as valuable as any other stakeholders' even when attempting to redress histories of oppression experienced at the hands of the state itself. Neoliberal governments often respond to such requests for historical redress by stating or implying that disadvantaged individuals could – in entrepreneurial fashion – somehow overcome their systemic disadvantages themselves. By extension, however, the failure of all to do so is portrayed as a sign of their lack of true desire and need, not of the system being rigged against them (Harvey, 2006: 152; Wacquant, 2009: 307).

In this sense, the legitimacy of the neoliberal state is more likely to depend upon the state *not* engaging with a dissenting minority. This is particularly true when doing so would directly obstruct market competition, but it is equally so in any instance where engagement (or 'surrender' to their demands) could be seen to disrupt or skew the process of 'context-free' self-interested individual advocacy that characterises neoliberal democracy. In this model, the state's job is no longer to redress historical inequalities but instead to be a neutral arbiter between competitors in the so-called political market. Crucially, this understanding of the state's relationship to collective action again mirrors and is constructed through the atomising and abstracting framework of the liberal legal form.

This shift has involved governments restricting or eliminating initiatives designed to encourage public debate and to foster participation of minorities in that debate, which had been built into many states in the Keynesian era (Aucoin and Turnbull, 2008). Governments are also seen more regularly (and perhaps more brazenly) to ignore collective dissent that they might previously have been politically obligated to engage with, including sustained social movements. In the UK, examples range from the Miners' Strike in 1984–5 to mass protest of the invasion of Iraq in 2003. One explicit and succinct example arose in 1996 when the Premier of the Canadian province of Ontario faced the largest political mobilisation the province had seen in 30 years in response to his 'quick-and-dirty' neoliberal restructuring of the province's public sector. When asked by media about the growing opposition, he replied simply, 'It doesn't matter really' and stayed his course (Spears, 1997: A1).

In addition to the form of law modelling the state's relationship to collective action, neoliberal governments are also mobilising law's indeterminacy to avoid their pre-existing legal commitments to progressive change without generating further dissent and opposition (Brabazon, 2013). For instance, neoliberal governments can be seen increasingly to treat laws more as a suggestion than as a mandate, selectively ignoring progressive legislation. In this approach, a law remains on the books, allowing the government to retain a symbolic commitment to the social concern that the law purports to address, but the government engages in various measures by which to ensure that it does not actually have to implement the provisions it opposes.

In its most overt form, this tactic includes an explicit suspension of existing law, often suspending civil liberties by declaring something to be an exceptional circumstance. Examples include immigration detention policies, counter-terrorism laws, and crowd control tactics at protests that suspend established legal principles and civil liberties (Daniels *et al.*, 2001;

AI *et al.*, 2011; NUPGE/CCLA, 2011). In other instances, neoliberal governments have avoided enforcing progressive laws more quietly. This has included passing symbolic laws that are never intended to be enforced (see Charles Hale's (2002, 2004) analysis of 'neoliberal multiculturalism'), or simply informally not enforcing existing laws. Examples of the latter include governments delaying and obstructing access to information requests; not fulfilling indigenous treaties; and starving the budget of government agencies to which they are opposed (Roberts, 2001; Rubin and Kozolanka, 2014).

Through this tactic of under-enforcement, the government takes advantage of law and the logic of the legal form in a way that insulates its policy decisions from public discussion. The liberal legal idea that laws are neutral, technical, and fixed apolitical facts eclipses law's indeterminacy and the fact that political will is required not just for laws to be enacted but also for laws to be enforced. This image allows a government's failure to enforce a law to appear to be a circumstantial bureaucratic error, rather than a concerted political choice, which leaves little recourse. This move can be seen as an appropriation of the legal realist use of legal indeterminacy for progressive social ends in the post-war period.

This 'fast and loose' use of law might appear contradictory given the emphasis in neoliberal theory on the law, and indeed the orientation of neoliberalism around an expansion of the rule of law. Borrowing from Tzouvala's analysis of a similar inconsistency in her chapter, this disjuncture arises from contradictions between neoliberalism's theoretical ideals and its political project to reassert class interests: in this case, whilst the neoliberal theoretical project subordinates the political sphere to law and the market, the neoliberal political project subordinates even this theoretical imperative to politics, trumping both law and market. Yet, the grandeur, indeterminacy, and mystifying capacity of the legal form helps to conceal such contradictions and political interests. The legal form provides a model of social interaction that weakens the relationship between the state and the progressive demands of the political left. This model has helped to detach the state's legitimacy from its responsibility to engage dissent and has enabled neoliberal governments to avoid the political contestation that might otherwise be engendered by such disjunctures, and by the contradictions between neoliberalism's theoretical and political imperatives that they signal.

Reframing social concerns

The fourth and final shift is a reframing of the social concerns held by dissenters, again by structuring them increasingly around the logic of law. Kerry Rittich (2006) has argued that law has been used to reframe the social concerns that the neoliberal agenda purports to be incorporating as part of the cosmetic reconstitution it has undergone since the 1990s in response to growing opposition to neoliberal policy. Rittich and others have observed this reframing in changes to the international development agenda, arguing that law is now considered to be 'definitional' (205) and 'constitutive' (Trubek, 2006: 89) of development, which increasingly has become limited to 'a legal/institutional reform project' (Rittich, 2006: 205).

The increased emphasis on law in development reduces the extent to which development is conceived as a political matter in the sense of being publicly debatable and concerned with questions of distribution and power relations. Duncan Kennedy (2006) argues that the focus on legal institutional reform increasingly removes conflicts about the role and type of law espoused and promoted in development initiatives from the political sphere to the sphere of legal expertise (70), which makes it difficult to think of development in political terms (David Kennedy, 2006: 167). Again, the view of law as neutral, technical, and apolitical limits the opportunities for meaningful and effective debate and dissent.

The experience of Market-Led Agrarian Reform (MLAR) in Bolivia provides an illustration of how this reframing can depoliticise social concerns. MLAR was introduced across the global south in the 1990s at the behest of neoliberal governments and institutions such as the World Bank in response to growing pressure for land redistribution. MLAR revamps traditional agrarian reform by redistributing land not via state action but through market transactions (Akram-Lodhi, 2007; Lahiff *et al.*, 2007; Veltmeyer, 2007). That is, MLAR is not 'unduly confiscatory' (as critics of state-led agrarian reform argued) but instead is motivated by 'consensus' (International Fund for Agricultural Development in Bernstein, 2010: 99) in the form of voluntary market transactions between 'willing buyers' and 'willing sellers' (Akram-Lodhi, 2007: 1438). The primary aim of MLAR is not a just or equal distribution of land but an economically efficient one, and the role of the state is not to distribute land more equally in the public interest but to facilitate the efficiency of the land market.

The 1996 National Institute for Agrarian Reform law (known as the INRA law) was Bolivia's version of MLAR. Instead of wide-scale state-led land redistribution, the INRA law mandated an assessment and registration of all *existing* land titles in the subsequent 10 years. The emphasis of the INRA law on legal title over redistribution reframed the antagonistic relationship between large landowners and landless peasants into a technical matter of allocating title to stakeholders who held equal rights before the law. The actors involved were not referred to as 'landowners' and 'landless' but rather as 'buyers' and 'sellers' of land, which abstracted them from their historical contexts and from the economic and political power differentials between them – differentials which, unsurprisingly, persisted in influencing the outcomes of titling disputes (Akram-Lodhi, 2007). The presentation of landowners and landless as equal stakeholders independent from historical and political context hindered traditional attempts by landless peasants to articulate their claim for a broader redistribution of land in order to redress past wrongs. Moreover, the creation of a bureaucratic institution to adjudicate competing land claims and assign titles created the legalistic image of an autonomous 'third party' to whose independent reasoning and impersonal authority all citizens were equally subject, which further concealed the political nature of land disputes.

Instead of an equal distribution of land amongst Bolivians, this legalistic approach sought an equitable and impartial regulation of existing land ownership (Salvatierra, 2004; Vadillo interview, 2010; de Dios Fernandez interview, 2011): essentially to uphold the rule of law in land tenure. The legalistic logic characterising this version of agrarian reform hindered both land redistribution and public participation in its debate and critique. In fact, the INRA law exemplified Bolivia's ability in the mid- to late-1990s to display a 'sophistry of social solidarity with the poor' whilst enacting policy consistent with the neoliberal schema and maintaining an unusual level of political stability – an approach for which Bolivia was applauded by the World Bank and other international organisations (Brabazon and Webber, 2014). Versions of MLAR have been implemented across the South with little or no success at redistributing land (Lahiff *et al.*, 2007; Veltmeyer, 2007; Bernstein, 2010).

A juridical project

These four reframings suggest that the legal form plays a key role in enabling, constructing, and cohering the neoliberal political sphere not only through its coercive, facilitative, and ideological functions but also by modelling particular subjectivities and social relations. The legal form does not do so alone; these reframings are not reducible to merely juridical phenomena, but the specificities of the legal form enable law to play a unique and crucial role in this process.

As law increasingly mediates social relations, whether through private law or by framing the political sphere as a market, the legal form recasts social relations as depoliticised and dehistoricised interactions between atomised and self-interested rights-bearing individuals with no common social goal. This obscures power differentials between them and enables them to be presented as equal stakeholders, much like the formal equality of legal subjects under the rule of law. In the absence of collective political goals that could temper this formal equality, this rule of law-based conception of social interaction prevents the articulation and advancement of redistributive claims, instead perpetuating and accentuating substantive inequality and furthering neoliberalism's political project. The legal form also reframes the social concerns it mediates to appear as technical or administrative problems, which obscures their political nature and makes public participation in their resolution difficult to conceive. Moreover, the image of laws as fixed and apolitical eclipses their indeterminacy and the political will required to enforce them, and allows the deliberate under-enforcement of progressive laws to appear as mere bureaucratic failures.

These reframings also restrict the spaces and conceptual language through which dissent can be articulated. The increased mediation of social relations by private law in the private sphere, along with the shift of the state's mandate away from social change in the public interest toward administration of the market, transfer authority from public to private actors, which curtails possibilities for accountability and contestation through the state and depoliticises social relations themselves. This is further achieved by channelling dissent toward elections and legalistic institutional arenas such as human rights, in which social relations are reconfigured as abstracted relations between equal individuals and collective advocacy is delegitimised. This limits the potential for social change by ignoring power dynamics amongst individuals, by limiting the possible goals of social change to the institutionalisation of social concerns, and by limiting the extent to which claims to redress historical and systemic problems can be articulated and understood.

Not only do the reframings outlined above further the conceptions of a reduced political sphere advocated in neoliberal theory, but this reduced political sphere also advances neoliberalism as a political class project by constraining the possibilities for dissent to neoliberal restructuring. Moreover, the legal form, and particularly law's indeterminacy, has been useful in legitimising the departures of the neoliberal political project from neoliberal theorisations of the political sphere, as well as contradictions within neoliberal theory.

Returning to the promised caveat to my use of the term 'market' to describe the neoliberal political sphere, the analysis in this chapter offers an important reformulation of the position that neoliberalism involves a marketisation or economisation of all spheres of social life (Caliskan and Callon, 2009; Mirowski, 2009; Brown, 2015). First, key indicators of the 'economisation' that is identified in such analysis as 'the distinctive signature of neoliberal rationality' (Brown, 2015: 32) are in the first instance features of the legal form. For instance, Wendy Brown (2015) rightly observes that the

> disavowal of stratification and power differentials in the field of analysis and action is a crucial feature of neoliberal rationality, precisely

> the feature that discursively erases distinctions between capital and labor, owners and producers, landlord and tenant, rich and poor. (161)

However, she attributes this to an economisation of the political sphere rather than a juridification. As discussed earlier in the chapter, the abstracting and depoliticising capacity of formal equality that Brown describes is not specific to neoliberalism or to the economy but is a long-standing feature of the legal form.

Second, when the role of law in this marketisation or economisation is acknowledged, law tends to be seen as a vehicle for this process. Drawing from Foucault, Brown for instance argues that 'law and legal reasoning not only give form to the economic, but economize new spheres and practices. In this way, law becomes a medium for disseminating neoliberal rationality beyond the economy, including to constitutive elements of democratic life' (151). As demonstrated throughout this chapter, law and legal reasoning do give form to the economic, and they do *shape* other spheres and practices. However, to say that they marketise or 'economise' other spheres and practices does not fully acknowledge the extent to which law possesses its own form and logic which shape the market and economy.

Finally, this account of law in what is understood to be a new process of marketisation risks implying that law has recently entered the political sphere for the first time, whereas the account of juridification laid out in this chapter illustrates that the role of law in the political sphere has merely shifted, expanded, and intensified. For instance, the abstracting and depoliticising capacity of formal equality that Brown describes has long shaped the political sphere, as seen for example in the very concept of equal citizens as political subjects and the premise of the liberal democratic model on the principle of 'one citizen, one vote'.

More specifically, the processes of juridification discussed above do not mark a definitive break from the welfare state period as the legal form shaped the political sphere then as well. Legal indeterminacy and faith in the rule of law created an image of law as a force that could be harnessed just as equally for socially progressive aims as for maintaining status quo inequality. However, law's mystification of the constitutive role of its form (not just its content) in maintaining unequal capitalist relations also enabled and provided a model for the pursuit of progressive redistribution in a manner that remained limited to (albeit important) surface level changes without fundamentally altering the capitalist system. Its pursuit of substantive equality was always limited to what could be achieved without departing from the fundamental premise of formal equality and abstracted rights, including private property rights.

However, the welfare state system also pushed the limits of the legal form. Substantive equality itself (and social solidarities) was not a feature of the legal form but a political consideration made possible through the indeterminacy of the legal form. In this sense, the conception and role of law in the neoliberal period can be understood as truer to the liberal capitalist legal form, moulding and modelling all spheres of social life – including the political sphere – on the substantive core of the legal form. Further than this, it could be argued that the legal form is in fact more conducive to free market competition – a distinguishing focus of neoliberal economic theory – oriented as law is toward isolated adversarial cases with definitive winners and losers. It would seem that neoliberal economic and social relations are modelled more closely on the legal form than they were in the welfare state period, as now law is not only enabling the categories and framework for market and social interaction but is also modelling market and social interaction itself.

In this sense, whilst it is useful to conceive of the neoliberal political sphere as a market in many respects, it is important to note that the qualities of the market that characterise the process of *marketisation* or *economisation* commonly described in this narrative are often in fact juridical. Other spheres thus are not so much marketised or economised by law as they are *juridified*, just as the economy is juridified as it is shaped by the legal form, and this is not new but rather is occurring with an emphasis on different, more central, elements of the legal form and with a particular intensity in the neoliberal period.

This analysis of the increased juridification of the political sphere and the resulting restrictions on political debate and dissent raises questions about how neoliberal social relations might be resisted. If the avenues for dissent that remain are limited by their own juridification, is struggle on the legal terrain the only option? If so, does this not imply an acceptance of the premises of competition between atomised equals that only perpetuates neoliberal subjectivities and social relations? There are various approaches to answering this question (Miéville, 2005; Marks, 2007; Bowring, 2011; Knox, 2011; Brabazon, 2011). Given the centrality of the logic of the legal form to neoliberalism, this chapter suggests that resistance that acknowledges the power of this logic is liable to be generative. For instance, rather than using legal channels in order to legitimise and institutionalise counter-neoliberal goals, there is potential for law to be used in a manner that additionally exploits the ubiquity of the logic of the legal form, incorporating a critique of law into attempts to use legal channels subversively to debate and challenge neoliberalism (Brabazon, 2011, 2012, 2016).

The reframings and analysis discussed in this chapter suggest that neoliberalism is, at least in part, about the (conscious or not) realisation on the part of both neoliberal theorists and practitioners that the legal form is an essential constitutive element of capitalist social relations and that mobilising the legal form in certain ways can influence the dominant permutation of capitalist social relations. Specifically, the overlapping neoliberal theoretical and political projects mobilise the rule of law as the fundamental organising principle of social relations in the political and economic spheres. They further use law's indeterminacy to cohere contradictions in their efforts in practice. However, this analysis also lays the groundwork for the notion that resistance to neoliberalism can itself be cognizant of the centrality of the legal form to neoliberalism and, by incorporating challenges to the legal form, seek to delegitimise neoliberal legality and the neoliberal social relations dependent upon it.

References

Akram-Lodhi, A. Haroon. 2007. 'Land, Markets and Neoliberal Enclosure: An Agrarian Political Economy Perspective.' *Third World Quarterly* 28(8): 1437–1456.

AI (Amnesty International), Canadian Council for Refugees, Canadian Tamil Congress, International Civil Liberties Monitoring Group. 2011. 'Rights advocates decry detention of refugee claimants from MV Sun Sea.' Press release. 10 February.

Anghie, Antony. 2004. *Imperialism, Sovereignty and the Making of International Law.* Cambridge: Cambridge University Press.

Arthurs, Harry. 2003. 'Governing the Canadian State: The Constitution in an Era of Globalization, Neo-Liberalism, Populism, Decentralization and Judicial Activism.' *Constitutional Forum* 13(1): 16–23.

Aucoin, Peter and Lori Turnbull. 2008. 'The Democratic Deficit: Paul Martin and Parliamentary Reform.' *Canadian Public Administration* 46(4): 427–449.

Balbus, Isaac D. 1977. 'Commodity Form and Legal Form: An Essay on the "Relative Autonomy" of the Law.' *Law and Society Review* 11(3): 571–588.

Ban, Cornel. 2016. *Ruling Ideas: How Global Neoliberalism Goes Local.* New York: Oxford.

Bernstein, Henry. 2010. *Class Dynamics of Agrarian Change: Agrarian Change and Peasant Studies.* Halifax and Winnipeg: Fernwood Publishing.

Bowring, Bill. 2011. 'What is Radical in "Radical International Law"?' *Finnish Yearbook of International Law* 22: 4–29.

Brabazon, Honor. 2011. 'Legal Aspects of Agrarian Reform and Resistance in Contemporary Bolivia.' Paper presented at Toward a Radical International Law Workshop. Department of Law, London School of Economics and Political Science, London, UK. 6–7 May.

Brabazon, Honor. 2012. '"Les Carrés Rouges contre la loi": Understanding the Creative Use of Law by the Quebec Student Protests.' Paper presented at the Annual Conference of the Journal Historical Materialism. SOAS, University of London, UK. 8–11 November.

Brabazon, Honor. 2013. 'Juridification and its Discontents: How Neoliberal Legality Has Reframed Dissent and How Some Social Movements Are Responding.' Paper presented at *Understanding Neoliberal Legality Conference: Perspectives on the Use of Law By, For, and Against the Neoliberal Project.* University of Oxford, UK. 21 June.

Brabazon, Honor. 2016. 'Occupying Legality: The Subversive Use of Law in Latin American Occupation Movements.' *Bulletin for Latin American Research,* Special Section: Social Movements and Social Emancipation. Early view: http://online library.wiley.com/enhanced/doi/10.1111/blar.12527.

Brabazon, Honor and Jeffery R. Webber. 2014. 'Evo Morales and the MST in Bolivia: Continuities and Discontinuities in Agrarian Reform.' *Journal of Agrarian Change* 14(3): 435–465.

Brown, Wendy. 2015. *Undoing the Demos: Neoliberalism's Stealth Revolution.* New York: Zone Books.

Buchanan, Ruth and Sundhya Pahuja. 2004. 'Legal Imperialism: Empire's Invisible Hand?' In *Empire's New Clothes.* Ed. Paul Passavant and Jodi Dean. New York: Routledge.

Caliskan, Koray and Michel Callon. 2009. 'Economization, Part I: Shifting Attention from the Economy Towards Processes of Economization.' *Economy and Society* 38(3): 369–398.

Clarke, Harold D., Jane Jenson, Lawrence LeDuc, and Jon H. Pammett. 1996. *Canadian Electoral Politics in an Age of Restructuring.* Calgary, AB: Gage.

Clarke, John. 2012. (Founding member and lead organiser, Ontario Coalition Against Poverty.) Personal Interview. Toronto: 25 January.

Daniels, Ronald J., Patrick Macklem, and Kent Roach. 2001. *The Security of Freedom: Essays on Canada's Anti-Terrorism Bill.* Toronto: University of Toronto Press.

D'Arcy, Stephen. 2013. *Languages of the Unheard: Why Militant Protest is Good for Democracy.* Toronto: Between the Lines.

Dardot, Pierre and Christian Laval. 2009. *The Way of the World: On Neo-Liberal Society.* London and New York: Verso.

de Dios Fernández, Juan. 2011. (Secretary General, National Institute for Agrarian Reform (INRA).) Personal interview. La Paz, Bolivia. 20 January.

Dominiczak, Peter and Ben Riley-Smith. 2015. 'David Cameron tells Tory MPs: Ignore the "terrorist sympathisers" and vote for Syrian bombing.' *The Telegraph,* 1 December. www.telegraph.co.uk/news/politics/conservative/12028017/.

Duménil, Gérard and Dominique Lévy. 2011. *The Crisis of Neoliberalism.* Cambridge, MA and London: Harvard University Press.

Faundez, Julio. 2005. 'Community Justice Institutions and Judicialization: Lessons from Peru.' In *The Judicialization of Politics Latin America.* Ed. Rachel Sieder, Line Schjolden, and Alan Angell. New York: Palgrave Macmillan. 187–210.

Fine, Bob. 1984. *Democracy and the Rule of Law: Liberal Ideals and Marxist Critiques.* London and Sydney: Pluto Press.

Forcese, Craig and Kent Roach. 2015. *False Security: The Radicalization of Canadian Anti-Terrorism.* Toronto: Irwin Law Inc.

Glendon, Mary Ann. 1991. *Rights Talk: The Impoverishment of Political Discourse.* New York: The Free Press.

Goodale, Mark. 2005. 'Empires of Law: Discipline and Resistance with the Transnational System.' *Social and Legal Studies* 14(4): 553–583.

Hale, Charles R. 2002. 'Does Multiculturalism Menace? Governance, Cultural Rights and the Politics of Identity in Guatemala.' *Journal of Latin American Studies* 34: 485–524.

Hale, Charles R. 2004. 'Rethinking Indigenous Politics in the Era of the "Indio Permitido."' *NACLA Report on the Americas* 38(2): 16–21.

Harvey, David. 2006. 'Neoliberalism as Creative Destruction.' *Geografiska Annaler* 88(2): 145–158.

Hay, Douglas. 1975. *Albion's Fatal Tree: Crime and Society in Eighteenth-Century England.* New York: Pantheon Books.

Hayek, F.A. 1944. *The Road to Serfdom.* London and New York: Routledge.

Huneeus, Alexandra, Javier Couso, and Rachel Sieder. 2010. 'Cultures of Legality: Judicialization and Political Activism in Contemporary Latin America.' In *Cultures of Legality: Judicialization and Political Activism in Latin America.* Ed. Javier A. Couso, Alexandra Huneeus, and Rachel Sieder. Cambridge: Cambridge University Press. 3–21.

Isin, Engin. 1998. 'Governing Toronto without Government: Liberalism and Neoliberalism.' *Studies in Political Economy* 56: 169–191.

Jessop, Bob, Kevin Bonnett, Simon Bromley, and Tom Ling. 1988. *Thatcherism: A Tale of Two Nations.* Cambridge, MA: Polity Press.

Kennedy, David. 2006. 'The "Rule of Law", Political Choices, and Development Common Sense.' In *The New Law and Economic Development: A Critical Appraisal.* Ed. David Trubek and Alvaro Santos. Cambridge: Cambridge University Press.

Kennedy, Duncan. 2006. 'Three Globalizations of Law and Legal Thought: 1850–2000.' In *The New Law and Economic Development: A Critical Appraisal.* Ed. David Trubek and Alvaro Santos. Cambridge: Cambridge University Press.

Klare, Karl. 1979. 'Law-Making as Praxis.' *Telos* 40: 123–135.

Klare, Karl. 1982. 'The Public/Private Distinction in Labor Law.' *University of Pennsylvania Law Review* 130(6): 1358–1422.

Knox, Robert. 2009. 'Marxism, International Law, and Political Strategy.' *Leiden Journal of International Law* 22: 413–436.

Knox, Robert. 2010. 'Strategy and Tactics.' *Finnish Yearbook of International Law* 21: 193–229.

Knox, Robert. 2011. 'What is to be Done (with Critical Legal Theory)?' *Finnish Yearbook of International Law* 22: 31–47.

Koskenniemi, Martti. 2005a. 'By Their Acts You Shall Know Them (and Not by Their Legal Theories).' *European Journal of International Law* 15: 839.

Koskenniemi, Martti. 2005b. *From Apology to Utopia.* Cambridge: Cambridge University Press.

Kuhling, Clarice and Alex Levant. 2006. 'Political De-Skilling/Re-Skilling: Flying Squads and the Crisis of Working-Class Consciousness/Self-Organization.' In *Sociology for Changing the World: Social Movements/Social Research.* Ed. Caelie Frampton, Gary Kinsman, A.K. Thompson, and Kate Tilleczek. Halifax: Fernwood Publishing.

Lahiff, Edward, Saturnino M. Borras, Jr, and Cristobal Kay. 2007. 'Market-Led Agrarian Reform: Policies, Performance and Prospects.' *Third World Quarterly* 28(8): 1417–1436.

Langille, David. 1987. 'The Business Council on National Issues and the Canadian State.' *Studies in Political Economy* 24: 41–85.

Ligue des droits et libertés. 2015. *Manifestations et repressions.* Montreal: Ligue des droits et libertés.

Marks, Susan. 2007. 'International Judicial Activism and the Commodity-Form Theory of International Law.' *International Journal of International Law* 18(1): 199–211.

Merry, Sally. 2005. 'Human Rights and Global Legal Pluralism: Reciprocity and Disjuncture.' In *Mobile People, Mobile Law: Expanding Legal Relations in a Contracting World*. Ed. Franz von Benda Beckman, Keebet von Benda Beckman, and Anne Griffiths. Aldershot, UK: Ashgate. 215–233.

Miéville, China. 2004. "The Commodity Form Theory of Law: An Introduction." *Leiden Journal of International Law* 17(2): 271–302.

Miéville, China. 2005. *Between Equal Rights: A Marxist Theory of International Law*. Chicago: Haymarket Books.

Mirowski, Philip. 2009. 'Postface: Defining Neoliberalism.' In *The Road from Mont Pèlerin: The Making of the Neoliberal Thought Collective*. Ed. Philip Mirowski and Dieter Plehwe. Cambridge, MA and London: Harvard University Press. 417–445.

Mirowski, Philip. 2013. *Never Let a Serious Crisis Go to Waste*. London and New York: Verso.

NUPGE/CCLA (National Union of Public and General Employees and Canadian Civil Liberties Association). 2011. *Breach of the Peace. G20 Summit: Accountability in Policing and Governance*. Proceedings of public hearings held 10–12 November, 2010. Ottawa: National Union of Public and General Employees and Canadian Civil Liberties Association.

Oliver, Hugh. 1989. 'The Labour Caucus and Economic Policy Formulation, 1981 to 1984.' *The Making of Rogernomics*. Ed. Brian Easton. Auckland: Auckland University Press. 11–52.

Palmer, Bryan. 2005. 'System Failure: The Breakdown of the Post-War Settlement and the Politics of Labour in our Time.' *Labour / Le Travail* 55: 334–346.

Panitch, Leo and Donald Swartz. 1993. *The Assault on Trade Union Freedoms: From Wage Controls to Social Contract*. Toronto: Garamond Press.

Pashukanis, Evgeny. B. 1978[1929]. *Law and Marxism: A General Theory*. London: Ink Links Ltd.

Piore, Michael J. 1995. *Beyond Individualism*. Cambridge, MA: Harvard University Press.

Rajagopal, Balakrishnan. 2003. *International Law from Below*. Cambridge: Cambridge University Press.

Riles, Annelise. 2000. 'An Ethnography of Abstractions? Encountering the New Legal Formalism.' *Anthropology News* 41(6): 100–101.

Rittich, Kerry. 2006. 'The Future of Law and Development: Second-Generation Reforms and the Incorporation of the Social.' In *The New Law and Economic Development: A Critical Appraisal*. Ed. David Trubek and Alvaro Santos. Cambridge: Cambridge University Press.

Roberts, Alasdair. 2001. 'Structural Pluralism and the Right to Information.' *University of Toronto Law Journal* Summer: 243–271.

Rose, Nikolas. 1997. 'Governing "Advanced" Liberal Democracies.' In *Foucault and Political Reason: Liberalism, Neo-Liberalism and Rationalities of Government*. Ed. Andrew Barry, Thomas Osborne, and Nikolas Rose. Chicago: University of Chicago Press. 37–64.

Rubin, Ken and Kirsten Kozolanka. 2014. 'Managing Information: Too Much Publicity, Not Enough Public Exposure.' In *Publicity and the Canadian State*. Ed. Kirsten Kozolanka. Toronto: University of Toronto Press.

Salvatierra, Hugo. 2004. 'Tierra: Propiedad y Función.' In *La Reforma Agraria desde las Regiones: Tierra y Territorio. 50 Años de Reforma Agraria en Bolivia.* CIDES. La Paz: Plural Editores.

Sieder, Rachel, Line Schjolden, and Alan Angell. 2005. 'Introduction.' In *The Judicialization of Politics Latin America.* Ed. Rachel Sieder, Line Schjolden, and Alan Angell. New York: Palgrave Macmillan. 1–20.

Smulovitz, Catalina. 2005. 'Petitioning and Creating Rights: Judicialization in Argentina.' In *The Judicialization of Politics Latin America.* Ed. Rachel Sieder, Line Schjolden, and Alan Angell. New York: Palgrave Macmillan. 161–186.

Spears, John. 1997. '"No" to Megacity if Taxes Unprotected: Poll.' *Toronto Star* 1 March: A1.

Tate, C. Neal and Torbjörn Vallinder, eds. 1995. *The Global Expansion of Judicial Power.* New York: New York University Press.

Thompson, E.P. 1975. *Whigs and Hunters: The Origin of the Black Act.* Harmondsworth, UK: Penguin Books Ltd.

Thorburn, Hugh, ed. 2001. *Party Politics in Canada.* Toronto: Prentice-Hall.

Tigar, Michael E. with Madeleine R. Levy. 1977. *Law and the Rise of Capitalism.* New York and London: Monthly Review Press.

Trubek, David. 2006. 'The "Rule of Law" in Development Assistance: Past, Present, and Future.' In *The New Law and Economic Development: A Critical Appraisal.* Ed. David Trubek and Alvaro Santos. Cambridge: Cambridge University Press.

Trubek, David and Alvaro Santos. 2006. 'Introduction: The Third Moment in Law and Development Theory and the Emergence of a New Critical Practice.' In *The New Law and Economic Development: A Critical Appraisal.* Ed. David Trubek and Alvaro Santos. Cambridge: Cambridge University Press.

Vadillo, Alcides. 2010. (Regional Director of Fundación Tierra in Santa Cruz, former National Director of the National Institute for Agrarian Reform (INRA).) Personal interview. La Paz, Bolivia. 20 October.

Veltmeyer, Henry. 2007. *On the Move: The Politics of Social Change in Latin America.* Peterborough, ON and Orchard Park, NY: Broadview Press.

Wacquant, Loïc. 2009. *Punishing the Poor: The Neoliberal Government of Social Insecurity.* Durham, NC and London: Duke University Press.

Wood, Ellen Meiksins. 2009. 'Peasants and the Market Imperative: The Origins of Capitalism.' *Peasants and Globalization: Political Economy, Rural Transformation and the Agrarian Question.* Ed. A. Haroon Akram-Lodhi and Cristóbal Kay. London and New York: Routledge. 37–56.

Chapter 9

Alegality: outside and beyond the legal logic of late capitalism

Vanja Hamzić [1]

Introduction

In times when state violence and law's covert or overt complicity in it seem more evident than ever, exacerbated and epitomised in contemporary conflicts such as those in Iraq, Libya, Mali, Syria, Palestine and Ukraine, it seems pertinent to re-examine the prospect of a radical re-imagination of the paradigm of law and legality. My intention is not to reprise some of the commonplace stands in Marxist legal thought, which tend to oscillate between two seemingly opposite poles. On the one end, common accounts uphold a commitment to the perceived counter-hegemonic and emancipatory aspects of law and legality, in which re-appraisals of human rights somehow always manage to take centre stage. In contrast, on the other end, common accounts re-enact the classic prophecy in Marx, Engels and Pashukanis that both state and law ought to and will eventually wither away. Meanwhile, between these two extremes is a curious space full of indecisiveness, inconsistency, 'bad faith' and other post-utopian 'maladies'.

If this were an essay about such common stands, I could hardly find any reason not to agree with those left with little or no faith in law and legality, *tout court*. As sombre works such as China Miéville's *Between Equal Rights: A Marxist Theory of International Law* (2005) demonstrate all too well, '[a] world structured around international law cannot but be one of imperialist violence. The chaotic and bloody world around us *is the rule of law*' (ibid: 319). Indeed, in the present-day capitalist mode of economic, cultural and political production, it is difficult to perceive or recuperate *any* law and law-making activity – either on national or supranational levels – as not *always already* neoliberal. That is, the very production of law and

1 Senior Lecturer in Legal History and Legal Anthropology, SOAS, University of London (vh1@soas.ac.uk). I am grateful to Safet Hadžimuhamedović and Grietje Baars for their insightful comments on an earlier version of this chapter. I would also like to thank Honor Brabazon for her magisterial editorial work and for making the writing and publishing of this piece an all-round enjoyable experience.

legality[2] is an integral part of the economic, cultural or political logic of late capitalism (cf. Jameson, 1991). Even the few remaining sites of anti-capitalist legality, such as those produced and maintained in certain Latin American states, increasingly find themselves unable to subvert the dominant, globalised logic of neoliberal legality. While I take the point of those who claim that this might be a reductive (e.g. Stone, 1985; Vincent, 1993) or overly doctrinaire vision (Carty, 2008) – one that potentially lacks the sophistication of everyday (legal, political, social, economic) life – I am reluctant to denounce the importance of its stark pessimist overtone. Quite the contrary, it could be the very same unceasing pessimism, which had ultimately made Miéville and a number of other legal prodigies leave legal writing *altogether*, that compels my search for spaces *outside* or *behind* the prevalent legality. For, even if law *as such* is *undesirable* at this or any future point, it strikes me that its *material* zones of influence and realisation, i.e. social, political and even economic human relations, are *still* capable of resisting its omnipresent neoliberal turn.

The usual way to approach this capacity to resist a dominant form of legality is to analyse the dyad of legal–illegal relations, for an active opposition to law is almost always taken for granted as *formally* illegal. In this brief piece, I would like to propose that this is an incomplete picture of the terrain *affected by law*, and that what usually gets lost is the aspect of *alegality*, a capacity to be neither legal nor illegal, an ability to exist and act in the interstices, or perhaps beyond or outside, the dominant (capitalist) modes of legal production.

I begin by sketching out a trajectory of legal and political writing on the question of alegality. In these works, alegality remains a legal phenomenon, i.e. an occurrence firmly within the domain of law, legal theory and practice. In order to test this supposition, I revisit seminal Marxist interpretations of alienation and resistance to account for both emancipatory and anti-emancipatory potentials of the alegal space. This experimentation reveals an array of underexplored issues concerning alegality and leads me to the next step, which is a search for material accounts of the alegal in spaces and communities that resist the law as well as the dyad of legal–illegal relations. Relying on certain instructive sociological and anthropological studies on the matter and my own ethnographic experience in Pakistan, I propose that strategies for alegal self-governance – that

2 *Legality* is commonly understood to denote the quality or state of being in accordance with the law. The term's antonym – *illegality* – is, thus, the quality or state of being in discordance with the law to a degree deemed proscribed by the same (system of) law. This chapter's intervention mainly revolves around the space (or quality or state) outside of the domains of legality and illegality, which I call *alegality*. We can presume, at the outset, that alegal space harbours and is governed by normativities that surpass or escape the logic of the law, be it municipal, international or any other law or legal system sanctioned by governing elites of the state.

is, for communal normative life outside the law – invite an analysis that is both spatial and discursive. In other words, what alegality produces is often both a geographic terrain and a corresponding discourse in which the dominant legal–illegal relations are replaced with alternative regulative frameworks. After a brief visit to several examples of spatial alegality, I move to a closer examination of discursive alegality, with a particular focus on what James C. Scott calls 'the infrapolitics of the powerless' (Scott, 1990: xiii): the clandestine practices of resistance – in our case, to the law – that may or may not erupt into a full-fledged proletarian uprising. I argue, apropos, that any theorisation of discursive resistance to neoliberal legality in our time has to take into account the relationship between capitalism and alegality as well, given the centrality of global capitalism in the production cycles of neoliberal political economy. I continue by attempting just that – a brief account of how capitalism fares in the present discussion on alegality. I revisit, on the one hand, Marx's theory of primitive accumulation (Marx, 1961 [1867]: 713) and capital's 'colonial anomalies' (ibid: 765) and, on the other hand, Thomas Piketty's popular call for a renewed analytical focus on the distribution of wealth (Piketty, 2014 [2013]: 15), to account for a continuous alienation of the powerless by both capital and law. I argue that this modality of capitalist and neoliberal social, economic and legal accumulation can be productively (en)countered by taking *pessimism* seriously, as an instance of *critique* of life under capitalism in which the alegal and the infrapolitical constitute invaluable sources of everyday anti-capitalist struggle. I conclude by interrogating a disconcerting example of a new *global* neoliberal and, curiously perhaps, neo-Roman legality. Both local and global planes reveal a necessary *turn* towards further studies of the alegal – a turn that is both epistemic and methodological in nature. For, it is our system(s) of knowledge as well as disciplinary (academic) production that need changing in our commitment to the radical potential of alegality.

Alegality: what's in a name?

It may come as a surprise that legal theorists have generally eschewed dealing with the question of alegality. What has prevailed, instead, at least in most influential accounts, is an unwillingness to recognise that there could exist social spaces and contexts *outside* the law, or outside legal systems. Hans Kelsen, for example, maintains that *all* 'legal norms' belong to a certain 'legal order' (*Rechtsordnung*)[3] and that the task is, quite simply, to sort them accordingly:

3 It is instructive to recall that the German word *Recht*, much like its cognates in many other Germanic and, indeed, Romanesque and Slavic languages, does not only denote 'law' but also 'right' and is therefore often used to describe normative configurations of justice.

> The law *qua* system – the legal system – is an order of legal norms. The first questions to answer here have been put by the Pure Theory of law in the following way: what accounts for the unity of a plurality of legal norms, and why does a certain legal norm belong to a certain legal order?
>
> (Kelsen, 2002 [1934]: 55)

There is significant disagreement amongst the likes of Kelsen, H.L.A. Hart and Ronald Dworkin – to name but a few prominent thinkers – as to *how* a *Rechtsordnung* comes into being. Hart, for example, famously distinguishes between 'primary' and 'secondary' rules and vests the latter with the all-important ability to congeal a legal system (e.g. Hart, 1994 [1961]: 103), whilst Dworkin insists that, apart from rules, there are other constitutive elements of a legal order, such as 'policies' and 'principles' (e.g. Dworkin, 1977 [1967]: 38). However, there is little or no consideration in these works of spaces that might exist outside the legal–illegal paradigm that is manifested in the plurality of legal norms and systems they discuss.

More thoughtful accounts of alegality have only begun to emerge in the present century. Hans Lindahl seems to have blazed a trail with his conceptualisation of alegality as a space *in between* the legal–illegal distinction:

> To the extent that human behaviour does not simply fall tidily on either side of the divide between legality and illegality, legal closure manifests itself primordially in challenges to the ways in which legal orders draw the boundary between legality and illegality: *a-legality*. Spatially speaking, a-legality manifests itself in forms of behaviour that intimate a place that has no place within the distribution of legal places a collective calls its own, yet ought to in some way. So described, a-legality points to a primordial form of spatial closure which is constructive of all legal orders: the distinction between a familiar distribution of places – an inside, and a strange place – an outside. In this fundamental sense, all legal orders are localised, emplaced.
>
> (Lindahl, 2010: 31)

Poised though he may be to address 'a strange place – an outside' of the legal–illegal dyad, all Lindahl ultimately does is to account for the 'placedness' or 'situatedness' – comparable in use and meaning to Hegel's *Sittlichkeit* (Hegel, 1991 [1820])[4] – of alegality that is of necessity local(ised), i.e.

Thus, a *Rechtsordnung* can mean much more than a 'legal order' or, conversely, it can signal a multiplicity of justice and rights claims underpinning a legal order.

4 Hegel's *Sittlichkeit* denotes, primarily, an 'ethical life' as one of the 'spheres' of *Recht* (i.e. Law/Right) in which collective and individual justice claims are negotiated and harmonised. The same is, in a way, both a desideratum and necessary outcome of any *Rechtsordnung* for Lindahl.

constitutive and dependent upon spatially cohesive legal and social collectives. Note that the 'unity' of a legal order is not broken by this intervention. On the contrary, it is reaffirmed by allowing the presumptive 'grey area' between legal and illegal of a *Rechtsordnung* to be locally negotiated and defined. For Lindahl, alegality 'denotes behaviour that calls into question the distinction itself between legality and illegality as drawn by a legal order in a given situation' (Lindahl, 2013: 30–31), principally by *revealing* 'the capacity of behaviour to draw boundaries [between legal and illegal] otherwise' (ibid: 37). But, while such boundaries can be locally redrawn over and over again, they still remain firmly emplaced *within* the relevant legal order.

Lindahl's theory of alegality has been particularly instructive to an emergent group of political scientists, spearheaded by Andrew Schaap, who strive to re-employ the Ancient Greek concept of the *agon* (*ἀγών* – 'struggle', 'contest') in order to articulate a conflict theory of politics, in opposition to dominant liberal-republican consensus theories:

> Far from being a legally mediated reciprocal conflict among equals …, the agon resides in the asymmetrical relation between 'alegal' acts that politicize a legal order and the legal response to such acts through the (re)enforcement and/or (re)constitution of the boundaries of the legal order. This relation is asymmetrical because a legal order can only respond finitely to the political acts that contest it, i.e. by representing struggle as *internal* to the social unity that is at stake. In other words, a legal order can only respond to political agonism by rendering conflict meaningful in terms of the distinction between legal and illegal that the struggle would otherwise contest.
>
> (Schaap, 2009: 4)

In this account, then, alegality is imbued with the capacity to 'politicise' (or, presumably, 'give agency to') legal orders and, mediated by the power of the *agon* (conflict), disturb the boundaries between legal and illegal *within* them. The legal orders' typical response to such acts is primarily *epistemological*, and reactionary. This is an important insight in as far as it assumes a *systematic corrective reaction* of the paradigmatic collective, in this case a *Rechtsordnung*, to an act of contestation stemming from a *body politic* cognisant of the limitations of that very legal order. In that sense it is comparable to Marx's fundamental discernment, in his famous 'Preface' to *The Critique of Political Economy*, that '[i]t is not the consciousness of men that determines their existence, but, on the contrary, their social existence determines their consciousness' (Marx, 1911 [1859]: 12). Thus, we can assume that alegality as a form of insurrectionary 'social consciousness' contrary to that produced by a dominant legal order can be conceived as politically – ideologically – *different* to that order, but neither Lindahl nor

Schaap attempts to construe it as a phenomenon putatively *separate* or *separable* from the abiding plurality of legal orders, governed by a spatial logic of its own. Instead, alegality is given an 'agonistic' injection only in as much as it can engender contestations and changes within the irreplaceable paradigm of a *Rechtsordnung*. Its agony is, ultimately, inconsequential, since the most it can do is to cause the internal boundaries of a legal order to shift, or to replace one legal system with another.

Important for our discussion is, also, Fleur Johns' recent project, which sets out to problematise 'a vocabulary of non-legalities (namely, illegality, extra-legality, pre- and post-legality, supra-legality and infra-legality)' (Johns, 2013: 1). In her attempt to critically interrogate an 'expanded repertoire' of non-legal moves attributable to the jurisprudence and practice of international law, Johns reflects upon a number of dissonant discourses emerging around the phenomena that do not quite square with what she terms 'prevailing "usable knowledge" of and about international law' (ibid: 217). In order to showcase such dissonance, she compares, for example, the theme of torture with the idea of illegality (ibid: 32–68) and the question of Guantánamo Bay with the notion of extra-legality (ibid: 69–108). The end product of these iterations seems to be '[a]n accentuation of international law's negative spaces – attention, that is, to international legal makings of the non-legal' – which Johns claims 'could embolden the sort of experimentation these questions imply without necessary recourse to some higher or lower ground of assurance or initiative' (ibid: 223–224). In other words, Johns seems convinced that the discursive *opening* she performs by exposing certain 'negative spaces' of international law can, in itself, generate further *spaces* of contestation, critique and cross-pollination primarily in amongst the existent fields of international legal scholarship (cf. ibid: 224). This is a valiant attempt, which nonetheless remains but an initial step towards a more nuanced catalogue of alegal phenomena.

In the context of Guantánamo Bay, for example, the notion of extra-legality is described by Johns as paradoxical, i.e. as 'highly regularised through legal work and writing' (ibid: 71). Johns is careful not to fall in the classic Schmittian trap, in which the *nomos* (*νόμος* – 'norm', 'law') – Carl Schmitt's own conception of norm – 'is described as a deliberately alegal, antipositivist figure' (Augsberg, 2010: 382), albeit one which has, 'in the course of time, already in the ancient world, lost its original meaning, and has at last sunk to an insubstantial, general designation for every normativist regulation and adjustment' (Schmitt, 1988 [1950]: 36). The alegal, historically deteriorated *nomos* and its 'normativist' followers are for Schmitt none other than Jewish law – *halakha* – and its adherents, observant Jews (Schmitt, 1993 [1934]: 9). Johns' extra-legality, epitomised in the Guantánamo Bay detention camp, is a more complex state of exception than that of Schmitt, because it 'emerge[s] on all scales throughout legality' (Johns, 2013: 108) and is, to wit, not so exceptional after all.

Rather, it is an exception *regulated* by 'legal workings' that are 'dedicated as much to the annihilation or codification of the exception as to the assertion of exceptional extra-legality' (ibid). In that sense, extra-legality is a legal product *par excellence*, however ambiguous and self-contradictory.

If we assume that, so defined, the concept of extra-legality is the closest in amongst her categories to what Johns would consider an alegal space, then it is a notion wholly subsumable under the concept of legality. Because it is 'regularised' by law, it cannot exist outside the law's domain, despite its 'extra-legal' label. As such, it is, at worst, a form of discursive deception, and, at best, an emanation of the heterodox nature of contemporary juridical interventions – otherwise evidenced in phenomena such as 'legal pluralism' or the 'fragmentation of international law'. But it is not in any way outside or beyond the all-defining and all-governing gaze of law.

Alegality reconsidered

It is probably not a coincidence that 'neither Marx nor Engels had a positive normative theory of law' (Vincent, 1993: 371). Marx's writings are a case in point, for his jurisprudential thought is commonly considered to have been 'often premised upon a critique of law per se, and what he has to say tends to be overwhelmingly negative in character' (ibid). Both the 'younger' and 'older' Marx, so epistemologically divided since Althusser's seminal musings on the matter (Althusser, 2005 [1965]), did not consider the bourgeois law/morality/justice – so neatly conjoined into the single German word *Recht*[5] – to be worth preserving in any shape or form. For Marx and Engels, as well as for a range of Marxist legal thinkers coming after them (e.g. Pashukanis, 2001 [1924]; Renner, 1949 [1929]), the ultimate goal of the socialist revolution was the withering away of the *Recht*, as a less-than-helpful capitalist legacy. This resolute stance towards legality might partly explain 'the paucity of Marxist jurisprudence until modern times' (Collins, 1982: 10), while subsequent generations of radical thinkers may have been additionally encouraged to steer away from law in the face of Stalinist atrocities committed in the name of 'Soviet socialist law' – the very antithesis of the earlier Marxist rejection of legality.

I would like to suggest that the scarcity of Marxist law is a good sign; moreover, it is a sign that holds out the promise of alegality. It has been argued that law is inextricably connected to the dominant concept of the state in times of late capitalism, economically (through the demands of capital), socially (via the class society it reinforces and reproduces), politically (by lending its direct or indirect support to bourgeois ideologies and structures of governance) and even linguistically (e.g. the notion of *Recht*).

5 See supra note 3.

If this is true, then it is more pertinent than ever for today's radical thinkers to instigate an *epistemic shift* toward the sites of the alegal, i.e. the contemporary social phenomena that are lacking a legal sense or that successfully remain outside or beyond the legal–illegal dichotomy.

Alegality, in a Marxist sense, could be construed as a potentially emancipatory space in which a law's subject, whether individual or collective, resists the domination of a capitalist society by the sheer force of that subject's *otherness*, or *outsideness*, to the (spatial and otherwise) legal regulation that is enabled by the legal–illegal distinction and other modes of legal production prevalent in that society. I say a 'potentially emancipatory' space because alegality, *as such*, guarantees neither classlessness nor freedom from many other social malaises. What it does provide, however, is a type of *anomie* (cf. Durkheim, 2002 [1897])[6] in which one can experiment with and engage in, at least to a degree, social relations free from the grip of legality.

The material alegal spaces are, almost by definition, *messy*. It would be misleading and a little too hopeful to consider them, *a priori* or *causa sui*, immune to the various forms of *alienation* (in Marx: *Entfremdung, Entaüsserung* or *Vergegenständlichung*) – such as through labour, politics or sheer existential struggle (cf. Axelos, 1976) – that those who inhabit such spaces experience in their daily lives. Besides, alegal spaces are quite different from one another, in that they seem to encompass – as we shall soon see – quite a wide range of alegal sociality and harbour both insurrectionary 'subaltern' agency and the will to dominate and oppress, depending on which extreme end of the gamut is considered. In fact, it is possible to speak of both *proletarian* and *bourgeois* alegality, with these classic terms somewhat broadened to include today's more complex understanding of the categories of labour and class.

The spectrum of alegality

In one of his early socio-legal essays, Boaventura de Sousa Santos observes the state of legality in a Rio de Janeiro *favela*, which he gives the fictitious name of Pasargada,[7] arguing that this poor 'squatter' settlement benefits from a curious 'legal' system of its own:

> As I concentrated my research on the dispute prevention and dispute settlement mechanisms associated with the Pasargada Residents'

6 Following Émile Durkheim, *anomie* denotes a 'condition in which society provides little moral guidance to individuals' (Gerber and Macionis, 2010: 97). For our purposes, the word 'moral' can easily be replaced with the word 'legal' in the above definition.

7 This name is hardly a coincidence. In 1930, the celebrated Brazilian poet Manuel Bandeira published a poem – *Vou-me embora pra Pasárgada* (*I will go away to Pasargadae*) – in which the ancient city of Pasargadae, the birthplace of the First Persian Empire (550–330 BCE), was re-imagined as a utopian city.

> Association I came to conceive of these mechanisms and their institutional setting as forming an unofficial legal system, which I called Pasargada law. I then analyzed this law in its dialectical relations with the Brazilian official system, as an instance of legal pluralism.
>
> (de Sousa Santos, 1977: 7)

However, what de Sousa Santos has stumbled upon in Pasargada seems to be precisely the kind of alegality associable with city slums *everywhere*:

> Because of the structural inaccessibility of the State legal system, and especially because of the illegal character of these communities, the dominated classes living in [the *favelas*] devise adaptive strategies aimed at securing the minimal social ordering of community relations. One such strategy involves the creation of an internal legality, parallel to (and sometimes conflicting with) State legality – a kind of popular justice.
>
> (ibid: 5)

In his later writings, de Sousa Santos recognises the lack of nuance in such accounts, giving the 'internal legality' of the *favelas* a broader sociological scope:

> The legal and the illegal are the only two relevant forms of existing before the law and, for that reason, the distinction between the two is a universal distinction. This central dichotomy leaves out a whole social territory where the dichotomy would be unthinkable as an organizing principle, that is, the territory of the lawless, the alegal, the nonlegal, and even the legal or illegal according to nonofficially recognized law.
>
> (de Sousa Santos, 2007: 48)

De Sousa Santos' gradual coming to terms with the idea of alegality seems to be guided by his later more in-depth experience with the urban poor and the forms of social normativity they develop in opposition to and on the outside of state legality. In my own ethnographic research of the inner city slums of Lahore, Pakistan's ancient cultural and urban centre, I came face-to-face with a number of social properties that designate such spaces firmly outside the (official) law-governed social structures, including: (1) specific forms of labour, such as sex work, begging for 'money gifts' (*wadhaian*) or ritual dancing, based on a wide range of 'informal economies'; (2) specific forms of sociality, such as master-disciple (*guru-chela*) and mother-daughter (*ma'an-dhi*) relations amongst the Pakistani gender-variant subjectivity known as *khwajasara*, which stem from an alternative kinship system of this community; (3) specific forms of communal living, in which a *khwajasara* household (*dera*), amidst a busy lower-class neighbourhood, simultaneously and harmoniously dubs as a family house, brothel, dance studio, beauty salon, kindergarten and bank-like depository of *community* cash and other worthy possessions. Some of these idiosyncrasies are proscribed but the majority of them remain wholly unregulated by Pakistani law. What is more, Pakistani law is most of the time even *physically* absent from the inner city slums, with law-enforcement forces having a very complex relationship with their residents – one that involves violence, coercion and extortion, to be sure, but also one that obeys an 'unconstitutional' but 'customary' 'right' of these residents: the right to be left alone, as much and whenever possible, except in times of wider 'moral panic'.

In the delicate 'ecosystem' of an inner city slum, *norms abound*, but they do not coalesce into an abject 'formal' legality; they are outside the 'system-productive' limelight of the state and the macro-political; they have been fought for and against, preserved and reshaped on a daily basis, in continuum yet with some paradigmatic shifts every now and then, for centuries. They are laboured from within the *body social*, from its material and immaterial contingencies and its manifold understandings of its own past. Thus, the prevalent social experience, the very *art* of living, in the slum is both proletarian and alegal. It may not be *fully* free from the violent sway of the state, but it does resist and is by and large self-regulated outside the state law and legal system.

The precariousness of such social arrangements is sometimes overstated. If one sees only the 'abject', 'marginal', 'deprived' and 'violent' side of alegal slum life, one is bereft of its many imaginative, egalitarian, self-liberating and symbiotic aspects. At any rate, such lifeworlds have chiefly developed their own epistemologies, which often place the yardstick of a/the 'good life' beyond the reach of an outsider's pool of knowledge. In this they echo Marx in as much as 'their social existence determines their consciousness' (Marx, 1911 [1859]: 12). The idiosyncratic reality of their daily life constitutes their equally idiosyncratic understanding and enjoyment of that very life.

However, the spectrum of the alegal does not quite end within the purview of the urban poor. In sharp contrast to alegality of the proletariat, there also exist the forms of alegality that are clearly designed to overcome the power of the *Recht* for the sake of elite, bourgeois interests. The profit- and power-centred rationalities of social and economic phenomena, such as the 'corporate culture' and 'supra-legal'[8] *modi operandi* of a great deal of multinational corporations, suggest both the ever so adaptive nature of global capitalism and an aberration of its prevalent legal logic that is still

8 The 'supra-legal' denotes here the commonplace corporate practice to place certain business relations and dealings 'above the law', i.e. to avoid legal regulation and control of such relations and dealings.

statist in nature. Could it be that such phenomena signal a new, *post-legal*, phase in late capitalism, in which the Occupy movement and Wall Street share an uncanny resemblance in that they both produce and operate from at least partly alegal spaces? Or, is it more probable that bourgeois alegality simply suggests that certain high capitalist classes can be, and often are, *above* the law, whatever the popular perception of law's omnipresence? Whatever the case, the further *transformation* of nation-state sovereignty, a trend directly related to global capitalism, whether conceived as the steady erosion of such sovereignty (cf. Brown, 2010) or its re-orientation towards a more 'market-friendly' phenomenon (as argued elsewhere in this book), is likely to produce new forms of neoliberal legality – and alegality. This necessitates an inquiry into the relationship between alegality and capitalism proper, to which I turn later in the present chapter.

So far, I have examined the examples of alegal life that require a certain *physical space* in order to develop and thrive, but what of the occurrences of the alegal that do not necessarily require such territorial designation because they are, *principally*, discursively produced and perpetuated?

Discursive alegality

Owing primarily to the influence of Foucauldian discourse analysis, especially as postulated in *Archaeology of Knowledge* (Foucault, 1969) and *The Order of Discourse* (Foucault, 1971), most social scientists nowadays tend to assume that a discursive practice does not have to have a physical base (i.e. it can be dispersed across spaces) nor does it have to *produce* a space of its own. In the case of alegality, it seems that this Foucauldian logic holds water in as much as it points to what James C. Scott, a noted anarchist scholar, calls 'the infrapolitics of the powerless' (Scott, 1990: xiii). Relying on his ethnographic work amongst poor Malay peasants and a series of theoretical and historical insights, Scott defines infrapolitics as 'the strategic form that the resistance of subjects must assume under conditions of great peril' (ibid: 199). This resistance, for Scott, is *primarily discursive*, and it takes form of the *hidden transcript*. By this he means that this resistance 'takes place "offstage", beyond direct observation by powerholders', and 'consists of those offstage speeches, gestures, and practices that confirm, contradict, or inflect what appears in the public transcript' (ibid: 4–5). Moreover, the hidden transcript is not only used by the powerless:

> Every subordinate group creates, out of its ordeal, a 'hidden transcript' that represents a critique of power spoken behind the back of the dominant. The powerful, for their part, also develop a hidden transcript representing the practices and claims of their rule that cannot be openly avowed.
>
> (ibid: xii)

If applied in the context of alegality, Scott's insights suggest, *mutatis mutandis*, that law's public, official face always already has other, hidden sides. That is, there are *rules* about how one *governs* through law and, alternatively, how one silently *resists* and resents law, even if these rules are 'only' discursive and of necessity known to some yet not to all. Such infrapolitics are alegal in nature, and are especially significant when they empower the 'powerless' to engage in more visible – revolutionary – modes of defiance and 'lawlessness':

> Social scientists, not to mention ruling elites, are often taken by surprise by the rapidity with which an apparently deferential, quiescent, and loyal subordinate group is catapulted into mass defiance. That ruling elites should be taken unaware by social eruptions of this kind is due, in part, to the fact that they have been lulled into a false sense of security by the normal posing of the powerless. Neither social scientists nor ruling elites, moreover, are likely to fully appreciate the incitement a successful act of defiance may represent for a subordinate group, precisely because they are unlikely to be much aware of the hidden transcript from which it derives much of its energy.
>
> (ibid: 224)

Defiance, then, presupposes a phase of secretive 'soul-searching' that may or may not be followed by more self-evident forms of social unrest. It is a phase free from law's 'public force', from law's *official* (i.e. publicly officiated) legality, but it is not necessarily bereft of knowledge about law and governance altogether. It is not rule-free. What is more, despite its intrinsic messiness, derived in part from the clandestine nature of its 'rules of engagement', discursive alegality of the powerless appears to be a prime depository of their insurrectionary knowledge, an agential time bomb waiting to explode as soon as circumstances permit.

Capitalism and alegality

We have seen how certain forms of alegality can exist *outside* the domain of the legal–illegal dyad, both spatially and discursively. But can they be conceived outside capitalism proper, too? And, if so, what does it tell us about the relationship between neoliberal legality and capitalism in its current phase? Are the emerging examples of *capitalist* alegality, such as those signalling Wall Street's deliberate 'lawlessness' in dealing with increasingly 'vulnerable' institutions of national and international law, constitutive of a certain nascent form of capitalist production that no longer requires law to function?

Paradigmatic for these quandaries are Marx's brief deliberations, towards the end of the first volume of *Capital*, on the so-called 'primitive accumulation' preceding capitalist accumulation (Marx, 1961 [1867]: 713–716) and on certain difficulties European capitalists were facing in the mid-nineteenth century in their overseas colonies (ibid: 765–774).

In the first example, Marx sketches out his theory of primitive accumulation to account for 'the historical process of divorcing the producer from the means of production' (ibid: 714), the very 'starting-point' of the capitalist mode of production and political economy's undeniable 'original sin' (ibid: 713). Because a 'capitalist system pre-supposes the complete separation of the labourers from all property in the means by which they can realise their labour' (ibid: 714), the proto-capitalist accumulation presumed the making of two classes of 'commodity-possessors' – 'the owners of money, means of production, means of subsistence, who are eager to increase the sum of values they possess by buying other people's labour-power' and 'free labourers, the sellers of their own labour-power, and therefore the sellers of labour' (ibid). Of course, the making of these two classes had as its inevitable consequence the alienation of free labourers from the product of their labour.

Let us now presuppose that a similar process precedes the advent of capitalist law and legality. If one substitutes labour-power with legal power and the two classes of 'commodity-possessors' with the owners/buyers of legal power and those who are bound to sell it, one is left with a convenient formula for capitalist alienation by law. Because the commodification of legal power, and law proper, in a capitalist society relies on such alienation being performed and reproduced in perpetuity, it creates an artificial *demand* for capitalist legality – one that unconditionally vests the capitalist with the right and means to legal power, despite such power being formally a purview of 'all people'. But what if capitalism has entered a stage in which it no longer requires legal power to thrive?

To address this question we must briefly turn to Marx's second example – that in which he discusses capitalism's 'colonial anomalies'. It is in the colonies, Marx avers, that 'the capitalist régime everywhere comes into collision with the resistance of the producer, who, as owner of his own conditions of labour, employs that labour to enrich himself, instead of the capitalist' (ibid: 765). Moreover, the producer there seems to have 'discovered that capital is not a thing, but a social relation between persons, established by the instrumentality of things' (ibid: 766). If one replaces 'the colonies' with 'post-colonial societies' or, indeed, any society in which alegal life is possible, either spatially or discursively, and once again supplants labour-power with legal power, Marx's nineteenth-century analysis of the difficulties the European coloniser was facing in transplanting capitalist production reveals an enduring legacy – and *limitation* – of capitalism. Wherever the legal subject of capitalist law can exit, if only for a while or partially, the 'vicious circle' (ibid: 713) of capitalist accumulation that perpetually reproduces capitalist legality, that subject can realise that such legality, or law in general, is also 'not a thing, but a social relation between persons, established by the instrumentality of things' (ibid: 766). This is of immense importance, for this is precisely how alegal resistance to neoliberal legality is often conceived. In Lahore's inner city as well as in de Sousa Santos' Pasargada or Scott's accounts of the proletarian hidden transcript, alegal spaces and discourses create opportunities to conceive alternative forms of (normative, insurrectionary, etc.) social relations.

But the same is true for decidedly *capitalist* forms of alegal life, some of which, such as the Wall Street example, seem curiously *post-legal*. Thomas Piketty's bestseller, *Capital in the Twenty-First Century* (Piketty, 2014 [2013]), is but one of numerous influential testimonies that capitalism is changing, too. If anything, Piketty's analysis reveals an even more drastic alienation that the current phase of capitalist accumulation is based on, most readily visible in the resulting global wealth and income inequality – greater than ever before. There appear to be numerous instances where designing and leveraging specific laws is no longer fully required to secure the proliferation of those and other forms of capitalist inequality. But this does not mean that neoliberal legality is about to wither away, especially since it firmly remains in service of global capitalist production. Indeed, even if individual laws are not always mobilised, the liberal legal *form* is mobilised increasingly in the production of neoliberal capitalist relations, as previous chapters have demonstrated. Rather, this is to say that specific laws and legal mechanisms are no longer required *at all times* and can, if need be, be supplanted with *other* forms of capitalist subjugation.

Therefore, there *can be* (and there are) instances of both capitalist and non-capitalist alegality. The alegal space *can*, but does not always, provide a refuge of sorts not *just* from capital's vicious legal power but from its relentless commodification of labour-power, too. Such instances presuppose the unmaking of the two classes of 'commodity-possessors' *to the extent possible* – an action (and 'consciousness') immensely difficult to realise, given the perturbing ballasts of life under capitalism (almost) everywhere.

Pessimism and alegality

As we have just seen, for all their revolutionary potential, contemporary alegal social practices of the oppressed – whether they are spatial and/or discursive, open and/or underground – take place in a time of rampant global capitalism. It seems to me that, in such grave conditions, one is best off to cautiously embrace pessimism as a *critical stance*, not as a mode of desperation, and to acquiesce to an uneasy realisation that one cannot but live a life that is *damaged* by capitalist production in one way or another.

Writing in the aftermath of World War II from his American exile, Theodor Adorno famously captured the sombre lifelessness of life under capitalism:

> What the philosophers once knew as life has become the sphere of private existence and now of mere consumption, dragged along as an appendage of the process of material production, without autonomy or substance of its own ... Our perspective of life has passed into an ideology which conceals the fact that there is life no longer.
>
> (Adorno, 2005 [1951]: 15)

Adorno's is not the mere hopelessness of an émigré, nor is it *just* an admonishment of early Fordist America. He is acutely – and bitterly – aware that 'the relation between life and production', which in his account undoubtedly denotes capitalism, 'in reality debases the former to an ephemeral appearance of the latter' (ibid). Thus,

> [o]nly by virtue of opposition to production, as still not wholly encompassed by this order, can men bring about another more worthy human beings. Should the appearance of life, which the sphere of consumption itself defends for such bad reasons, be once entirely effaced, then the monstrosity of absolute production will triumph.
>
> (ibid)

The ugly lifelessness of life entrapped in capitalist production is reflected, perhaps better than in any other context, in the domain of legality, which renders all jurisprudence – to echo Pierre Schlag – *jurisprudence noire* (cf. Schlag, 2001), and all today's lawyers 'at home in their alienation, comfortable in their anomie' (ibid: 1733). The totality of capitalism and neoliberal legality calls into question the utility of an *optimistic* engagement with both life and law. Instead, a darker critique seems to be required, followed by an equally sombre politics, which, as Slavoj Žižek suggests, forbears unpremeditated action:

> The first task today is precisely *not* to succumb to the temptation to act, to directly intervene and change things (which then inevitably ends in a cul-de-sac of debilitating impossibility: 'what can one do against global capital?'). Rather, the task is to question the hegemonic ideological coordinates or, as Brecht put it in his Me Ti, 'Thought is something which precedes action and follows experience'. If, today, one follows a direct call to act, this act will not be performed in an empty space; it will be an act *within* the hegemonic ideological coordinates.
>
> (Žižek, 2001: 194)

Viewed from the angle of *analytical pessimism*, as one could call this strand of critical theory, alegality and infrapolitics *make sense* as they defy – however macabrely – both the logic and totality of life under late capitalism.

Global legality and epistemic shift

One of the peculiar features of neoliberal legality in the twenty-first century is its turn towards *global law*. As a paradigm for worldwide legal transformations that have been ignited by the spectacle of the latest capital-driven globalisation, global law has become an enormously popular analytic frame for rethinking the future of both international and municipal law, and their discontents. 'Global' legal research centres are being opened at universities with a correspondingly 'global' remit and ambition; new 'global' legal degrees and scholarships are being offered to future law students, or rather, law students of *the future*. Meanwhile, the leading academic publishers are contemplating specialised publication series to account for a sharp surge in writing about this, well, seemingly *global* phenomenon. But, amongst a myriad of ideas about global law, a distinct *locality* has emerged as a new focal point for an *ancien régime* of legal imperialism: the locality of *Europe* as a 'new-old' global legal hegemon.

The leading representative of the newest iteration of European 'civilisatory' thought that has been repackaged for global consumption is Spanish jurist, legal theorist and professor of law Rafael Domingo. His *magnum opus*, titled *The New Global Law* (Domingo, 2010), is probably the clearest manifesto of this discourse. The book presents an upbeat, unashamedly straightforward call to reinstate the absolute primacy of Roman and later European law on a global scale. 'Globalization', argues Domingo, 'commands a reformulation of the law, an appropriate legal response to changing times to avoid becoming hostage to outmoded, transient paragons. It is a moral obligation' (ibid: xiv). The change, Domingo suggests, must, as it were, run in the family. The 'three legal domains (the law of nations, international law, and [the new] global law)', he explains, 'are like grandfather, father, and grandson, respectively. They are part of one and the same family' (ibid). But this is not *just* a dim rumination about the necessity to return to the 'grandfather', the *ius gentium europaeum* (the European law of nations). Rather, for Domingo, it is the case of *ex Roma ius* (cf. Domingo, 2005).[9] Thus, he asks rhetorically:

> Is it possible to understand Grotius without at least Gentili or Vitoria, Vitoria without Thomas Aquinas, or Aquinas without Isidore of Seville? Can we understand St. Isidore without first knowing Ulpian, Ulpian without Gaius, Gaius without Cicero, the great Roman orator without the Stoics, and stoicism without Socrates? ... Of course not.
>
> (Domingo, 2010: xv)

9 Domingo's quip, translatable as 'the law comes from Rome', based on the Latin maxim *ex Roma lux* ('the light comes from Rome').

In Domingo's account, the primacy of the European genealogy of law is both an inescapable 'cosmopolitan destiny' (ibid: xvii) and promise for success of the 'new global law'. In his 200-page defence of this project, the only *other* legal tradition mentioned is that of Islamic law and its 'law of nations' (*siyār*). Domingo provides a two-page account of this tradition, only to swiftly conclude that its 'imitation or transplantation' into the 'new global law' would be 'impossible' (ibid: 19–21). The intrinsically *violent* nature of his global law project is not concealed. On the contrary, Domingo explains: 'The *ius* needs force – coercion – to prevail, and force is, in the final analysis, more political than juridical' (ibid: xvii). It is, perhaps, for this reason that Domingo, in the closing passages of his book, beseeches the United States to 'follow the path of justice' and join 'the global law initiative' (ibid: 198). Ultimately, Domingo's vision is that of one law (*ius*), one government (*gubernatio*) and one people (*populus*) – a vision of an *imperium europaeum* frightful enough to conjure up an entire pandemonium of not-so-friendly ghosts from Europe's not-ever-so-distant past.

Domingo's is, of course, but one of many accounts of legal imperialism in its twenty-first century apparitions. Faced with such disconcerting discursive practices, left-leaning scholars have proposed a number of oppositional strategies, primarily in the sphere of legal education and research, i.e. the sphere central to knowledge production. Boaventura de Sousa Santos, for instance, has called for a turn towards 'vernacular epistemologies' of the global South, which should gradually displace the primacy of 'Northern epistemologies' (e.g. de Sousa Santos, 2006). Sally Engle Merry has made a similar case for 'vernacularisation', with an even more pronounced sensitivity towards locale-specific knowledge systems, including those pertaining to and/or formative of local legalities (e.g. Engle Merry, 2000). For John and Jean Comaroff, such an epistemic shift would be constitutive of a 'theory from the South', whose geo-political location would primarily serve to *de-universalise* global Northern knowledge production (Comaroff and Comaroff, 2011) towards what Raewyn Connell, another proponent of 'Southern theory', calls 'the self-knowledge of society' (Connell, 2007: vii). Whilst the interest in what Clifford Geertz has dubbed 'local knowledge' (Geertz, 1983) is, of course, not new, especially in the fields of anthropology and sociology from which these authors invariably intervene, a call for its primacy in other-than-local contexts (including political, educational, legal and other aspects) is in itself an *epistemic shift*, and one in which some overarching Marxist terms-of-art, such as 'class consciousness' (cf. Lukács, 1999 [1923]), could find a renewed use.

In the sphere of legal studies, it seems to me that this move necessitates not only a turn towards the alegal as an analytical category, but also a *methodological* shift of sorts, with a dual emphasis on alegal ethnography and critical theory, as the means to traverse the problems that will inevitably occur, such as those of *scale* (i.e. whether a certain form of 'local' alegality can be comparable to other 'local', 'regional', 'trans-local' and potentially 'global' alegalities), *political context* (which, as the phenomena such as the 'Arab Spring' attest, can be difficult to gauge in that it contains a range of historical and ideological idiosyncrasies) and *technology* (e.g. the alegality of certain internet forums and their relationship with physical locales).

Another question altogether would be how to carve a space within higher education systems to study and teach alegality. If *alegal studies* were subsumed under the more general umbrella of legal education, would it lose its necessary critical (and methodological) edge and be considered but another strand of studies *about the law*, albeit from a new angle?

The central argument of this chapter has been that alegality should be understood as an important exploratory site for the future anti-capitalist modes of resistance and counter-production, through which neoliberal spaces and spectres of law can be challenged and both spatially and discursively *displaced* by the emergent, hidden or revealed, scripts for (class, gender, anti-neo-colonial, epistemic, etc.) *struggle* in late capitalist societies. Whilst the role of academia 'on the left' should not be underestimated in this process, it is certainly not the only aspect – and promise – of a sustained but pessimistically wise social action.

References

Adorno, Theodor, *Minima Moralia: Reflections from Damaged Life* (London: Verso, 2005 [1951]).

Althusser, Louis, *For Marx* (London: Verso, 2005 [1965]).

Augsberg, Ino, 'Reading Law: On Law as a Textual Phenomenon' (2010) 22(3) *Law and Literature* 369–393.

Axelos, Costas, *Alienation, Praxis, and Technē in the Thought of Carl Marx* (Austin: University of Texas Press, 1976).

Brown, Wendy, *Walled States, Waning Sovereignty* (Cambridge: MIT Press, 2010).

Carty, Anthony, 'Marxist International Law Theory and Hegelianism' (2008) 10(1) *International Studies Review* 122–125.

Collins, Hugh, *Marxism and Law* (New York: Oxford University Press, 1982).

Comaroff, Jean and Comaroff, John L., *Theory from the South: Or, How Euro-America is Evolving Toward Africa* (Boulder, CO: Paradigm Publishers, 2011).

Connell, Raewyn, *Southern Theory: The Global Dynamics of Knowledge in Social Science* (Cambridge: Polity Press, 2007).

de Sousa Santos, Boaventura, 'The Law of the Oppressed: The Construction and Reproduction of Legality in Pasargada' (1977) 12(1) *Law & Society Review* 5–126.

de Sousa Santos, Boaventura, *Another Production is Possible: Beyond Northern Epistemologies* (Verso: London, 2006).

de Sousa Santos, Boaventura, 'Beyond Abyssal Thinking: From Global Lines to Ecologies of Knowledges' (2007) 30(1) *Review (Fernand Braudel Center)* 45–89.

Domingo, Rafael, *Ex Roma ius* (Pamplona: Thomson Aranzadi, 2005).

Domingo, Rafael, *The New Global Law* (Cambridge: Cambridge University Press, 2010).
Durkheim, Emile, *Suicide: A Study in Sociology* (London, Routledge, 2002 [1897]).
Dworkin, Ronald, 'Is Law a System of Rules?' in Ronald Dworkin (ed.), *The Philosophy of Law* (Oxford: Oxford University Press, 1977 [1967]), 38–65.
Engle Merry, Sally, *Colonizing Hawai'i: The Cultural Power of Law* (Princeton: Princeton University Press, 2000).
Foucault, Michel, *L'archéologie du savoir* (Paris: Gallimard, 1969).
Foucault, Michel, *L'ordre du discours* (Paris: Gallimard, 1971).
Geertz, Clifford, *Local Knowledge: Further Essays in Interpretative Anthropology* (New York: Basic Books Inc., 1983).
Gerber, John J. and Macionis, Linda M., *Sociology* (7th edn; Toronto: Pearson Canada, 2010).
Hart, H.L.A., *The Concept of Law* (Oxford: Clarendon, 1994 [1961]).
Hegel, Georg Wilhelm Friedrich, *Elements of the Philosophy of Right* (Cambridge: Cambridge University Press, 1991 [1820]).
Jameson, Fredric, *Postmodernism, Or, The Cultural Logic of Late Capitalism* (Durham, NC: Duke University Press, 1991).
Johns, Fleur, *Non-Legality in International Law: Unruly Law* (Cambridge: Cambridge University Press, 2013).
Kelsen, Hans, *Introduction to the Problems of Legal Theory* (Oxford: Clarendon, 2002 [1934]).
Lindahl, Hans, 'A-Legality: Postnationalism and the Question of Legal Boundaries' (2010) 73(1) *Modern Law Review* 30–56.
Lindahl, Hans, *Fault Lines of Globalization: Legal Order and the Politics of A-Legality* (Oxford: Oxford University Press, 2013).
Lukács, Georg, *History and Class Consciousness: Studies in Marxist Dialectics* (Cambridge: MIT Press, 1999 [1923]).
Marx, Karl, *Critique of Political Economy* (Chicago: Chicago University Press, 1911 [1859]).
Marx, Karl, *Capital, Volume I: A Critical Analysis of Capitalist Production* (Moscow: Foreign Languages Publishing House, 1961 [1867]).
Miéville, China, *Between Equal Rights: A Marxist Theory of International Law* (Leiden: Brill, 2005).
Pashukanis, Evgeny, *The General Theory of Law and Marxism* (Somerset: Transaction Publishers, 2001 [1924]).
Piketty, Thomas, *Capital in the Twenty-First Century* (Cambridge: The Belknap Press of Harvard University Press, 2014 [2013]).
Renner, Karl, *The Institutions of Private Law and Their Social Functions* (London: Routledge & Kegan Paul, 1949 [1929]).
Schaap, Andrew, 'Introduction' in Andrew Schaap (ed.), *Law and Agonistic Politics* (Surrey: Ashgate, 2009).
Schlag, Pierre, 'Jurisprudence Noire' (2001) 101(7) *Columbia Law Review* 1733–1741.
Schmitt, Carl, *Der Nomos der Erde im Völkerrecht des Jus Publicum Europaeum* (Berlin: Duncker & Humbolt, 1988 [1950]).
Schmitt, Carl, *Über die drei Arten des rechtswissenschaftlichen Denkens* (Berlin: Duncker & Humbolt, 1993 [1934]).

Scott, James C., *Domination and the Arts of Resistance: Hidden Transcripts* (New Haven, CT: Yale University Press, 1990).
Stone, Alan, 'The Place of Law in the Marxian Structure–Superstructure Archetype' (1985) 19(1) *Law & Society Review* 39–68.
Vincent, Andrew, 'Marx and Law' (1993) 20(4) *Journal of Law and Society* 371–397.
Žižek, Slavoj, 'Have Michael Hardt and Antonio Negri Rewritten the Communist Manifesto for the Twenty-First Century?' (2001) 13(3) *Rethinking Marxism* 190–198.

Index

acquired rights doctrine 50, 54–5
administrative agencies 67–70, 72
administrative law 70
agency 4, 194, 197
agonistic politics 13, 85, 90, 194–5
agrarian reform 9, 27, 180–1
alegality 19, 191–201, 203–4, 207
alienation 18, 114, 191–2, 197, 202–4
anomie 197, 204
anti-statism 5, 14, 25, 93, 109, 147
Arab Spring (2011) 207
Argentina 54n37
Asian Financial Crisis (1997) 30–1
austerity 38, 120, 128
Australia 54n58, 158, 163
Austrian-Libertarian tradition 24
authoritarian statism 120, 133–4
authoritarianism 9, 84, 142
authority 43, 46–53, 64, 67, 69, 147, 150, 153, 168–9, 173, 181–2

base 79, 168
bilateralisation 43, 45
Bolivia 9, 16, 180–1; Market-Led Agrarian Reform 180–1
Brazil 198
Bretton Woods institutions 24, 34n67

capitalism 4, 6–8, 15–16, 19, 22n2, 73n46, 81, 89, 93–5, 101–2, 111–16, 126, 133–4, 143, 168, 190–2, 196, 199, 200–4
capitalist legal form 2, 168–9, 171, 184
capitalist legality 119, 202
Chicago, University of 3, 65, 132
Chile 24, 63n6, 132
China 132
citizenship 78, 98n3, 141, 145, 147, 154
civil liberties 31, 178–9
class 3–5, 8–9, 11–12, 15, 17–18, 25, 28n35, 80, 84, 87–8, 92–5, 99–102, 106, 108, 110–15, 119–21, 125, 131–2, 134–5, 144–5, 155, 167, 179, 182, 196–8, 200, 202–3, 206–7
classical liberalism 4–5, 9, 62, 65–6, 71, 74, 78, 119, 125, 131, 145, 172; *see also* liberalism
closed shop 96, 99, 103–5
coercion 45, 84n13, 114, 120, 122–3, 134–5, 168, 199, 206
collective action 8, 12, 18, 110, 124, 177–8
collective agreements 97–9, 108, 110
collective bargaining 10, 94–6, 98–9, 101, 105, 108, 110, 113, 120, 124, 129, 136
collective laissez-faire 18, 94, 97–101, 104–10, 112–16; *see also* laissez-faire
collective subjectivity 18, 100–2, 107–16; *see also* subjectivity
colonialism 14, 142, 146–8, 151–2, 163
common law 67, 68, 96, 98
communism 70
competition 5, 8, 16, 38–9, 63, 70, 80–1, 85–8, 90, 93, 101–2, 130–2, 144, 172–5, 178, 184
constitutional law 54
content of law 136
contract law 17, 34, 54, 87–8
contracts 9–10, 16–17, 32–3, 35, 43–5, 47–8, 51–8, 68, 79, 83, 84n13, 86–9, 96–7, 104
corporations 15, 47, 79, 153, 157, 161, 199; *see also* multinational corporations
counter-terrorism 179

courts 6, 34–5, 46, 50, 52, 67, 69, 71, 79, 88, 105, 109, 112, 128, 130, 168, 176
criminal justice system 78
critical legal studies 70, 109n6
cultural rights 142–3, 148–9, 158–9, 161
customary international law 49

decolonisation 23, 51–2
democracy 3, 8, 12, 35, 71, 102, 107, 147, 155, 175, 177–8
depoliticisation 9, 18–19, 23, 84–5, 89–90, 109n6, 110, 169, 173, 180–3
deregulation 28, 30, 68, 109, 144–5
development 1, 5, 10, 12, 14–17, 22–31, 33–7, 39, 52, 72, 147, 149–53, 160–1, 180; *see also* international development
disciplinary social policy 78, 84
dissent 11–12, 19, 26, 168, 171, 174, 176–80, 182, 184

economics 1, 6, 9, 12, 14–15, 17, 26n18, 29, 32, 45, 56, 67, 71–2, 74, 77–8, 81, 99, 101, 108, 176
Ecuador 56
education 27, 32, 65, 72, 82, 84–5, 145, 150, 159, 206–7
efficiency 5, 12, 22, 32, 38, 47, 56, 65–9, 180
empire 1, 51, 146
entrepreneurialism 16, 23–4, 36–7, 93, 178
environmental regulation 48
equality 2, 5–10, 12, 18, 35, 51, 55, 68, 87–8, 90, 100, 114, 149, 151, 154–5, 157, 170, 172, 175–6, 181, 183–4
essential industries 124, 129–30
European Union 53, 63, 108
exchange 5, 9, 28–9, 32, 34, 83, 101, 103, 113n8, 114, 125, 131, 168–9
extra-legality 195–6

Falklands War 104
favelas 197–8
feudalism 168–9
financial crisis of 2008 38, 131–2
flexicurity (Scandinavia) 132
Ford Foundation 23
foreign investment 10, 17, 25, 43, 45, 49–50, 53, 55
formal equality 7, 10, 18, 87–8, 90, 114, 170, 181, 183
France 53
free market 5, 24, 27, 36–7, 62, 93, 144–5, 184
freedom 3, 5, 9, 45, 55, 62–3, 65–6, 80, 83–4, 88, 90, 114, 123, 144, 154, 156, 175, 197
Freiburg School 62
Friedman, Milton 28, 122, 131
functionalism 37

Germany 53, 63
global administrative law 54
global value chains 44
globalisation 1, 36, 63, 70, 105, 145, 148, 205
governmentality 43, 45, 48, 135
Greece 6, 8, 16, 18, 119, 125–6, 128–30, 135, 137; constitution 18, 126–8, 130; military dictatorship 126–7, 133; reforms of 2010 128, 130, 135
Guantanamo Bay 195
Guatemala 159, 161

Halakha 195
Hayek, Friedrich von 24n10, 27, 63–6, 67n23, 80, 82, 107, 121–5, 136, 170, 172
health care 17, 77, 80, 85–6, 89–90
hegemony 2, 23, 26, 119, 126
homo economicus 156–8
housing law 77
human rights 12, 14, 16, 35, 140–3, 145–52, 154–7, 160–2

immigration detention 178
import substitution industrialisation 23
indigenous rights 8, 15, 18–19, 140–4, 148–63, 179
individualism 32, 93, 136, 147, 154, 175
industrial action 6, 8, 94–9, 101, 103–9, 111, 113, 127, 129
inequality 5–7, 9, 12, 25–7, 45, 168, 170, 182–3, 203
inflation 36, 102, 122
informal economies 198
infrapolitics 192, 200–1, 204
International Conference on Indigenous Peoples of the Americas (1977) 149
International Court of Justice 51
international development 1, 14, 16, 22–3, 180; *see also* development

International Fund for Agricultural Development 180
international law 15, 22, 49, 51–2, 55–7, 140, 142, 146–7, 154–5, 162–3, 190, 195–6, 201, 205
International Monetary Fund 24, 72, 144
investment 10, 17, 23, 25, 33, 36, 40, 45–6, 48–50, 53–6, 82, 132n57, 140, 153, 155
invisible hand 62–3
Iraq 178, 190
Islamic law 206

Jacobins 95
Japan 26
juridical relations 6, 16, 169
juridification 6, 11–12, 15, 19, 22n2, 110, 168, 171, 183–4

Keynesianism 11, 15, 52, 120, 121n3, 122, 124, 126, 130–1, 133–5, 144, 167, 171–2, 178

La Paix du Travail 1937 (Switzerland) 121
labour 6, 8–9, 15, 18, 35, 38, 81–2, 84–5, 92–7, 101–2, 104–5, 107–8, 110–15, 121–6, 128–30, 136–7, 144, 150, 155, 172, 175, 177, 197–8, 202–3; *see also* organised labour
labour law 95–7, 111–12, 129
laissez-faire 3, 14, 38, 78, 97, 101, 119, 131, 136, 172; *see also* collective laissez-faire
landless peasants; *see* peasants
Latin American debt crisis (1980s) 70
law and development movement 23, 25
law and economics 14, 17, 31–2, 36, 56, 61, 65, 68–9, 70n35, 71, 74
lawyer/policy analysts 72
left 9, 12, 125–6, 177, 179, 206–7
legal form 2, 5–7, 9–10, 12–13, 16–19, 22n2, 61, 87–8, 90, 97, 101, 114–15, 131, 134, 154, 167–71, 173–4, 176–9, 181, 185; *see also* liberal legal form
legal framework 11, 19, 79–80, 85, 90, 110, 119–20, 125, 127, 130–1, 140, 162
legal indeterminacy 10–11, 120, 170n2, 179, 183
legal order 2, 43, 49, 55, 57, 63, 65–6, 109, 192–5
legal pluralism 196, 198
legal realism 43–4, 69
legal subjects 7–9, 16, 87, 168, 170, 173–4, 176–7, 181, 202
liberal legal form 18, 61, 88, 125, 135–6, 173, 176, 178, 203; *see also* legal form
liberal legality 2, 74, 131
liberalism 3–4, 78, 92, 98, 119, 125, 131, 145; *see also* classical liberalism
liberty 3, 62–4, 80, 82, 90, 124, 132, 147, 149, 157

market 1, 3, 5–6, 8–12, 16, 23–5, 27–30, 32–9, 44, 47, 49, 57, 62–6, 68, 70, 72, 74, 78–82, 84–8, 90, 93, 101, 122, 123n11, 132, 144–5, 153, 155–8, 171–84, 200
market order 78–80, 85
marketisation 11–12, 77, 140, 182–4
Mexico 49, 55, 160
microeconomic rationality 43
middle class 93
militancy 95, 102, 113, 125, 130
monopolies 15, 78, 120–5, 133
Mont Pelerin Society 24, 64, 121, 144
moral panic 199
multiculturalism 140, 143, 158, 179; *see also* neoliberal multiculturalism
multinational corporations 47, 199; *see also* corporations
mystification 183

nationalisation 93, 126
natural law 47, 49
Nazi regime 63
neoclassical economics 78
neoinstitutional economists 44, 53
neoliberal economists 28
neoliberal legality 1, 2, 7, 9–13, 15–17, 23, 31, 35–9, 43, 47–8, 53, 56–7, 74, 119–20, 125, 130–1, 133, 137, 185, 191–2, 200–1, 203–5
neoliberal multiculturalism 143, 158, 179; *see also* multiculturalism
neoliberal project 2, 18, 23, 49, 81, 140, 142, 145, 162, 167
neoliberal rationality 19, 93, 142, 182–3; *see also* rationality
neoliberal subjects 4, 16, 93–4, 104, 143, 184; *see also* subjectivity
new institutional economics 14, 28
nomocracy 7, 80

nomos 195
non-governmental organisations (NGOs) 20, 140, 146, 148–9, 159, 161
non-legalities 195
non-state forums 167

Occupy movement 200
ordoliberals 3, 62–3, 65–6
organised labour 18, 92–5, 104, 121, 123n13, 125, 128, 130; *see also* labour
Organization for Economic Cooperation and Development (OECD) 72

pacta sunt servanda 48–9, 51, 54, 57, 82, 88
Pakistan 16, 191, 198–9
peasants 9, 180–1, 200
Permanent Court of International Justice 50
pessimism (as critique) 191–2, 203–4, 207
Pinochet, Augusto 24
policy entrepreneurs 72
political sphere 12, 15, 19, 101, 167–8, 170–4, 176, 179–84
positivism 63, 195
Posner, Richard 22–3, 31, 65–6, 67n23, 68–9
post-colonial 14, 52–3, 146–7, 202
post-war period 4, 18, 23, 44, 52, 63, 94, 97–9, 101–2, 107, 112, 133, 167, 172–4, 177, 179
primitive accumulation 192, 202
prisons 78, 86n17
private authority 46
private law 11, 17, 47, 55, 80–1, 87, 90, 132, 173, 181–2
private property 10, 16, 23, 31, 33–5, 43, 45–9, 51, 88, 93, 112, 144, 183
private sphere 11, 154–5, 172–3, 182
privatisation 15, 17, 25, 28–9, 36, 47, 77, 124, 129–30, 171–3
production 84, 88, 101–2, 111, 113, 144, 168–9, 190–2, 197, 201–4, 206–7
profit 4–5, 46, 50, 86–9, 92, 119, 125, 144–5, 153, 157, 199
property 9–10, 16–17, 22–3, 30–1, 33–5, 38, 43–51, 54, 56–7, 67–8, 79–80, 93, 111–12, 113n8, 127, 144, 150, 157, 159, 168–9, 202
property rights 1, 5, 10, 22, 25, 29, 32–5, 37, 43, 46–7, 50, 52, 63, 78, 88, 126, 153, 155, 157, 183
property-sovereign paradigm 45, 57
protest 6, 109, 121, 129n30, 157, 162, 175, 177–9
public authority 43, 153
public good 15, 18, 70, 125, 130, 135
public interest 7–8, 88, 154, 172–4, 177, 180, 182
public law 43, 127, 132, 173
public sector 85, 128, 130, 172, 178
public sphere 154, 172
public utilities 46, 70
public–private partnerships 86

rationality 2, 4, 17, 19, 32n52, 39, 43, 61, 64–6, 69, 81–2, 84, 87, 90, 93, 102, 120n1, 132, 143, 145, 155–6, 176, 182–3; *see also* neoliberal rationality
Reagan, Ronald 92, 144
Rechtsordnung 192–5
regulation 3, 5–6, 10–11, 17, 26, 32–3, 35, 37–9, 44, 46–9, 52–3, 61–2, 64–74, 79, 97, 101, 104–5, 109–10, 114–15, 119–20, 143, 148, 175, 181, 195, 197, 199n8
regulatory capture 71
regulatory law 61
regulatory theory 61
repression 97, 110, 125, 169, 175
resistance 11–13, 15, 19, 23–4, 46, 48, 53, 68, 112, 128, 135, 141, 143, 157, 159, 161–3, 168, 176, 184–5, 191–2, 197, 199–203, 207
resource control 44
responsibility 78, 82
right to strike 6, 18, 98, 103, 119–20, 123–7, 130, 135; *see also* strikes
rights *see* acquired rights doctrine; cultural rights; human rights; indigenous rights; property rights
rule of colonial difference (Chatterjee) 142, 156
rule of law 1, 7–9, 11, 22, 30–1, 33–5, 37–8, 64, 66, 74, 122, 124, 133, 144, 156, 170–1, 179, 181, 183, 185, 190
rules of just conduct 64, 80
Russia 28

semi-autonomous regulatory agency 13, 17, 70, 72, 74
sex work 198

Smith, Adam 125
social contract 87, 135
social democracy 102, 107
social insurance 87
social justice 7, 72–3, 102, 107, 151, 172
social law 80, 87–90
social movements 8, 16, 146, 148, 162–3, 177–8
social organisation 5, 12, 24, 64, 80, 93, 101, 114
social policy 17–18, 47, 77–8, 80–1, 83–5, 90
social relations 3–4, 6–7, 9–13, 16, 18–19, 27, 37, 39, 78, 82, 90, 93, 95, 104, 112–14, 155, 168–71, 173, 176, 181–2, 184–5, 197, 202–3
social services 77, 85, 145, 171
socialism 3, 126, 133, 175n3, 196
sociology 15, 26n18, 77–8, 191, 198, 206
solidarity 8–9, 87–9, 94, 99–102, 105–6, 121, 177, 181
sovereignty 10, 17, 43–5, 47–9, 51–2, 55–7, 62, 133n38, 146, 158, 200
Soviet Union 28
special interests 8, 107–8, 174
stakeholders 8, 174, 177, 180–1
state 5–7, 9–12, 14–17, 19, 23–5, 27–30, 33–9, 44–57, 62–74, 77–90, 93, 97–103, 110, 120, 128, 132–6, 140–1, 143–8, 150–1, 153–63, 167, 171–3, 176–80, 182–4, 190, 191n2, 196, 198–200
state of exception 131, 195
strikes 15, 92, 97–100, 103–5, 111, 120, 125–30, 135–7, 177–8, 191; *see also* right to strike
structural adjustment 23–4, 26–7, 39, 144
subaltern 12, 174, 197
subjectivity 3–5, 7, 9, 12–16, 18, 39, 78, 82, 90, 92–5, 100–2, 104–5, 107–16, 167, 169, 171, 173, 177, 181, 184, 198; *see also* collective subjectivity, neoliberal subjects
superstructure 6, 79, 168
sustainable development 29, 31, 33, 153
Switzerland 121
symbolic laws 11, 179

tariffs 23, 26, 46
taxation 48
teleocracy 80
Thatcher, Margaret 94, 99, 102, 107, 124, 144
torts 67–8, 96–8, 103, 122
totalitarianism 3
trade 23–6, 36, 50, 53, 144; trade liberalisation 36
trade unions 6, 10–11, 15–16, 18, 92–115, 120–6, 128
transnational 10, 55
transplant effect 73

Ukraine 190
unemployment 9, 18, 27, 80–5, 90, 122
unions see trade unions
United Kingdom: Conservative Party 102–3; Employment Act 103–4; General strike of 1926 97, 100; Golden Formula 96–7, 103, 105; health care 77, 85–6, 89–90; Labour Party 95, 101, 107–8, 110, 115; Miners' Strike of 1984–5, 92, 104, 178; National Union of Mineworkers (NUM) 92, 104; Primary Care Trusts (UK) 85–6; Social Contract 103; Taff Vale Case 96, 103; Trades Union Congress 99, 107; Winter of Discontent 103–4, 113
United Nations 141, 146–9, 151–2
United States 3, 46, 49, 53, 64, 68–9, 112, 144, 146, 167, 206
United States Agency for International Development (USAID) 23

Washington Consensus 23, 25–6, 36, 70
welfare 9, 16–18, 63, 67–8, 77, 80–3, 85, 87, 111, 135, 155
welfare state 3, 4, 11, 15–16, 18, 25, 38, 87–8, 98–9, 133–4, 143–4, 171–2, 177, 183–4
Westphalian model 49
Wolfensohn, James 30, 33
workers' movement 120–1
workfare 8–9, 17, 78, 80–5, 89–90
working class 8, 15, 18, 25, 93–5, 99–102, 108, 110–15, 135, 144